Abstraction Level	Development Phase	Structural Model	Function...	
System (problem domain)	**System Requirements Specification**	System context diagram	System u... diagram a... use cases	use cases (scenarios)
Subsystem	**System Architecture**	Subsystems diagram	Specified in the analysis functional models of subsystems ↓	Specified in the analysis dynamic models of subsystems ↓
Class	**Subsystem Analysis**	Class diagram and class description table	Subsystem operation sheets	Subsystem event list and event groups diagram and event sheets and statecharts and actions table and significance table and (compound events) and scenarios
Object	**Subsystem Design**	Class outlines and process outlines and inter-process message outlines	Outlines of member function which merge into the outlines in the structural model ←	Object interaction threads and event threads and object groups

OCTOPUS roadmap

OBJECT-ORIENTED TECHNOLOGY FOR REAL-TIME SYSTEMS:
A PRACTICAL APPROACH
USING OMT AND FUSION

Maher Awad
Juha Kuusela
Jurgen Ziegler

For book and bookstore information

http://www.prenhall.com

PRENTICE HALL PTR
UPPER SADDLE RIVER, NJ 07458

Library of Congress Cataloging-in-Publication Data

Awad, Maher.
    Object-oriented technology for real-time systems : a practical approach
using omt and fusion / Maher Awad.
    Juha Kuusela, Jurgen Ziegler.
        p. cm.
    Includes bibliographical references and index.
    ISBN 0-13-227943-6
    1. Object-oriented programming (Computer science)   2. Real-time
data processing.   I. Kuusela, Juha.   II. Ziegler, Jurgen.
    III. Title.
    QA76.64.A93   1996
    005.2--dc20   95-39004
                                          CIP

Editorial/production supervision/design: Patti Guerrieri
Cover director: Jerry Votta
Cover designer: Anthony Gemmellaro
Manufacturing buyer: Alexis R. Heydt
Acquisitions editor: Paul W. Becker
Editorial assistant: Maureen Diana

The publisher offers discounts on this book when ordered in bulk quantities. For more information, contact: Corporate Sales Department, Prentice Hall PTR, One Lake Street, Upper Saddle River, NJ 07458, Phone: 800-382-3419, Fax: 201-236-7141, e-mail: corpsales@prenhall.com

SMALLTALK-80 is a registered trademark of ParcPlace Systems, Inc. Paradigm Plus is a registered trademark of ProtoSoft Inc. ObjectMaker is a registered trademark of Mark V Systems Limited. Visio is a registered trademark of Shapeware Corporation. OMG is a registered trademark of Object Management Group, Inc. Ada is a trademark of Ada Joint Program Office, DoD, US Government. Paradigm LOCATE is a trademark of Paradigm Systems. XRAY MasterWorks is a trademark of Microtec Research, Inc. Use Case is a trademark of Telefonaktiebolaget L M Ericsson. All other products are trademarks of their respective companies.

Printed in the United States of America
10 9 8 7 6 5 4

ISBN   0-13-227943-6

Prentice-Hall International (UK) Limited, *London*
Prentice-Hall of Australia Pty. Limited, *Sydney*
Prentice-Hall Canada Inc., *Toronto*
Prentice-Hall Hispanoamericana, *S.A., Mexico*
Prentice-Hall of India Private Limited, *New Delhi*
Prentice-Hall of Japan, Inc., *Tokyo*
Simon & Schuster Asia Pte. Ltd., *Singapore*
Editora Prentice-Hall do Brasil, Ltda., *Rio de Janeiro*

To Heli and my parents with love,
MA

To Vuokko, Matias and Turkka with love,
JK

To my parents, my children Lasse, Kirsi and Mikko, and to Marja-Liisa with love,
JZ

TABLE OF CONTENTS

FOREWORD

As the advantages of object technology have become more widely known, objects are being applied in more and more diverse areas. One very important area, where there is a large amount of experience, is real-time systems. Till now, unfortunately, there has been little published about how to apply object-oriented technology in this domain. In this book, Maher Awad, Juha Kuusela and Jurgen Ziegler have crystallized the experience of many real-time object-oriented projects into a systematic approach to software development using the OCTOPUS method. A great strength of the book is that the authors have not sought to innovate for innovation's sake. OCTOPUS is a natural extension to OMT and Fusion, two of the most popular mainstream object-oriented methodologies.

The authors are to be congratulated on pushing out the boundaries of object-oriented methodologies in such a clear, concise and accessible manner. This book should be invaluable to everyone interested in a systematic and practical approach to real-time object-oriented software development.

Derek Coleman
Palo Alto
October 1995

PREFACE

Audience

This book is a practical guide for engineers and managers of software development projects, particularly for embedded real-time systems. It offers two case studies that demonstrate how to master the complexity of these systems. The book is most useful for readers interested in the crossover of object-oriented technology and real-time systems. Anybody seeking knowledge in the two areas will also find it worthwhile.

It can be used in undergraduate and graduate courses on real-time systems and object-oriented software development.

Basic knowledge about object-oriented concepts and C++ is useful, but not essential. It also helps if the reader has some background in real-time systems. Otherwise, the book is self-contained.

Background

Embedded software has a special characteristic which distinguishes it from other branches of software: it is tightly connected to its physical environment through sensors and actuators. Normally, it is real-time software because it has to react to many events within specified time limits.

Object-oriented technology helps in the development of embedded real-time systems in a way that naturally maps to the inherent nature of the systems being built, while providing benefits such as reuse, increased extendibility, and robustness, already well known in the development of other branches of software.

The OCTOPUS Method

Because of the diverse needs of different application domains, an efficient method for software development has to be domain-specific, focusing on the important aspects of its intended application domain. OCTOPUS provides a systematic approach for developing object-oriented software for embedded real-time systems. It provides solutions to many important problems such as concurrency, synchronization, communication, interrupt handling, ASICs, hardware interfaces and end-to-end response time through the system.

OCTOPUS has a well-integrated development process covering the major phases of software development. From requirements specification to implementation, the models are continuously and clearly linked. Incremental development of the software system is supported.

The OCTOPUS approach also supports the development of heterogeneous systems where the object-oriented solution is a part of a non-object-oriented system. A conventional real-time operating system is used as an implementation platform. The dilemma of merging processes with objects is solved by a systematic and efficient procedure that maps objects into processes.

The OCTOPUS method adopts, as far as possible, the notations of the well-known OMT method, and applies standards. OCTOPUS introduces additional notations only when required by the special constraints of embedded real-time systems.

OCTOPUS is the marriage of object-oriented techniques with real-time systems; it bridges the gap between them. It can help real-time system designers to model, design, and implement their system faster. The resulting system is robust and reliable.

Book Outline

Chapter 1 is an introduction to real-time systems and concurrency models, and includes a comparison to other object-oriented approaches as well as an introduction to the case studies. The OCTOPUS method in a nutshell is the subject of Chapter 2, whereas Chapter 3 deals with the requirements specification, how to apply use cases to capture requirements and how to build a system context model. Chapter 4 deals with the system decomposition: how to divide a large system into a number of manageable subsystems, how to define the interfaces between them and how to develop them incrementally.

Analysis and design of a subsystem is described in Chapters 5 and 6, respectively. The analysis chapter emphasizes the dynamic model and the linkage to the object model. The design chapter provides a clear transformation of the analysis results to a description of the solution. It explains the mapping between objects and processes and the design of the hardware wrapper.

Chapter 7 discusses issues which affect the configuration of the software system, such as priorities of processes and the verification of the timing requirements. Chapter 8 treats detailed design issues and implementation aspects that are specific to embedded real-time systems when using the C++ programming language.

Application of the OCTOPUS method is practically demonstrated in two case studies in Chapters 9 and 10. The first is based on a real telecommunication product and the second is the popular Cruise Control system. The latter can be used to compare OCTOPUS to different methods. The reference manual of this book, Chapter 11, includes a notation summary and OCTOPUS roadmap.

This book can be used in different ways. An efficient way may be to read the whole book from start to finish first and, after that, depending on the phase of the project, to use it as a guide on theory, process and application of the OCTOPUS method. After some time, when the reader is familiar with the method, the case studies and the reference manual of this book are the chapters to which he or she will refer frequently, retrieving some detail.

Acknowledgments

We are very grateful to our employer, Nokia Corporation. Nokia has always achieved its greatest success by innovative application of new technologies in its products. This gave us the opportunity to develop the approach presented in this book and to introduce it successfully in real applications. We are also very grateful to our colleagues in the Software Technology Laboratory at Nokia Research Center for their confidence, continuous support and constructive criticism.

Projects applying the OCTOPUS method were carried out at Nokia Telecommunications and Nokia Mobile Phones. Other projects are still ongoing, and new ones are being planned. We wish to thank all members of those projects for their valuable feedback.

We wish to thank Pertti Lounamaa, head of the laboratory, who has made this book possible by giving us the opportunity and the facilities to develop and experiment with the ideas presented here.

Many individuals helped in the review of the manuscript, but in particular we wish to thank Jorma Kuha and Laszlo Huray. Their ideas and comments are much appreciated. Jorma Kuha also helped a great deal by thoroughly checking all the C++ listings for syntactic and semantic errors. He also helped us in developing macros which facilitated the writing of the book.

We used a CASE tool called KISS, developed at Nokia Research Center. Our thanks to Antero Taivalsaari and to the developers of KISS.

We also would like to thank Mohammed Fayad for triggering us to write this book at a workshop at the OOPSLA '94 conference.

Finally, and most important, we wish to thank our families for their patience and encouragement during the many long weekends and evenings that went into the writing of this book.

Maher Awad
Juha Kuusela
Jurgen Ziegler
Helsinki, Finland
September 1995

1

INTRODUCTION

Software is used to implement more complex behaviors than other technologies, and its development is constrained more by our mental capabilities than physical processes. It is not the technology itself but the conceptual complexity of its application domains that causes problems. Development of software for real-time systems make even harder demands because of their puzzling interaction with the physical world, and the timing constraints and continuous service required.

This chapter briefly introduces real-time systems, discusses object-oriented methods and deduces the rationale for developing the OCTOPUS method. The chapter concludes by a brief introduction to the case studies which are used in examples throughout the book.

1.1 Real-time Systems

Embedded real-time systems support various aspects of modern life. The increased power of microprocessors and steadily falling prices have made digital control systems technically attractive and highly cost-effective. Television sets, cars, instruments and telecommunication equipment are controlled by microprocessors and the related software, which is embedded into the product itself. The user does not see or feel this software. The only indication of its existence is the large set of operations provided by the product.

1

Embedded software has a special characteristic that separates it from other types of software: it is tightly connected to its physical environment. Through sensors and actuators, the control software senses and changes the state of its environment. Embedded software is normally real-time software, because it has to react to many events within the specified time limits.

Real-time software controls the behavior of a real-time system, which must perform the main part of its operation within given time requirements. Accordingly, real-time systems are classified as *hard real-time systems* and *soft real-time systems.* In hard real-time systems, a late response is treated as an error and may cause loss of life or property. Conversely, a response may also be erroneous if it is returned too early. Hard time constraints appear often in control applications, such as sophisticated fly-by-wire systems in aircraft, arm controllers in industrial robots, or automatic braking systems in cars. In soft real-time systems, a late response is normally acceptable. Typical examples of soft real-time systems are communications equipment, such as digital telephone exchanges.

Performance issues are critical in all real-time systems. In the case of soft real-time systems, performance considerations are related to the capability to adequately handle the external load on the system. In hard real-time systems, performance requirements mean the ability to meet all the specified deadlines.

Typically, a real-time system has to perform several different tasks. Some of these tasks are periodic, that is, they are executed at regular time intervals. Other tasks are aperiodic, that is, the need to execute a task may occur at any arbitrary point in time. A real-time system that is able to react to aperiodic requests within given time limits is called *reactive.* Most embedded real-time systems are reactive; that is, they have to be able to react to new events, even if the system is still processing earlier tasks. Thus, competing requests are processed concurrently.

Since embedded systems are connected to the surrounding real world, processor overload may occur. In an overload situation, the performance degradation of the system should take place gracefully. During the shortage of resources caused by an overload situation, some tasks will have to wait for processing. Tasks have been classified into critical, essential, and nonessential. Critical tasks have deadlines that must be met. Essential tasks also have deadlines, but failure to meet them will not cause severe problems. Nonessential tasks are allowed to wait without any specified time limit.

This book addresses the software development of embedded real-time systems. These systems are characterized by soft time requirements. They may contain several processor boards and the development work is done by medium-size, or large teams. If hard time constraints are required, they affect a limited part of the system only.

1.2 Object-Oriented Methods

The object-oriented approach to building a system is based on the definition of a set of communicating entities called *objects*. The object-oriented technology originates from simulation applications [Dahl '69], where real systems are naturally modeled by the simulation software. Through the introduction of Smalltalk [Goldberg '83] and its programming environment, the applicability of object-oriented methods to the development of user interfaces was demonstrated. For some time object-oriented technology was seen as an implementation technique, and it was developed alongside programming languages.

Object-oriented technology has increasingly gained wider interest, and the need to change the focus from implementation issues to software design has become evident. The first step in this direction was taken by the Ada-language community. Booch introduced his method for software design [Booch '87]. On the basis of that work and the ideas behind structured analysis [DeMarco '78], Sally Shlaer and Stephen Mellor introduced their object-oriented analysis (OOA) method in 1985 [Shlaer '85].

The above-mentioned OOA method stimulated a collection of other methods in which the system is based on a conceptual model of the application domain. Such an abstract model clarifies the application by formally organizing and structuring all the relevant information. This model consists of entities, attributes, and relationships. Accordingly, it is called an entity-relationship (ER) graph [Chen '76]. These ER graphs are capable of representing static relationships. However, they are weak in describing other aspects of the application domain. In order to overcome this difficulty, the OOA uses state automatons to describe the dynamic behavior of the system, and data flow diagrams to describe the functionality. All three of the models are similar to structured analysis, although the modeling proceeds in a reverse order.

Among the many derivatives of OOA, the Object Modeling Technique (OMT) [Rumbaugh '91] has been very successful. The OMT relaxes the completeness requirements of OOA and covers the whole life cycle of the system developed by giving guidelines for design and implementation.

Behavior-based methods have been developed as alternatives to the methods based on conceptual models. The underlying idea behind these methods is simple: communication aspects are analyzed first, because in the final stage the system will be composed of a collection of communicating objects. Among the behavior-centered methods, Class-Responsibility-Collaboration (CRC) cards [Wirfs-Brock '90] is the most well known. Object-Oriented Software Engineering (OOSE) [Jacobson '92] can also be seen as a behavior-centered method, because it strongly emphasizes use cases.

The Fusion method [Coleman '93] combines the above-mentioned aspects. It emphasizes the role of entity-relationship graphs in the analysis phase, and the behavior-centered view in the design phase.

The OMT and Fusion methods are the basis for the development of OCTOPUS. The object model notation of the OMT enables compact expression of all the necessary details, and the separation of structural, functional and dynamic aspects makes the models easier to build and understand. Basic separation between the analysis phase, concentrating on describing the external behavior, and the design phase, concentrating on the internal behavior of the application, is borrowed from the Fusion method.

The good features of the OMT and Fusion are maintained in OCTOPUS as far as possible, and combined with techniques that are able to cope with the characteristic problems of software development for embedded real-time systems. In particular, the aspects related to reactive behavior, time domain, and concurrency have been taken into account. OCTO-PUS is not the only attempt to introduce object-oriented methods for real-time systems. We would like to mention CODARTS [Gomaa '93] and ROOM [Selic '94].

CODARTS has its roots in structured analysis and design. Recently, it has been complemented by a component called the *domain model* [Gomaa '95] which adds some more object-oriented flavor. The domain model defines several viewpoints for the analysis of the system. In one of these views, the data flow diagram notation is used to develop object communication diagrams. This shows the flow of data and control between nodes that are called *concurrent objects*. Although positioned in the domain model, the object communication diagram makes a design of the system. Consequently, the design phase starts immediately with structuring the system into tasks, for which CODARTS gives good guidelines. The focus on tasks, and separately on information-hiding modules, matches well with the features of the Ada programming language. Thus, an Ada-based architectural design is the natural result.

ROOM is based on a modeling language that allows building formal design models. A ROOM model consists of actors interacting using messages. Interaction takes place through ports. Each port defines a protocol: the input and output messages and their legal ordering. Since each actor can have multiple ports, ports can also be used to reflect different roles of actors. Composition and layering support the development of more complex systems. ROOM is not a general-purpose method. It is most effective in control-centered applications modeled with static structure.

1.3 Concurrency in a Real-time System

Concurrency aspects always occur in embedded real-time systems. The reason is that concurrency is an inherent feature of real-time applications, and it must be included in every modeling effort. External events may occur at any point in time, even simultaneously, and they must be queued and handled within preset time limitations.

This can be demonstrated by a simple example, which has enough features to enable the demonstration of the concurrency requirements and also assist in the discussion of different ways to model it. Traditionally, concurrent programming was developed for two reasons:

1. Concurrency enables an efficient utilization of the underlying hardware.

2. The concurrency approach helps the designer decompose a single program into separate activities, without being concerned with the exact sequencing of these activities.

These reasons are both important in practice. However, they are defined in the solution domain and do not reflect the inherent concurrency of the application.

Our view of concurrency is demonstrated by the following example. Let us assume that a system S has to react to two different events called E1 and E2 (see Figure 1-1).

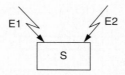

Figure 1-1. System with two events.

To be able to analyze the interleaving of simultaneous tasks, it is necessary to make assumptions regarding the atomicity and duration of the operations performed by the system. The following assumptions are made:

- System S reacts to event E1 by performing a sequence of three unbreakable operations, T1, T2 and T3, each of them requiring one time unit.

- System S reacts to event E2 by performing a sequence of two unbreakable operations, T4 and T2, both of them requiring one time unit.

In addition, let us assume that in both cases the first operation in the sequence is critical, but the succeeding ones are only essential.

- At the occurrence of each event, the system shall start processing the first operation within one time unit, and complete it no later than two time units after the occurrence.

- System S must complete operation T3 no later than six time units after the occurrence of E1. Operation T2 must be completed no later than four time units after the occurrence of E2.

The sequences of operations are assumed to be independent of each other.

Suppose that the following situation appears:

1. At time 0   event E1 occurs

2. At time 1.5   event E2 occurs

3. At time 3.5   event E1 occurs

Any system that reacts to this situation in the required manner is *concurrent*. It must simultaneously handle more than one sequence of operations. If the system is *ideally concurrent*, it is able to process any number of independent operation sequences. An ideally concurrent system reacts to the given conditions by performing the specified sequence of operations immediately after the occurrence of each event (see Figure 1-2).

However, an ideally concurrent system cannot be implemented. Even the approximation of an ideally concurrent system requires vast resources. Embedded systems do not normally have such overwhelming resources due to economic constraints. Thus, it is meaningful to assume that the system contains only one processor, which can only perform one atomic operation at a time. In such a system, overlapped processing is not possible, and the operations must be performed sequentially. The order of the operations in this sequence totally

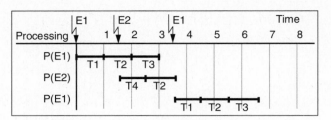

Figure 1-2. Ideally concurrent system.

determines the performance of the system. If the events are handled in a first-in first-out order, the previously given time requirements are not satisfied (see Figure 1-3)

Thus, the system must be able to break the processing of a operation sequence at the completion of any single operation and start processing another sequence of operations, if necessary to meet the time requirements. If this break is made in the manner shown in Figure 1-4, the time requirements can be satisfied even with a single processor.

A system is called *quasi-concurrent* if it meets the concurrency requirements by postponing the processing of one operation sequence in order to process another sequence. In the example, quasi-concurrency of a single processor sufficiently solves the problem and fulfills the requirements.

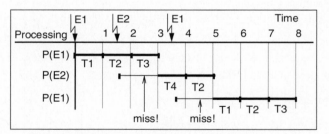

Figure 1-3. No interleaving of processing.

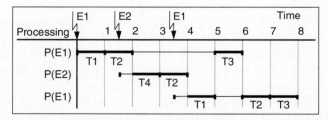

Figure 1-4. Quasi-concurrent system.

1.4 Object-Oriented Concurrency Models

Software development methods are based on modeling. Throughout the development phases a set of models are built, starting from the requirements specifications of the system and gradually adding more details until the system is finally ready for use. In a good method, each model concentrates on the essential characteristics of the system.

Because concurrency is inherent in all real-time systems, it must be included in the model. The development of an object-oriented method requires the modeling of objects. The basic difficulty of applying object-oriented methods to the development of real-time systems is how to combine the concepts of concurrency and object.

An object-oriented approach to concurrency modeling is to use either an *explicit concurrency model* or an *implicit concurrency model*. These two models differ in how and when concurrency is taken into account during the software development work.

The *implicit concurrency model* delays the design of concurrency. The object model as such is the basis of computation. As long as the implementation level is not approached, each object is considered as an autonomous unit, which performs specific actions concurrently with the actions of other objects. Thus, the system is first analyzed and designed as if each object had its own processor providing a thread of execution (see the left side of Figure 1-5). Each external event entering the system is seen as a processing request that broadcasts to some objects, which in turn may request further processing from other objects. Conceptually, any number of objects may actually do some processing in response to a single request. The realization of concurrency is addressed later in the design phase and relies on scheduling of the operations of objects.

The *explicit concurrency model* addresses concurrency first and describes concurrency separately from the objects by using the notion of processes as supported by real-time

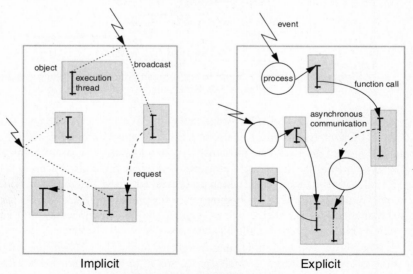

Figure 1-5. Concurrency models.

operating systems (see the right side of Figure 1-5). This model contains two abstraction levels, objects and processes, addressing first the decomposition of the system into quasi-concurrent processes. Inside each process, object-oriented technology is applied to replace the conventional functional decomposition and procedural programming techniques. The interaction of objects is seen and implemented as nested function calls. Explicit synchronization mechanisms, such as locks, monitors, and semaphores, have to be added to ensure the integrity of objects where necessary.

The explicit concurrency model can be applied to the previous example. For that purpose, the system must be decomposed into a set of processes that are able to model the concurrency as required. Initially, two processes are taken to describe the concurrency:

- Any occurrence of event E1 invokes a new incarnation of a process P1, which processes the operations T1, T2, and T3.

- Any occurrence of event E2 invokes process P2, which processes the operations T4 and T2.

The operating system is assumed to be preemptive, and the processes are assumed to have fixed priorities. Process P2 is set at a higher priority level than P1. In addition, the operations must be made unbreakable by the explicit use of the synchronization means of the operating system. These assumptions are described in Figure 1-6.

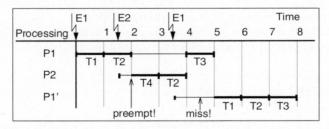

Figure 1-6. A failed attempt to use process priorities to interleave processing.

The first occurrence of E2 is handled correctly. However, when E1 occurs once more, the chosen approach fails, because process P1' cannot preempt its earlier occurrence having the same priority. This difficulty can be avoided by separating the first time-critical operation from the subsequent processing of event E1. This is accomplished by dividing P1 into two processes: P11, which processes operation T1, and P12, which processes T2 and T3. Similarly, P2 is divided into P21 for processing T4, and P22 for processing T2. If higher and equal priorities are assigned to the start-up processes, P11 and P21, the system is able to correctly handle all scenarios of event occurrences (Figure 1-7).

The above example shows that the use of the explicit concurrency model implies the division of the system into many processes in order to meet the external requirements. While this division may benefit functional decomposition, it is harmful for object-oriented

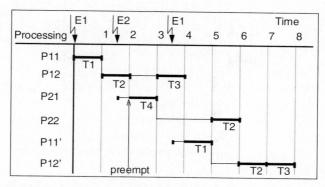

Figure 1-7. Correct use of process priorities to interleave processing.

analysis. Since the division is based on the concurrency requirements, not on the concepts of the application domain, object-oriented technology can be applied only to a limited extent.

What would this example look like if an implicit concurrency model were constructed? The necessary operations are already known. Each operation can naturally be encapsulated as an operation of a single object, resulting in objects O1, O2, O3 and O4 that perform operations T1, T2, T3 and T4, respectively. Furthermore, event E1 requests object O1 to perform operation T1, and O1 in turn requests the execution of T2 from O2, which in turn requests T3 from O3. Similarly, event E2 requests T4 from object O4, which in turn requests T2 from O2. In this way both events provoke a sequence of object interactions, as shown in Figure 1-8.

The implicit concurrency model allows the processing power of each object to be taken for granted. Therefore, concurrent actions between groups of objects do not create any

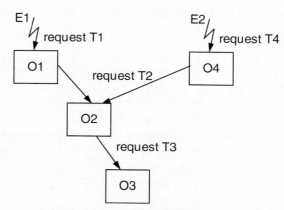

Figure 1-8. Object interaction sequence.

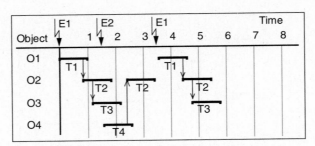

Figure 1-9. Ideally concurrent object system.

problem. At an early development stage, the processing in the system can be envisioned as in Figure 1-9.

Later in the development cycle, one must admit, true parallel processing is not possible with only one processor. To solve this problem, it is necessary to determine how processor time is multiplexed between the objects. The most straightforward solution is to make each operation a unit of processor switching, and to switch the processing at the completion of each operation. In this way, the operations automatically become indivisible. If priorities are assigned so that O1 and O4 are on a higher level than O2 and O3, the processing scenario shown in Figure 1-10 can be deduced.

In this case, only the distinct sequences of object interactions interleave with each other. Thus, these sequences can be regarded as quasi-concurrent. The actions of the objects, as such, are mutually exclusive (i.e., no single action can be preempted). Nevertheless, the resulting concurrency model meets the previously specified time requirements without requiring any additional synchronization means. It should be noted that the requests between the objects, represented by the thin arrows in Figure 1-10, are asynchronous. Either they have to be implemented using the support functions of the underlying operating system, such as a capability of asynchronous message exchange, or the objects themselves are enabled to receive and buffer requests, and to switch the processor between them.

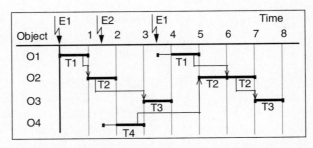

Figure 1-10. Quasi-concurrent object interaction threads.

The multiplexing of processor time between several operations is seldom as easy as in the previous example. The complexity of the scheduling depends on the objects that have been defined. For a given application problem, there may be many object designs that yield a correct description of the system. However, only a few of them have suitable processing characteristics.

In conclusion, the main difference between the implicit and explicit concurrency models is the timing of combining the objects and processes. The explicit model combines them at an early stage. It removes concurrency from the object level by putting processes above objects. This keeps the object domain sequential. The disadvantage is an early need to partition the application into processes. The implicit model postpones the difficulty of implementing quasi-concurrency. This simplifies the analysis phase, but in the design phase the process structure has to be formulated and the synchronization resolved.

The OCTOPUS method uses the implicit concurrency model in the analysis phase (Chapter 5). In the design phase, the concurrency is gradually made more explicit. This simplifies the analysis and still facilitates an efficient implementation. A stepwise procedure is presented for transforming the implicit concurrency model into an explicit model (Chapter 6).

1.5 Levels of Concurrency

In addition to the general capability of modeling concurrency, object-oriented technology enables the definition of three distinct levels of concurrency:

- *Low*: object-interaction concurrency

- *Medium*: interobject concurrency

- *High*: intra-object concurrency

Typically, a higher level includes the lower levels. Figure 1-11 illustrates the differences of the three levels.

An object-oriented system serves external service requests by performing a sequence of interactions between the objects. *Object-interaction concurrency* means concurrent execution of the sequences of these interactions. In its basic form, it is the most restrictive level of concurrency. It means that when an object completes the processing of a request, any other object with a request pending may gain access to the processor next, regardless of where the request of that object originated. Of course, this second object completes the processing of its request before other requests are processed. If several sequences of object interactions are currently running, they may interleave one another according to their priorities. The previous example demonstrated object-interaction concurrency.

Interobject concurrency appears between distinct objects. It means that an operation may be interrupted at some undetermined point when an operation of another object starts running. This includes the case where the objects are instantiated from the same class.

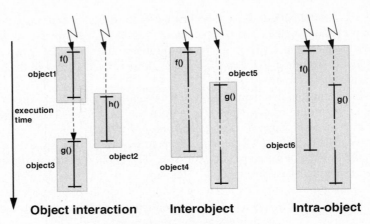

Figure 1-11. Levels of concurrency.

Intra-object concurrency occurs in the same way as interobject concurrency, except that it relates to the operations of a single object. It is the most enhanced level of concurrency.

Any approach to introducing concurrency can be classified [Karaorman '93] into three groups on the basis of the following principles:

- Design of a new concurrent object-oriented language (e.g., POOL [America '87], ABCL [Yonezawa '87])

- Extension of an existing object-oriented language (e.g., Actor [Agha '86], ACT++ [Kafura '89], CEiffel [Lohr '92], Eiffel// [Caromel '93])

- Use of an existing object-oriented language and the addition of a special class library for implementing the concurrency mechanisms (e.g., Choices [Campbell '92], [Colin '91], ROOM [Selic '94]).

Concurrency is a powerful concept that solves some problems of real-time systems. On the other hand, it creates new problems regarding the consistency of data, because the same data can be simultaneously accessed by two concurrent requests on the same object. As the level of concurrency increases, the synchronization problems increase as well. In the case of object-interaction concurrency, one need only deal with synchronization, which is inherent in the external requests. Interobject concurrency requires special caution when accessing global resources. Intra-object concurrency creates the most problems, since it affects the internal consistency of the objects. Whenever operations of the same object are executed concurrently, each operation can proceed properly only if the others maintain the consistency of the internal state of the object. The most obvious solution is to avoid intra-object concurrency by explicitly making the operations of each object mutually exclusive.

1.6 Design Criteria of OCTOPUS

At present, object-oriented methods meet the requirements of embedded real-time systems only to a limited extent. In contrast, OCTOPUS takes care of these requirements, especially reactivity, concurrency and processing of events.

The OCTOPUS approach also supports the development of systems where the object-oriented solution is possibly a part of a non-object-oriented system. A conventional real-time operating system serves as the implementation platform for both. This brings two distinct concepts together: process and objects. The dilemma of merging these concepts is solved by a systematic and efficient procedure that maps objects to processes (Chapter 6). Even if OCTOPUS took an alternative "object-only" approach to provide objects with processing capabilities, like ROOM is doing [Selic '94], the same basic difficulty would remain, because systems built with objects alone may still not be affordable in practice for some time. The decision to use a conventional operating system allows easy construction of a target system that, besides the part developed according to OCTOPUS, may comprise a conventional, non-object-oriented part, as demonstrated in Figure 1-12. This way, earlier investment in software development can be reused.

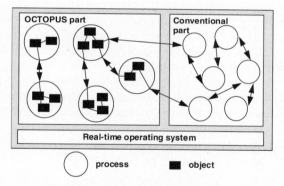

Figure 1-12. A hybrid application.

In the OCTOPUS approach, concurrency is considered as an inherent feature in the application domain. Modeling concurrency is simplified by making it implicit in the analysis phase. The subsequent design phase makes concurrency gradually explicit.

The method introduces additional notations only if required by the special constraints of embedded real-time systems. As a result, OCTOPUS can be supported by all CASE tools that allow adaptation of the notation.

OCTOPUS aims for a well-integrated incremental development process that also covers the requirements specification and the system architecture phase. It provides guidelines for dividing a large system into manageable and potentially distributed subsystems that can be developed in parallel, and for specifying the interfaces between them. The generated models serve essential purposes and complement each other. All that is independent of any implementation language. However, C++ influenced some concepts and terminology.

For practical reasons, distributed applications are not specifically addressed. However, the method can be applied in distributed systems based on a distributed operating system supporting location-transparent message-passing between the objects. Furthermore, OCTOPUS is not primarily intended for safety-critical, hard real-time systems. If, however, only a few hard time requirements exist, application of the method is still practicable and beneficial.

1.7 Introduction to the Case Studies

Throughout the book we use examples from two different case studies: the Subscriber Line Tester and the Cruise Control System. A short introduction to the case studies is given here. A detailed description can be found in Chapters 9 and 10.

Both case studies assume the typical software development situation for embedded systems. The software project is part of a broader system project that is already underway. The system project produced some system specifications, at least in an informal form, and most decisions regarding the software vs. hardware breakdown have been settled. Either the hardware of the microprocessor system and its interfaces to the environment already exist or the design is almost ready at the starting time of the software project. Consequently, those parts are not issues for a requirement analysis of the software project, they are just facts documented in detail elsewhere. The software project will take them into account. The documents of the software project will not recapture these requirements or design decisions, except for cases in which it would improve the result.

1.7.1 Subscriber Line Tester

Telecommunication networks evolve continuously. This evolution creates projects where some functionality needs to be added into existing systems. This case study is an example of such a project.

A subscriber line is a pair of wires. In order to function properly, these wires must be without faults. The Subscriber Line Tester (SLT) is able to measure the electrical characteristics of subscriber lines and to determine their condition based on the measured values. Faulty lines can be disconnected and maintenance action called for.

Subscriber lines used to be connected directly to telephone exchanges. In modern networks, many lines are often connected to remote digital transmission systems, which are digitally connected to telephone exchanges. The SLT described in this case study resides in such a remote digital transmission system (DTS), as shown in Figure 1-13. It is normally controlled remotely, but it can also be operated locally using a PC. The figure also shows a multiplexer unit (MUX) and channel units (CU).

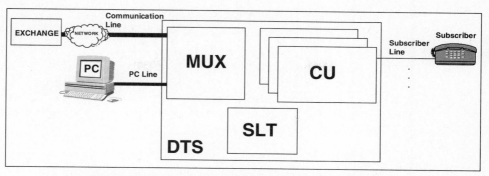

Figure 1-13. A remote digital transmission system (DTS).

1.7.2 Cruise Control System

A cruise control system maintains a car's speed, even over varying terrain, by controlling the throttle. The driver selects the desired speed or auto-accelerates to it but can regain manual control at any time (see Figure 1-14).

Cruise control is a standard example of an embedded real-time system that has been used many times in the literature [Ward '85, Booch '87, Hathley '87, Hoza '89, Pesonen '93 and Gomaa '93] for demonstrating the techniques of different methods. It is interesting to compare those with the application of OCTOPUS and to look at the differences.

The Cruise Control case study found in Chapter 10 covers all phases and components of the OCTOPUS method and produces a complete software system design, including the complete development process at a level of detail that sometimes may seem overly complete for the given level of complexity. However, this nicely demonstrates the OCTOPUS method in all respects.

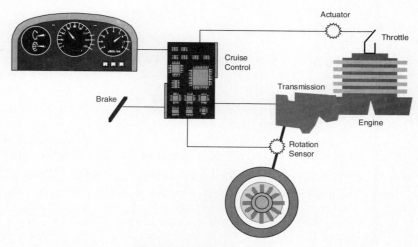

Figure 1-14. Cruise Control.

2

OVERVIEW OF THE OCTOPUS METHOD

This chapter outlines the major aspects of the OCTOPUS method and helps in building an overall picture of it. For a full reference on the method, please refer to the rest of the chapters in this book.

Adopting object-oriented technology can help in the software development of embedded real-time systems in a way that naturally maps to the inherent nature of the systems being built, while providing benefits similar to those already well known and widely reported for the development of other branches of software, such as increased extendibility, reuse and robustness. OCTOPUS applies object-oriented techniques and addresses important problems in real-time systems such as concurrency, synchronization, communication, handling of interrupts, ASICs, hardware interfaces and end-to-end response times. The OCTOPUS method is based on the popular OMT [Rumbaugh '91] and Fusion method, [Coleman '93], but provides additional innovative solutions that ease the application of object-oriented concepts in embedded real-time systems (see Figure 2-1).

Because of the diverse needs of different application domains, an efficient method for software development has to be domain-specific, focusing on the important aspects of its intended application domain—one method for database applications and another for user interface applications. OCTOPUS provides a systematic approach for developing object-oriented software for embedded real-time systems.

Many years of experience in the development of software for embedded real-time systems in a wide range of applications have made valuable contributions to OCTOPUS. Moreover, it has already been successfully applied to many projects in the telecommunications industry.

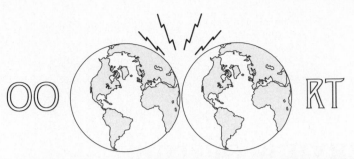

Figure 2-1. Object-oriented concepts are not easily integrated with real-time systems.

OCTOPUS is the marriage of object-oriented techniques and real-time systems. This method can help real-time system engineers to model, design and implement their real-time systems faster. The resulting systems are robust, flexible and reliable.

We selected *OCTOPUS* as the name of the method because an octopus resembles both a software context diagram and a typical real-time system which has a microprocessor and a number of interfaces operating concurrently. OCTOPUS also has two Os.

2.1 The Roadmap and Structuring the Development Process

OCTOPUS has structural, functional and dynamic models at the system, subsystem, class and object abstraction levels. These levels are distributed among the different development phases:

- The system requirements phase (Figure 2-2, Table 2-1) describes the structure of the system's environment by a context diagram, and its functional and dynamic behavior by a use case diagram and a number of use cases. Use cases may be complemented by scenarios between the system and its environment to show the dynamic behavior. The system in this phase is a black box.

- The system architecture phase (Figure 2-2, Table 2-1) describes the structure of the system by a subsystems diagram. The major interfaces between the subsystems are indicated on it as associations. The functional and dynamic models in this phase are delayed to the next phase of software development. They are specified by the functional and dynamic models of all the subsystems this architecture comprises. A subsystem in the system architecture phase is a black box.

- The subsystem analysis phase is done for every subsystem (Figure 2-3, Table 2-1). The structural model is a class diagram of the subsystem supplemented by a class description table. The functional model is a set of operation sheets. The dynamic model contains an event list, an event groups diagram, event sheets, statecharts, actions table, a significance table and possibly a list of compound events. Both the functional and dynamic models treat the subsystem as a black box but can make references to the classes in the structural model.

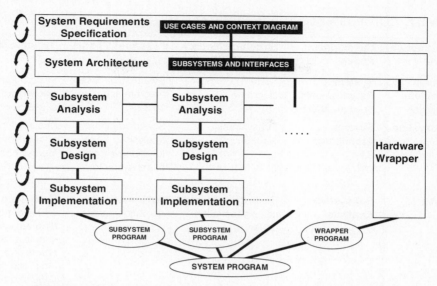

Figure 2-2. Structure of the development process of a software system.

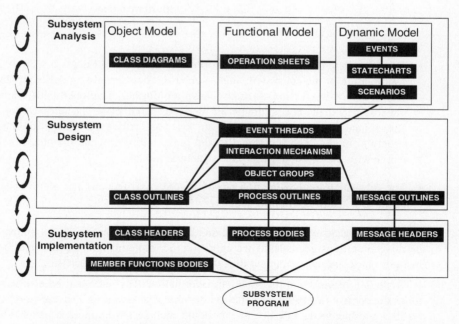

Figure 2-3. Structure of the development process of a subsystem.

Table 2-1. OCTOPUS roadmap.

Abstraction Level	Development Phase	Structural Model	Functional Model	Dynamic Model
System (problem domain)	System Requirements Specification	System context diagram	System use case diagram and use cases	System use case diagram and use cases (scenarios)
Subsystem	System Architecture	Subsystems diagram	Specified in the analysis functional models of subsystems ⇓	Specified in the analysis dynamic models of subsystems ⇓
Class	Subsystem Analysis	Class diagram and class description table	Subsystem operation sheets	Subsystem event list and event groups diagram and event sheets and state charts and actions table and significance table and (compound events) and scenarios
Object	Subsystem Design	Class outlines and process outlines and inter-process message outlines	Outlines of member function which merge into the outlines in the structural model ⇐	Object interaction threads and event threads and object groups

• The subsystem design phase is done for every subsystem (Figure 2-3, Table 2-1). It is a continuation of the subsystem analysis phase. The dynamic model is represented by a set of object interaction threads. These are further developed into qualified event threads, and then object groups are derived. From these the outlines for processes, classes and interprocess messages are systematically built. These outlines form the structural model. The functional model is the outlines of the member function which merge with the class outlines in the structural model.

• The subsystem implementation phase (Figure 2-3). The outlines are translated to code of the selected programming language.

The circular arrows in Figures 2-2 and 2-3 emphasize that the development process is iterative. Iterations decrease as we approach the implementation phase and the iterations inside a phase are more frequent than the iterations between the phases.

Table 2-1 summarizes the roadmap information. The table can be also used to determine the contents of different software documents. Assuming that each row in the table results in a document, that document should include all the models listed in that row in addition to some explanatory text.

2.2 System Requirements Phase

Developing an embedded system includes a large variety of activities not directly related to software, like hardware development, ASICs design, mechanics and many others. These activities take place in subprojects belonging to a master project. The software development is only one of these subprojects. Although software determines most of the functionality, the software subproject typically starts later than the others, and thus, software developers may not have participated in the product requirements specification. This situation typically results in a mixture of requirements documents containing scattered information. Most of the information has little value to the software developer, for example, details about the actual hardware of a system or the lower levels of a telecommunication protocol. For systems that evolve from earlier versions, implementation information often pollutes the requirements documents.

The term *system requirements specification* has been limited to recapturing the relevant requirements for the software. OCTOPUS applies use cases [Jacobson '92] because they allow capturing the requirements in a structured way. We have extended use cases to also cover the autonomous activities, that is, internal activities in the system not explicitly requested by a user of the system (Chapter 3). Use cases are useful in discussions with the developers and managers of other subprojects, and with customers. As Jacobson points out, only through exhaustive examination of the use cases can one be certain that the system provides the required behavior and no undesirable behavior.

In addition, OCTOPUS structures the use cases of the system in a use case diagram which shows the relationships between the use cases. Figure 2-4 is an example from the Subscriber Line Tester (SLT) system.

A use case has a specific structure, as shown in Figure 2-5 with a concrete example, and is built using natural language. A use case can be supplemented by other illustrations, such as scenarios between the system and its users. Use cases are built for all important and nontrivial usages of the system.

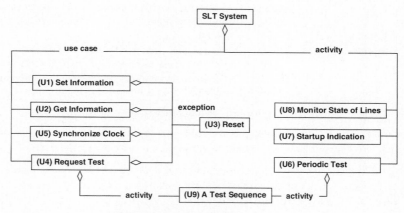

Figure 2-4. SLT use case diagram.

The requirements specification phase concludes by building the system context diagram based on the information from the use cases about the system operations and its actors. The context diagram is a top-level structural view of the problem domain. It shows the relationships between the system and its environment. OCTOPUS extends the context diagram to express important relationships between the actors themselves and uses for that purpose the class diagram notation (Figure 2-6). Relationships are often named after the use cases.

Use Case	*Name of the use case, e.g.,*
	(U4) Request test of a selected subscriber line (voltages, resistance and capacitance).
Actors	*External requesters of the system services or an autonomous activity, e.g.,*
	exchange or PC.
Preconditions	*Conditions that need to be satisfied to do the use case, these do not guarantee that the use case will be successfully completed, e.g.,*
	SLT is running and the requested subscriber line has a test permission.
Description	*Short statement describing the use case including time requirements and exceptions that could happen, e.g.,*
	actor requests the SLT to test a selected subscriber line.
	The SLT responds within 50 ms by an acknowledgment (Accepted | No Test Permission). The SLT then starts a test sequence on the line if it is idle, otherwise it will try later. If a test result is inside the fault limits, then the SLT sends a fault indication to the exchange and PC. Also a failure to establish a connection to a line is reported as a fault as described in U9.
	The request from the exchange must be always serviced first. If a line is being tested because of a request from the PC or periodically, the ongoing test must be postponed and the exchange request serviced.
Subuse cases	
Exceptions	*How the system responds to the exception cases indicated in the Description field, e.g.,*
	exception, no response within the time out: The actor waits another additional 50 ms, if still no response, the actor resets the SLT as in U3.
Activities	(U9) A line test sequence.
Postconditions	*Conditions after the use case is successfully completed and the conditions that apply if the use case is terminated due to an error, e.g.,*
	requested lines are tested and the test results are updated in the memory of the SLT. Any fault found is indicated to the actors.

Figure 2-5. A use case sheet with an example.

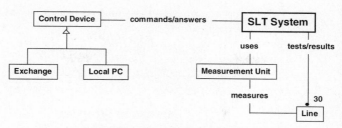

Figure 2-6. SLT system context diagram.

2.3 System Architecture Phase

To handle the complexity of large systems, the system is divided into a number of smaller and more manageable subsystems. The knowledge gained from the use cases describing the system operations and its users, from the system context diagram, from the implementation platform and from the experience in the application domain aids in decomposing the system into subsystems. A subsystems diagram which uses the class diagram notation is used to present the architecture (Chapter 4).

Decomposition into subsystems may reduce the time needed to complete a software project because subsystems can be developed in parallel. It also promotes reuse at a higher and more useful level than at a class level. A whole well-designed subsystem can be reused in another system.

Decomposition into subsystems is not without cost. It necessitates the specification of the interfaces between the subsystems. Therefore, having subsystems that are highly dependent on each other may not be justified. OCTOPUS recommends analyzing the subsystems in parallel before designing and implementing any of them in order to clearly specify the interfaces between them and to verify the system architecture.

A large software system must be developed incrementally. A system increment is composed of one or more subsystems which, when fully implemented, produces a partially operational system that can be tested [Sixtensson '93]. Naturally, the increments are implemented in an order that matches their relative importance. The core increment is implemented first. It is the one on which other increments depend, and without it the system cannot run. An increment can be added to the previously implemented increments until a fully operational system is reached.

Embedded system software typically runs on non- or semi-standard hardware. The structure of the hardware should not drive the design of the software. To reverse the order, OCTOPUS isolates the actual hardware behind a layer of software called the hardware wrapper (Figure 2-7). In an embedded system, a hardware wrapper subsystem always exists. It is treated just as other application subsystems and can be developed in parallel with them.

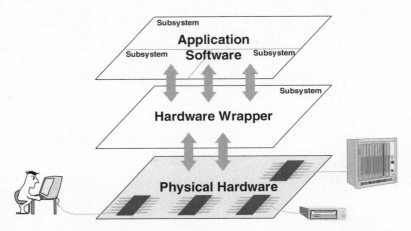

Figure 2-7. The hardware wrapper interfaces to the hardware and application subsystems.

The hardware wrapper contains objects to handle ASICs and other kinds of chips and peripherals. These objects are able to write outputs to these devices and to receive inputs from them. This is based on either polling or interrupts. Interrupt service routines belong to the hardware wrapper (Chapter 5). Other objects in the hardware wrapper provide services to the application subsystems. For example, when an interrupt occurs from a serial line, the hardware wrapper picks the received data from an input register. If the data is not the end of command control character, it is accumulated in a buffer. When the end of command control character is received, the hardware wrapper sends the accumulated buffer contents to the application for interpretation.

2.4 Subsystem Analysis Phase

In the analysis phase, the analyst models the problem to be solved. He specifies the subsystem using the terms and concepts of the problem domain and tries to avoid constructing solutions. All object-oriented analysis models view the subsystem as a composition of objects. These analysis objects are specified only through their classes, and often there is no differentiation between a class and an object of that class. Analysis objects are the concepts of the problem domain.

Analysis objects are able to perform specific actions concurrently with the actions of other objects. Any external event entering the subsystem is seen as a processing request that is broadcast to all objects. All processing is assumed to occur in parallel and in zero time. This view is called the implicit concurrency model. The realization of concurrency is addressed later in the design phase.

In the analysis phase, OCTOPUS uses a similar set of models as that used in OMT. These are the object model, functional model and dynamic model. The three models complement each other. Their different viewpoints enable the analyst to concentrate on one

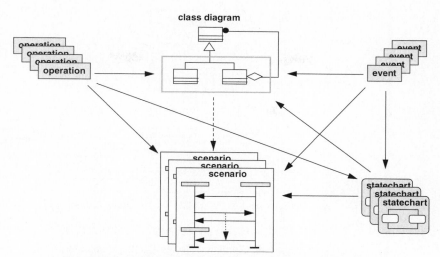

Figure 2-8. Analysis models are associated with each other.

aspect at a time. The relationship between the models is expressed by using the same names of the same components that may appear in different models, and by associating the components of the functional and dynamic models with the classes of the object model (Figure 2-8). Each model uses a set of appropriate notations.

The analysis phase is described model by model. In practice, the order of developing these models is not fixed, and the analyst is free to change his attention from one model to another.

The *object model* defines the static structure of the application being analyzed. It describes the objects of the domain, the relationships (e.g., associations, aggregations, specialization) between them and the relevant attributes of the objects. The object model is central in the analysis, since it defines the common terms that the functional and dynamic models use. The class diagram notation is the standard way to express the object model in a graphical form, as shown in the example in Figure 2-9. The class diagram also shows the boundary between the subsystem and its environment. The analyst describes shortly every class that appears in the class diagram. The descriptions are recorded in a class description table (Chapter 5).

The *functional model* describes the functional interface of the subsystem. This interface consists of a set of named services provided by the subsystem to other subsystems and external agents. A service may require complex interactions between the user and the provider of the service. The functional model does not specify dynamics, that is, when and why the operations are activated, whether they terminate on their own or not and whether they can be carried out in parallel or not. In the functional model, the analyst develops operation sheets to describe the operations of a subsystem (Figure 2-10). These are similar to the operation model schema used in the Fusion method. OCTOPUS does not use the data flow diagrams (DFD) of the OMT method [Rumbaugh '91] because the sheets are easier to build, understand and maintain than the DFD diagrams.

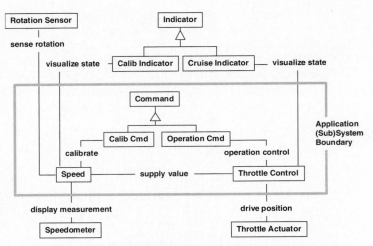

Figure 2-9. Simplified Cruise Control class diagram.

Operation	Name of the operation, e.g.,
	Calculate the actual speed of a car.
Description	*Short statement describing the operation, e.g.,*
	The cruise control system senses rotation pulses. Counting them in a known time interval allows calculation of the car's speed.
Associations	*Associations to the classes and objects and possibly also to the events and states to which it is related, e.g.,*
	class Speed, rotation pulse event.
Preconditions	*Conditions that need to be satisfied to start the operation, these do not guarantee that the operation will be successfully completed, e.g.,*
	measurement rate = 20 Hz.
	> 2 measurement periods completed since start-up.
	kilometer count (KC), either default value or from calibration.
Inputs	*Arguments that an operation needs to perform its intended function, e.g.,*
	rotation pulses.
	rotation pulse count (RC1) of the last measurement period.
Modifies	*What modifications the operation cause on its arguments or on common data in the subsystem? e.g.,*
	Increments rotation pulse count (RC0) of this measurement period.
Outputs	*What information the operation needs to supply its client? e.g.,*
	actual speed (SA), when the measurement period elapses.
	with SA = 10000*(RC0+RC1)/ KC [m/sec]
	Note: SA is average of last two periods.
Postconditions	*Conditions after the operation is successfully completed and the conditions that apply if the operation is terminated due to an error, e.g.,*
	RC1 = RC0

Figure 2-10. An operation sheet with an example.

The *dynamic model* describes the operation of the subsystem across its application boundary and addresses the real-time, reactive aspects. It explains under what conditions the operations are performed and how long they are allowed to take. It captures the order of interactions between the subsystem and its environment needed to perform an operation, and shows what operations are possible in different states and how different operations affect each other. It maintains the benefits of object-oriented analysis and includes other descriptions commonly used in real-time systems. It has steps, and in each step a number of related components are produced:

- Analysis of events: event list, grouping of events, and event sheets

- Analysis of states: concurrent statecharts and actions table

- Further analysis of events and states: significance table and compound events

- Validation of the dynamic model: scenarios for the complex operations

All events are listed and their meanings briefly explained. The complexity resulting from a large number of distinct events is managed by grouping them into superevents. This grouping can be documented using class diagram notation. Figure 2-11 shows an example from the Cruise Control case study. A superevent has subevents and may belong to another superevent at a higher level in the hierarchy. The leaf boxes in the diagram represent the individual events.

A unified event sheet (Figure 2-12) is used to describe every event if there are additions or differences compared to its superevent. In Figure 2-11, for example, if all subevents of superevent **Operation Command** have the same properties, then it is possible to specify them in the event sheet of **Operation Command**, and there is no need to build an event sheet for every distinct operation command.

Dynamic modeling is continued by examining the states of the subsystem and by modeling the transitions between them. Harel's statechart notation [Harel '87] is used to

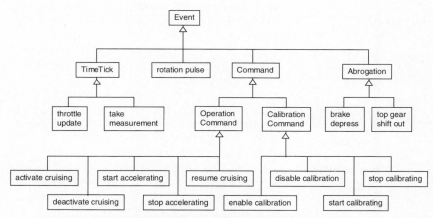

Figure 2-11. Example of grouping of events.

Event	Name of the event or event group, e.g., rotation pulse.
Associations	Associations to the classes and objects and possibly also to the operations to which it is related, e.g., class RotationSensor, class Rotationmeasure
Response	The desired end-to-end response from the (sub)system, e.g., update rotation counting
Source	The originators of the event, for example, other subsystems or the hardware wrapper, e.g., rotation of drive shaft.
Contents	Data attributes that an event may hold, e.g., nothing.
Response Time	The maximum and minimum time limitations concerning the giving of the response, e.g., 4 ms (= two thirds of max. rate).
Rate	The rate of occurrence that can be, for example, at startup, periodic every 10 minutes, timed at 8:00 AM and 2:00 PM, occasional etc., e.g., 0 to 1500 Hz

Figure 2-12. An event sheet with an example.

describe the state-dependent behavior. The notation allows the decomposition of states into substates, as well as allowing transitions to leave or enter states on any level. Figure 2-13 shows a sample statechart. The states in a statechart in which other states are not nested are called elementary states.

Although the use of statecharts reduces the well-known state-blowup phenomenon, modeling the subsystem with only one fully detailed statechart continues to be very difficult. OCTOPUS promotes a tailored use of statecharts that does not result in one complete, huge statechart describing the entire subsystem. A statechart is built wherever it improves

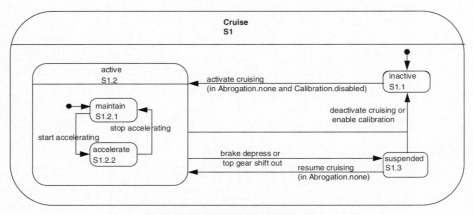

Figure 2-13. Statechart example.

the understanding of some important, sufficiently complex state-dependent behavior. Statecharts are built at different levels of detail, concerning different parts of the subsystem. One statechart may describe a subsystem at a broad level, while another describes a particular class in the subsystem in detail. OCTOPUS also limits the amount of information that is directly shown on the statecharts to prevent them from becoming overwhelming. For example, actions triggered by the events are recorded in a separate table. Statecharts are also associated with the object model.

How significant or important an event is depends on the state of the subsystem. Note, however, that the term *state of the subsystem* means a compound state, that is, a valid combination of the elementary states from all concurrent statecharts. Because the number of compound states can grow very rapidly, OCTOPUS uses an approach that is based on defining the significance of events only in each elementary state. The significance of an event in a particular compound state can then be calculated by multiplying the significance values of the event in the elementary states that make the compound state (Chapter 5). The analyst builds a significance table for the events against the elementary states and specifies in each cell an event significance value. The possible significance values are:

- *Critical (c)*: if the subsystem must handle the activities requested by the event within its time requirements and a failure is not acceptable

- *Essential (e)*: if the subsystem should handle the activities requested by the event but failure to do so is still acceptable

- *Ignored (0)*: if the event can be ignored in all compound states that include this particular state

- *Neutral (1)*: if the event significance value is to be determined by some other state

The dynamic model also includes enhanced scenarios between the subsystem and its environment, such as the one in Figure 2-14. An enhanced scenario shows the sequencing of the events, the timeouts between them, the changes in the subsystem states and the expected activities by the subsystem. The standard message sequence chart (MSC) notation [Z120 '94] is used to present the scenarios. Scenarios serve as a verification mechanism regarding the analysis of the behavior of the subsystem. They are also the starting point for building the object interaction threads in the design phase. The scenarios are built for complex operations of the subsystem, including the error cases where the handling of errors is nontrivial.

2.5 Subsystem Design Phase

The design phase in OCTOPUS is systematic and, after designing the event threads, can be automated. The design phase enables a controlled transition from the implicit concurrency model applied during the analysis phase to the explicit concurrency model, where

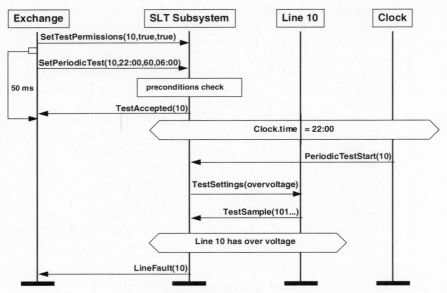

Figure 2-14. Example of a scenario.

objects are mapped to processes of a traditional operating system. The design phase has the following major steps, which are explained later:

1. Design object interaction threads based on the analysis models. Combine and expand them until they become event threads. Continue until the event threads of all events are designed. In parallel, record details in the class outlines.

2. Consider each interaction between the objects in every event thread and decide about the communication mechanism. Asynchronous interactions become interprocess messages, and synchronous interactions become member function calls.

3. Design the concurrency by grouping objects and developing the outlines of the processes associated with the object groups.

4. Verify steps 1–3 by removing inconsistencies, balancing the design decisions and determining how to synchronize the access to shared objects.

During the analysis phase a subsystem, as a whole, responds to events. In design, decide which object receives the event and how it interacts with other objects in order to provide the response (Chapter 6). An object interaction thread is a sequence of object interactions which has one trigger and can be traversed completely by only one thread of execution. If the trigger of an object interaction thread is an event, then it is called an event thread. It is absolutely necessary to build all event threads.

Figure 2-15 shows how the analysis models contribute to the design of event threads: an event starts an event thread, objects are instances from classes in the class diagram,

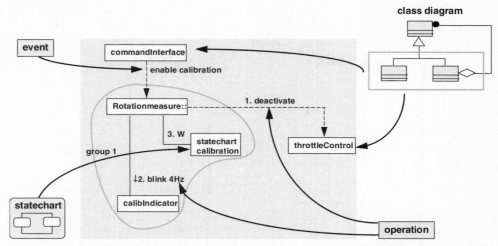

Figure 2-15. Usage of analysis models in the event threads.

operation sheets give indications about the objects responsibilities, and statecharts appear in the event threads and behave just like other objects. Remember also that event threads are the basis for all subsequent outlines of classes, interprocess messages and processes.

Object interaction graph notation [Coleman '93, Rumbaugh '95c] is used to express the interaction of objects in a concise, graphical way (Figure 2-16). OCTOPUS, however, makes a clear distinction between the notation of the graph and the content visualized by it. Object interaction graphs are also used for multiple, overlaid object interaction threads or event threads. Statecharts may appear in the object interaction graph, especially when they are accessed from many objects. The interactions with a statechart are labeled with read (R) or write (W). Figure 2-16 shows **calibration** and **cruise** statecharts alongside other objects.

The purpose of the object interaction graph is to give a high-level overview of the control flow between objects. Details, such as data flow, can be found in the class outlines which are always developed in parallel. Listing 2-1 shows a class outline based on the object interaction thread in Figure 2-16.

```
class Rotationmeasure
    int kilometerCount, calibrationCount; //shared by all subclasses
    int count;
    . . . .
    function disableCalibration()
        calibIndicator.off();
        statechart calibration = disabled;
    endfunction;
    function enableCalibration()
        throttleControl.deactivate();
        calibIndicator.blink(4 Hz);
        statechart calibration = enabled.ready;
    endfunction;
endclass;
```

Listing 2-1. Example of a class outline.

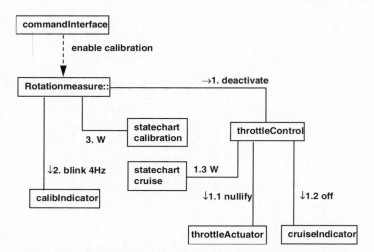

Figure 2-16. Example object interaction thread (event thread).

The event threads are the first step towards the explicit concurrency model. After that, each interaction between two objects is investigated, and a decision is made about the interaction mechanism: synchronous or asynchronous. The resulting event threads are called qualified event threads. The decision about the interaction mechanism is based on the information obtained during the analysis phase. The concurrency between the subsystem states, the time requirements of the events, the significance of events, the expected duration of the requested service and the communication with other subsystems are all factors that affect the decision.

A synchronous interaction is visualized in the object interaction graph by using a solid line, whereas any asynchronous interaction is visualized by using a dashed arrow (Figure 2-17). Asynchronous interactions are implemented using operating system messages. When an interaction that has a return value is converted to asynchronous, a new additional asynchronous interaction is required to carry the return values from the server object to the client object.

Once all event threads have been qualified, the design is continued by mapping the objects into object groups. Grouping is based on the interaction mechanism between the objects; all objects in an event thread which interact synchronously with each other are grouped into a single object group. Grouping starts from an event or an asynchronous interaction (Figure 2-18). This process is repeated for all the event threads in the subsystem. As a result, some objects may belong to more than one object group. The access to these shared objects must be synchronized. Several synchronization mechanisms are possible, and the selection between them is case-dependent (Chapters 6 and 8).

The execution threads of object groups are implemented using operating system processes for which process outlines are developed (Listing 2-2). A process receives the asynchronous messages, interprets them and performs the proper invocation.

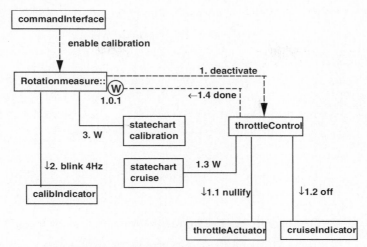

Figure 2-17. Example of a qualified event thread.

Class outlines are modified to reflect the decisions on interaction mechanisms. Wherever asynchronous communication has been introduced instead of synchronous, the original member function invocation is changed into a message to the target process. A return value can be awaited internally after the sending of the message or in the primary wait point of the process (Listing 2-2 and Chapter 6). Listing 2-3 shows the modified class outlines that correspond to Figure 2-18.

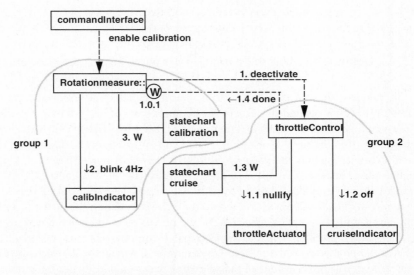

Figure 2-18. The object groups of the example event thread.

```
process function Calib //associated with group 1
    loop forever
       await commandMessage    // primary wait point
       switch commandMessage.id
       enableCalibration:  Rotationmeasure::enableCalibration();
       disableCalibration:  ...
       ...
       endswitch;
    endloop;
endprocessfunction;
process function Throttle  //associated with group 2
    loop forever
       await commandMessage ...
       if   commandMessage.id == calibDeactivate
       then throttleControl.deactivate();
            commandMessage.id = deactivateDone;
            send commandMessage to process Calib;
       else ...
    endloop;
endprocessfunction;
```

Listing 2-2. Process outlines of the example event thread.

```
class Rotationmeasure
    int kilometerCount, calibrationCount; //shared by all subclasses
    int count;
    . . . .
    function disableCalibration()
       calibIndicator.off();
       statechart calibration = disabled;
    endfunction;
    function enableCalibration()
       commandMessage.id = calibDeactivate;
       send commandMessage to process Throttle; //async interaction
       await commandMessage; //internal wait of return value
       if   commandMessage.id == deactivateDone
       then calibIndicator.blink(4 Hz);
            statechart calibration = enabled.ready;
       endif;
    endfunction;
endclass;
```

Listing 2-3. Class outline example with asynchronous communication.

   The process division that results from the object grouping procedure produces processes only where needed to achieve the required concurrency. Grouping objects minimizes the repetition of code in the processes because objects in different processes instantiated from the same class use the same code. A process executes a part of an event thread and encapsulates the parts of the objects covered by it. Therefore, a process can locally make decisions about accepting or rejecting new requests. Synchronization becomes simpler and localized. As a result, interprocess communication may decrease. In conventional functional process division, the access to shared resources is synchronized using an operating system mechanism, or the processes communicate with each other to control access to the shared resources. Figure 2-19 summarizes these differences.

   Once the processes of the system are determined, a systematic procedure enables the designer to derive the priorities of the processes that would best comply with the required

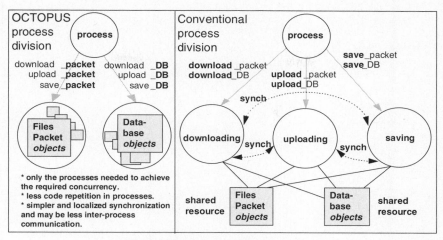

Figure 2-19. Different process divisions.

concurrency. The procedure is based on comparing the processes with each other in a pairwise manner. In each pair, one process is assumed to be running (Pr) and the other to be waiting its turn to run (Pt). In each pairwise combination, the designer decides whether Pt preempts Pr or not. Based on these pairwise decisions, the priorities of the processes can be derived (Chapter 7). Also, the timing and concurrency behavior of the system can be verified based on process priorities and the estimated time consumed by each process. The verification is done for the worst event sequence case before implementing the designs. The design solutions may need to be fine-tuned to achieve the desired behavior.

2.6 Subsystem Implementation Phase

The implementation phase is dependent on the programming language. The headers of the classes and the interprocess messages as well as the bodies of the member functions of the classes and the bodies of the processes are built based on their corresponding outlines from the design phase (Chapter 8). A CASE tool can automate much of this work.

3

REQUIREMENTS SPECIFICATION

Traditionally in the development of information systems, the requirements specification describes the software product to be developed. This description is used as a contract between the customer and the supplier on what the product is to do. Embedded systems are products of which the software is only one part and is made invisible to the user. Consequently, the *product requirements specification* describes the entire product in all its aspects, including electronics and mechanics. Although the software is expected to provide the required functionality using the available hardware resources, this product requirements specification usually ignores software.

The product requirements specification is centered around the user needs and the market situation. It describes manufacturing, pricing, physical appearance, mechanics, electronics, environmental conditions, packaging, operational availability and functionality of the product to be built. Often, external interfaces to other systems are important. In the telecommunications area, external interfaces can be defined by referring to standards of communication protocols. Performance is often also described by providing figures for speed, throughput, availability, and response time. Other nonfunctional requirements like correctness, portability and security are seldom quantified. Other software qualities, like reusability, modifiability and scalability, are only interesting to the provider and are rarely mentioned in the requirements specification document. If an organization attempts to develop a family of products, then requirements for the whole family should be defined so that the requirements for individual products might be seen as specialized cases.

This chapter describes how to represent the requirements in a way that supports software development. The corresponding description is called the *system requirements specification*. In an ideal situation, this is developed as part of the product requirements specification from the beginning. However, it is more realistic to assume that the software subproject starts late, and nobody has taken care that the requirements are in a form suitable for software development. Thus, the developer must extract the requirements specification from already existing documents and from other scattered information sources.

IEEE Recommended Practice for Software Requirements Specifications [IEEE '93] outlines several ways to structure requirements specification: system mode, user class, objects, features, stimulus, response, and functional hierarchy. If your project starts with existing system requirements specification, it could have been written according to the IEEE standard.

Figure 3-1 shows the focus of this chapter. The system requirements specification of the OCTOPUS method primarily includes a structured organization of *use cases* and the *system context diagram*.

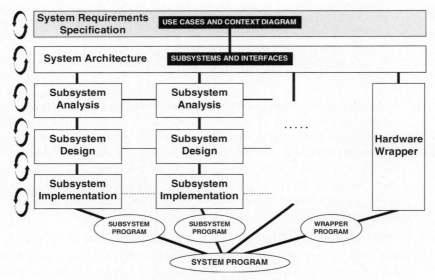

Figure 3-1. The system requirements phase.

3.1 Use Cases

Use cases have been advocated by Jacobson [Jacobson '92]. Now many methods, including OCTOPUS, capture the user's needs as a set of use cases.

Use cases are analogous to the script of a play. They describe the role of each actor in the play and how the actors behave in a scenario. Unlike plays, use cases are alternative and repetitive. However, it is often useful to check their completeness by combining them in a natural order and checking if they actually cover every way to use the system.

Use cases treat the system to be built as a black box. Each use case describes a particular way of using the system. Use cases are goal-oriented. They describe how the system can be used to achieve the desired results. Since any system has a finite set of goals to meet, the number of use cases is always limited.

A recommended practice for finding the use cases of a system is to consider all external agents that interact with it. These agents may be humans or other computers. While interacting with the system, each agent may play different roles. These roles may be very different, like the roles of a telephone user and an operator. An agent playing a role is called an *actor*. Since the role determines the context of usage, use cases are associated with actors. Therefore, start by finding all external agents and trying to distinguish their roles. Then consider their roles one by one.

Actors can be classified in several ways:

- *Active/Passive*: Each use case is initiated by one actor. Some of the actors are passive; they participate in use cases, but never initiate one.

- *Client/ Nonclient*: Actors either use the system for a certain purpose or just affect it. For example, failures of interacting components of a system force it to adapt to the new situation and report the problems. The client of this error recovery use case is often the operator actor, not the failed unit which was the reason for the report.

- *Primary/Secondary*: Secondary actors, like operators, only exist so that the primary actors can use the system. Requirements should be written from the primary actors' perspective in order to make the system user-centered.

Once actors have been identified and classified, consider each of them separately. Primary active client actors should be considered first. Ask yourself:

- What are the main tasks they want to perform?

- When are these tasks applicable?

- What are the exceptions?

- What is the effect of the task?

- What are the timing requirements?

The information about the usage of the system is recorded on a use case sheet such as the one in Figure 3-2. Use cases should show how the system works from the user perspective. Try to be precise and concrete. Emphasize the effects of the operation. Each use case is numbered to make referencing easier.

Use Case	Name of the use case.
Actors	External requesters of the system services.
Preconditions	Conditions that need to be satisfied to do the use case; these do not guarntee that the use case will be successfully completed.
Description	Short statement describing the use case, including time requirements and exceptions that could happen.
Sub Use Cases	References to sub use cases.
Exceptions	Responses to exceptions may refer to exception use cases.
Activities	References to use cases describing the activities taking place during each use case.
Postconditions	Conditions after the use is successfully completed and the conditions that apply if the use case is terminated due to an error.

Figure 3-2. Use case sheet.

Try to describe the intent of each use case clearly. Record any time requirements. Record the final effects of the operation in the postconditions. The preconditions should explain when the use case is applicable. If the preconditions are satisfied, the system will eventually fulfill the postconditions, unless some of the exceptions occur.

Let's consider the Cruise Control case study. The primary active client actor in a car is the driver, and most of the use cases are initiated by him. A secondary actor is the maintenance person.

Before considering individual use cases, their granularity must be decided. A good rule is to handle only one goal in each use case. The Cruise Control system provides three services: cruise control, distance measurements and speed measurement. Speed and lifetime measurements are ongoing activities, but measurement of relative distance is initiated by driver.

Figure 3-3 shows the description of **measure and show actual speed**. Since it is an autonomous activity, the system is the only actor. This is typical. Embedded systems often carry out activities, which are not initiated by actors. These autonomous activities can still be described using use cases. Autonomous activities either are continuous or take place during some user-initiated activity.

Use Case	(U4) measure and show actual speed
Actors	Autonomous activity of system
Preconditions	Engine is running.
Description	The normal speedometers on many cars are inaccurate, and so the system is to measure speed by counting pulses it receives from its own sensor on the drive shaft. Count-rate from this sensor corresponds to vehicle kilometers per hour through a proportionality constant. Based on the resulting value, the system continuously drives a speed-displaying unit at the driver's console either via an analog signal proportional to the speed or a digital output in 8 parallel lines.
Exceptions	(1) Engine is switched off: stops measurement.
Postconditions	Engine is running.

Figure 3-3. Services provided for driver.

3.2 Use Case Diagram

Use cases can be hierarchically composed from parts. Use cases not only have sub use cases, but they often share exceptions or subactivities. If this hierarchy is utilized, specification is shorter and easier to understand. Hierarchy can be visualized in a *use case diagram* using the notation of the object diagram (see Figure 3-4). The diamonds denote "parts of" relations and the names indicate whether the parts are sub use cases, subactivities or exceptions. The identification of use cases, the development of the structure of use case diagrams and the specification of use cases are interleaved activities. You may need to restructure the use cases later.

In the Cruise Control system, the services provided to the primary actors are collected into a use case diagram as shown in Figure 3-4.

In the case study, the role of the only secondary actor, the maintenance person, is to calibrate the system. Therefore, the use case **calibrate for 1 kilometer** is added.

The whole system can be described using only these use cases, but some of the use cases would be very complex and there would be much repetition. Notice that both **U2** and **U5** in Figure 3-4 depend on the **measure distance driven** activity. **U1** is the most complex use case and has to be decomposed.

The main activity of a cruise control system is to maintain the selected speed. However, the system is also able to automatically accelerate to a new cruise speed. This acceleration can be viewed as a sub use case of **U1**. Since the acceleration is constant, the sub use case has an independent activity, **maintain acceleration**. The result is summarized in Figure 3-5.

However, it is not enough to concentrate only on added functionality. You should also describe how the new functionality mixes with old services provided by the system. In this case, it is interesting to know how automatic speed control mixes with manual speed control:

• Intermediate accelerating with the pedal

• Intermediate reducing of speed with brake

• Suspension of cruise control by transmission

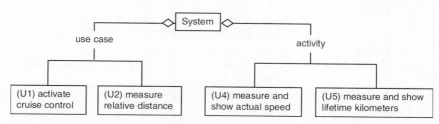

Figure 3-4. Services provided to the primary actor, the driver.

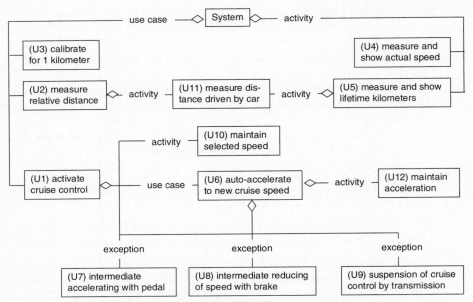

Figure 3-5. Decomposition of the functionality of the system.

These exceptions are common to both cruise control and auto-acceleration, so it is sufficient to specify them only once. Figure 3-6 shows an example of this. The activate cruise control consists of five different use cases which can also be seen in Figure 3-5.

Use Case	(U1) activate cruise control
Actors	Driver
Preconditions	Engine is running. Transmission is in top gear. The car's speed is at least 40 kilometers per hour. Brake is not pressed.
Description	When the driver gives an activate command, the speed at which the car is traveling at that instant is maintained.
	The driver may deactivate the cruise control at any time by a deactivate command. This returns control of the car's speed to the driver regardless of what has been done before.
Sub Use Cases	(U6) auto-accelerate to new cruise speed
Exceptions	(U7) intermediate accelerating with pedal
	(U8) intermediate reducing of speed with brake
	(U9) suspension of cruise control by transmission
Activities	(U10) maintain selected speed
Postconditions	Cruise control is active. Throttle is positioned unattended; pedal can be released.

Figure 3-6. The activate cruise control use case.

In a large system, it may be useful to decrease the amount of work by combining use cases. Similar use cases can be described on one sheet. In the SLT case study described in Chapter 9, the use cases **get information** and **set information** are examples of combined use cases. Use cases can also be extended. Extension adds new behavior into a complete base use case, without repeating the base case.

Each use case involves an interaction between the actors and the system. Interactions may be complex and may involve other actors. Each use case potentially describes a large set of different interaction sequences. Several different interaction sequences may achieve the correct result, and exceptional cases are often numerous. Since different interaction sequences are later analyzed in detail, it is not necessary to describe them in depth in the requirements specification.

3.3 System Context Diagram

Use cases help in specifying the functionality of the system. They also require the analyst to think and define what actors are using the system. This information is used to construct the system context diagram, which gives a structural overview of the system's environment. The context diagram shows the actors and how they are related to the system. OCTOPUS enhances the expressiveness of the context diagram, well known from structured analysis, by allowing it to show important relationships between the actors. This is easily achieved using the class diagram notation (Chapter 11).

Figure 3-7 shows the Cruise Control system context diagram, which demonstrates a number of interesting relationships between its actors. These relationships enhance the context diagram which become valid for different Cruise Control products with some variations in configuration. For example, the Cruise Control system has a console. By using the aggregation symbol we are able to express that a console is composed of a speedometer, two odometers and up to two indicators. The speedometer can be either analog or digital; this is expressed using the inheritance symbol. Also, if an actor plays different roles, it can be easily expressed using the inheritance symbol. Other relationships between the actors are shown as associations. For example, the driver actor uses the brake actor to reduce the speed. Associations are often named after the use cases.

The level of detail in the system context diagram can vary, but it should always contain all the actors mentioned in the use cases of the system. It does not matter if an actor is primary or secondary, active or passive, client or nonclient.

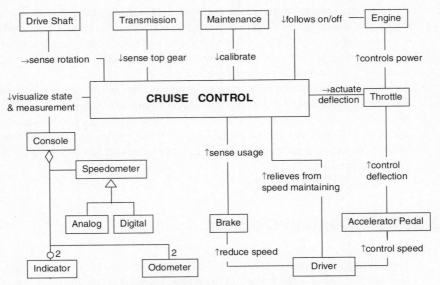

Figure 3-7. Cruise Control system context model.

4

SYSTEM ARCHITECTURE

System architecture has two parts: hardware architecture and software architecture. If the system is addressed as a whole, these architectures are developed together—hardware and software are codesigned. Hardware/software codesign is a complicated matter which involves integration of different modeling techniques [Kronlöf '93]. In practice, the software and hardware designs are often separated, and hardware design precedes software design. The use of standard hardware components or the use of hardware from earlier versions of the same product are often the reasons for this. Even if hardware is specially designed for the system, its design is often controlled by nonfunctional arguments like the cost or power consumption of the components. Software design affects the hardware structure only if it turns out to be unfeasible to implement the desired functionality on the given hardware. Most of the time, the hardware structure and its peculiarities are treated as additional constraints for software.

However, external requirements and hardware requirements have to be separated. Otherwise, the structure of the hardware would drive software design, and the design would become very sensitive to changes in the hardware. To reverse the order, the OCTOPUS method isolates the hardware behind a software layer called the *hardware wrapper*. Parts of the analysis and design of the hardware wrapper can be postponed until the requirements placed on it by application software are known. The hardware wrapper handles the hardware and provides services to the application subsystems (Figure 4-1). This is treated in detail in Chapters 5 and 6.

Embedded systems are often developed as a family of products. The products in the family may differ for unavoidable reasons, such as differences in communication stan-

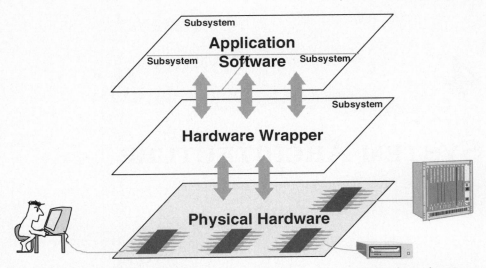

Figure 4-1. The hardware wrapper interfaces to the hardware and application subsystems.

dards, supply voltages or safety regulations. Often the differences are used to broaden the customer base by varying the functionality, capacity, outlook and price of the products. Despite these differences, it is essential to be able to develop the family as a whole. The inability to do so will radically increase the cost of development. This causes variance in the software controlling the product. If the product is developed as a family, software architecture is similar in all products. Architecture is design at the level of abstraction that focuses on the patterns of system organization which describe how functionality is partitioned and the parts are interconnected [Shaw '90].

Each product in the family has to satisfy its functional and nonfunctional requirements. The software must be efficient enough in terms of time and space; it must be as responsive and as reliable as required. Often, the nonfunctional and some of the functional requirements are similar throughout the whole family of products, and the architecture of the family must support these requirements. The architecture should also possess qualities related to the software development process. It should be easy to extend and modify the architecture to develop and test new products based on it. Qualities like extendibility, portability, or testability are determined by the architecture. Figure 4-2 shows the focus of this chapter within the software development cycle.

4.1 Modular Structure

Software architecture is traditionally understood as the modular decomposition of the system. Such a definition for software architecture has four parts:

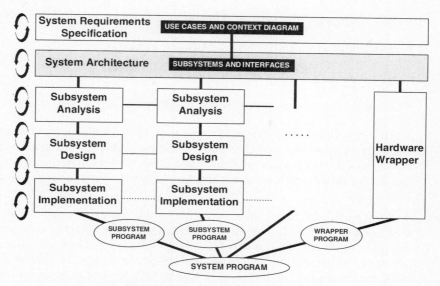

Figure 4-2. The system architecture phase.

- Modular structure of the system

- Module interfaces

- Communication mechanisms

- General control strategy

This top-down view of software architecture is very useful because it supports early separation of concerns. If modules are weakly coupled, they can be developed and tested almost independently. However, this definition of software architecture is restricted to high-level design. In reality, architectural decisions are made at all levels of detail, and often the fine-grained decisions determine the qualities of the system. Consider, for example, portability. The decisions that undermine portability include use of nonstandard language features, special operating system features and special hardware services. To achieve portability, these dependencies must be encapsulated behind a generic interface. There must also be a known policy to reduce dependencies, and it must be strictly followed. Since a very small detail may undermine portability, the policy is an essential part of a software architecture supporting high portability.

OCTOPUS contains a set of policies, and if these are followed as such, the resulting architecture will:

- Base modularization on concepts of the domain

- Use objects as a mechanism for structuring the software

- Use explicit concurrency in terms of light-weight processes

- Base the process structure on the time requirements of the external events

- Base control mechanism between processes on messages

- Base data sharing on the use of single address space

- Separate the hardware layer from the application

This architecture is applicable to many embedded systems. It provides efficiency and responsiveness, and it supports several decoupling mechanisms. Another architecture can be achieved if other policies are defined and followed. Note, however, that the further the architecture drifts from the one described above, the harder it becomes to use the OCTO-PUS method.

Since architecture determines the decomposition, interaction and overall control policies, it can be supported on the design and implementation levels by capturing the interaction and control mechanisms in a *framework*. A framework is a generic implementation which can be specified by adding the product-specific details. Techniques used in framework construction are described in [Johnsson '92]. Several frameworks for well-understood domains (like the graphical user interface) are available.

4.2 Early Division into Subsystems

In a large system it is desirable to share analysis work among several teams. This can be achieved by dividing the system into smaller subsystems, then analyzing and developing these subsystems independently. Early division involves risk. System-level requirements are not well defined before the division, and it may be difficult to satisfy them using the chosen subsystem structure. Early division also increases the work. Subsystems do not partition the conceptual space of requirements. The same requirements will be analyzed several times. Common concepts in different subsystems will result in multiple classes having similar names but different definitions, which is a problem for further evolution of the system. Also, the subsystem interfaces will evolve as understanding of the requirements increases.

If the analysis work has to be divided, a good way to ensure reasonable independence between subsystems is to use different domains as different subsystems. A domain is "a separate real, hypothetical or abstract world inhabited by a distinct set of objects that behave according to the rules and policies characteristic of the domain." In the object-oriented world, this concept is promoted by Shlaer and Mellor [Shlaer '92]. Since the concepts in a domain are defined within that domain and make sense only in that domain, domains partition the concept space. Moreover, since the domains are independent, subsystem division based on domains results in subsystems that can run independently and concurrently. They may potentially be distributed.

As an example of partitioning a system into subsystems based on domains, consider a system controlling a chemical process. You can immediately recognize the following domains:

- Chemical domain: model of the process to be controlled

- Device domain: sensors used to get feedback and actuators used to affect the process

- Operating system domain: concurrent processes, event handling and communication between processes

- Database domain: data storage and queries

- User interface domain: windows, menus, icons and dialog boxes

These domains can be analyzed separately and implemented as separate subsystems. However, since the domains are distinct, it is possible to provide separate support for them. Actually, all the domains listed above are general enough to be interesting in many applications; thus, operating systems, databases, user interface frameworks, device drivers and even chemical process modeling frameworks are available. The task of developing a system for such a process control can be seen as an integration task. Note also that the independence of domains promotes layered architecture (see Figure 4-3).

In the process of searching for different domains it is useful to consider services used by the application. If these services involve concepts which are not part of the application, they indicate the existence of a separate service domain. Most of the domains in the chemical process example are service domains.

Large domains are rather independent. They are routinely implemented as separate subsystems and have standard interfaces to other subsystems. In a large and complex system, it is also necessary to identify smaller domains like fault-tolerant computing, performance monitoring or alarm handling. These domains depend on the structure of other domains and will not be as independent as large domains. Since these domains are often not implemented as separate subsystems, they have no standard interfaces.

As an example, consider fault-tolerant computing. Embedded systems are often required to continue operation despite problems in their environment and even to sustain hardware failures to some extent. However, the domain of fault-tolerant computing is seldom separated. Instead, the recognition of the fault and the recovery actions are designed and implemented as parts of the application. Separation of this domain would ease the

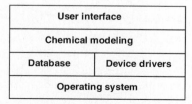

Figure 4-3. Layered architecture for control of chemical processes.

development of the application and would guarantee uniform behavior, but it is hard to provide widely acceptable support for fault-tolerant computing.

One possibility is to provide fault-tolerant processes on a multiprocessor network through replication of computing units and secure communication. Each fault-tolerant process runs on two different processor cards, and the replicas are kept in "hot standby" by also routing all the messages to the replicas. Once a computer unit fails, the replicas take over the role of the original processes on the failing unit. New replicas are initialized for them and alarms signaled.

The interface of this fault-tolerant subsystem consists of a simple registration procedure, but its structure is very much related to the structure of the overall control mechanism used in the system. No wonder fault-tolerance services are typically implemented as an addition to an operating system and not sold separately.

Once a domain has been identified, it can be tested by questioning its independence of other domains. If the domain is independent it should be possible to imagine several different implementations for it, and it should be possible to sell a package providing its services.

Before the analysis of domains is continued, the system decomposition into subsystems based on these domains should be considered. The control should be defined and the interfaces between the domains designed. The system can be shown as a set of subsystems connected by client/server relationships (see Figure 4-4). The arrows point to the server domains.

In practice, division into domains in not sufficient. Domains tend to be large, and often commercially available solutions exist for them. In our example, failure to reuse existing solutions for database, operating system and user interface parts would radically increase the cost of the system. However, the chemical modeling and device control parts are still large problems, and further subdivision is needed. Further division can be based on finding functionality clusters. The clusters of related functions are not as separate as domains, but will still give some division of work.

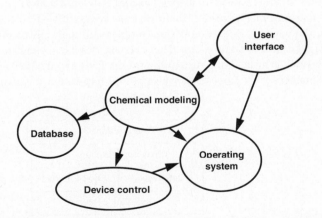

Figure 4-4. The relationships between the chemical plant process control system.

4.3 Subsystems Diagram

The object model notation can also be used to describe the decomposition into subsystems. As shown in Figure 4-5, OCTOPUS separates the hardware wrapper from the other subsystems. Client/server relations between subsystems can be shown as associations.

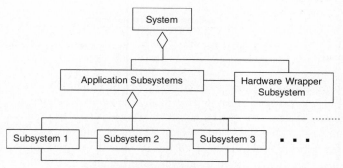

Figure 4-5. Subsystems diagram.

4.4 Incremental Development

Decomposition into subsystems may reduce the time needed to complete a software project because subsystems can be developed in parallel. It also has other positive organizational and management effects: the distribution of tasks to the project members becomes easier and more flexible. It is recommended that each subsystem be allocated to at least two designers [Sixtensson '93].

Decomposition into subsystems promotes reuse at a higher and more useful level than the class level. A whole, well-designed subsystem can be reused in another system. For example, a subsystem for remote downloading of files in a telecommunication network can be designed in such a way that the dependencies on the specific telecommunication protocol and the underlying hardware are implemented in their own subsystems. In this case, this download subsystem can be configured for use in different products and according to different telecommunication protocols.

Decomposition into subsystems is not without cost. It necessitates the specification of the interfaces between the subsystems. Therefore, having subsystems that are highly dependent on each other may not be justified. OCTOPUS recommends analyzing the subsystems in parallel before designing and implementing any of them in order to clearly specify the interfaces between them and to improve the original decomposition into subsystems. The responsibilities of some subsystems might change, two subsystems that are highly dependent on each other might merge, or new subsystems may be defined.

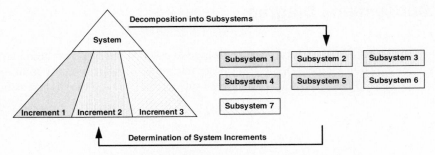

Figure 4-6. Subsystems and system increments.

A large software system must be developed incrementally. A system increment is composed of one or more subsystems which, when fully implemented, produces a partially operational system that can be tested [Sixtensson '93]. In Figure 4-6, for example, subsystems 1, 4 and 5 make up one system increment, and subsystems 2 and 3 another. A system can become usable even if all the increments are not implemented. Naturally, the increments are implemented in an order that matches their relative importance. The core increment is implemented first. It is the one on which other increments depend, and without it the system cannot run. An increment can be added to the previously implemented increments until a fully operational system is reached.

4.5 Interfaces

The architecture should be described in more detail. Several possible control and data flow mechanisms exist, and different mechanisms can be combined. Control can be either explicit or implicit, but it should be based on the use of operating system services if they are suitable. Data sharing can be based on messages, procedure calls or common memory. For different architectural alternatives you may refer to [Garlan '93]. Subsystems should be reasonably independent. Excessive communication is a warning sign.

The description of the interfaces should be tuned according to the control mechanism. Typical architecture for embedded systems is based on reactiveness: the control is often event-driven, and operating system messages are used to implement the events. Try to select the mechanism so that message encoding and decoding does not eat up the performance.

The subsystem interfaces are defined in the analysis. The functional model describes the services, and the dynamic model shows how the subsystems interact. There is also a relationship between the subsystem interface and its object model. The interface can be seen as a collection of services provided by the objects in the environment of the subsystem (see Figure 4-7). Relationships to other subsystems are visible in the object model as relationships to the objects in the environment. This makes it possible to show the

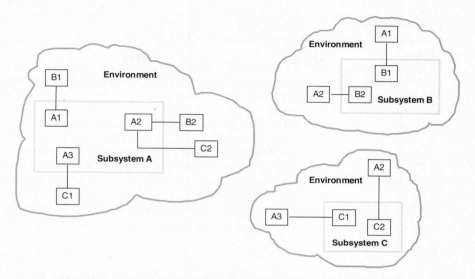

Figure 4-7. Subsystem interfaces as objects in their environments.

nature of the relationship between subsystems and, later, the exact interface needed by this relationship.

Since subsystem interfaces are described as a result of analysis, but subsystem division is determined before analysis, there is a need to iterate between architectural design and analysis. In particular, the groups analyzing subsystems in parallel which are known to be associated should coordinate their work.

The correctness of subsystem division can be checked by taking each use case of the system and drawing a message sequence chart showing how the subsystems communicate. It should be easy to understand the responsibilities of each subsystem. Pay attention to the coherence of services provided by subsystems.

4.6 Example

4.6.1 Decomposition into Subsystems

This example shows the subsystem division of SLT based on the domains covered by the system. The example is based on the requirements presented in Chapter 9. Division into subsystems before analysis involves a risk, and SLT is too small of a system to justify this, but larger systems are hard to fit into a book. The monitoring functionality (Figure 4-8) has been added to the requirements of SLT to make this example larger.

The problem statement shows that SLT has two external interfaces: exchange and PC. It also has internal interfaces to the channel units and to the measurement hardware. The

Use Case	Signal Monitoring
Summary	Starts and stops signal monitoring.
Actors	PC.
Preconditions	SLT is running and its clock is synchronized.
Description	The actor requests the SLT to monitor the signal bits of a selected number of lines. The requests also include the monitoring period (e.g., 1 minute).
	The SLT starts/stops monitoring the requested lines. When the SLT is monitoring, it sends the line numbers and their signals to the PC with a time stamp after each change in signal. The PC stores the sequence of signals in a file. The SLT must respond to the request within 10 ms.
Exceptions	Signal transfer not started within the time out: The actor waits another equivalent period. If there is still no answer, it resets the SLT.
Postconditions	Signal transfer is ongoing until stopped or monitoring period elapses.

Figure 4-8. Signal monitoring

use cases show that the main task of SLT is testing the lines. The other activities are signal monitoring, clock synchronization, reset, and storage handling. Since SLT reports the test results on request, it must store the results.

The separate domains covered are the protocols used in communication, the control of the hardware, the storing and retrieval of results, and measuring and monitoring (Figure 4-9). Measuring and monitoring are separate tasks, but they are not totally separate domains. They have some concepts in common, such as telephone lines.

The separation of the hardware control is built into the method (see Chapters 5 and 6). In this case study, storage handling is so trivial that separate analysis of the storage mechanism will hardly speed up the work. Storage handling will be considered within the Mea-

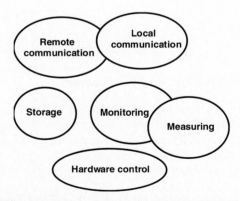

Figure 4-9. The domains covered by the SLT.

suring domain. The following subsystems result: Remote communication, Local communication, Monitoring and Measuring.

Other issues to consider in defining the subsystems are the overall control, interfaces between the subsystems and performance. This system is implemented using a single processor running a real-time operating system. The scheduling mechanism of that operating system can be used to implement the overall control.

Two communication mechanisms exist between processes: messages and shared memory. Since we decided to use the operating system for the overall control, we must use messages to control the execution order. Shared memory is an efficient way to transfer information if locking is needed only for an acceptable period. To make the system efficient enough, we decide to base the interfaces on shared memory whenever needed and use messages to pass commands.

The use cases get information, set information and synchronize the clock in the SLT set rather strict timing requirements for the system. They can be handled by directly accessing the information in the communication subsystems. Similarly, the status of the system can be directly accessed. The use cases left are Reset, TestLine and SignalMonitoring.

These use cases show that the commands issued by the PC and the exchange differ only in signal monitoring. Signal monitoring also causes other problems. It is continuous and cannot be handled by a collect-store-access pattern. We will need a mechanism to transfer the information from the Monitoring subsystem to the Local communication subsystem continuously. Whatever mechanism we use, it will make our system architecture more complex. If we use messages to pass the continuous flow we will tie the control of the Local communication and Monitoring together. These subsystems will lose their independence.

This complication can be avoided if we place monitoring in the Local communication subsystem. With this change we only have three subsystems left: Local communication, Remote communication and Measuring. We have also made the interfaces between Measuring and the other subsystems similar. At this point, we could decide to join the Remote communication and Local communication subsystems. Since these subsystems are rather large, independent and different, they will be kept separate (see Figure 4-10).

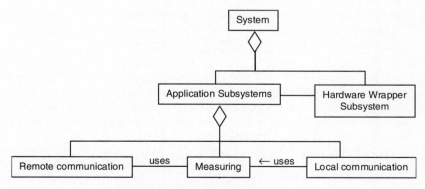

Figure 4-10. The subsystems of SLT.

4.6.2 Subsystem Interfaces

The information flow from the Communication subsystems (remote and local) to Measuring is straightforward. The test request and the reset request are passed on as commands. Settings are handled via shared memory.

The decision to use shared memory access to implement the *get information* use case takes care of almost all of the information flow from the measuring subsystem to the other subsystems. The only remaining information is the indication of a faulty line and the indication of an interrupted test. We could base that also on shared memory access by letting the interfaces continuously poll the status of lines. Such a solution would cause some execution inefficiency, and we would need a separate mechanism to prevent multiple indications of the same fault. More important, it would invalidate the command-driven nature that both interface subsystems currently have. We therefore decide to allow the measuring subsystem to notify us about the faulty lines and the termination of tests to the Communication subsystems.

The interfaces between the Measuring subsystem and the Communication subsystems are similar. They use the commands in Table 4-1 and access the shared information in Table 4-2.

Table 4-1. Commands to the Measuring and Communication subsystems.

From	To	Command
Communication	Measuring	Reset()
Communication	Measuring	TestLine(LineNumber:int,Request:[PC,Exchange])
Measuring	Communication	TestDone(LineNumber:int, Status:[Completed|Interrupted])

Table 4-2. Shared memory access to Measuring and Communication subsystems.

Read	Write	Information
Communication		Hardware and software IDs
Communication	Measuring	Test results
Communication	Measuring	List of faulty lines
Measuring	Communication	Fault limits
Measuring	Communication	Test permissions
Measuring	Communication	Periodic tests
Measuring	Communication	Clock settings

With these interfaces we have established a simple overall control for the SLT. The communication subsystems handle the interfaces. They are command-driven, and they are always able to respond immediately. The measuring subsystem schedules the test requests and performs the tests. Command interfaces are narrow, and information flow through shared memory is always unidirectional.

The resulting subsystems and their responsibilities are:

• Local communication—Interpreting the commands from the PC and answering immediately. Handling the signal monitoring.

- **Remote communication**—Interpreting the commands from the exchange and answering immediately.

- **Measuring**—Scheduling the test requests, measuring and storing the results. Announcing completion or termination of tests to the communication subsystems. Also perform the periodic tests.

Later in the analysis of the **Measuring** subsystem, we found a logical conflict in the interface provided by the SLT. The requirements are written so that the exchange does not need to recognize any local operation activated through the PC. However, it is also possible to issue the reset command from the PC, and during the reset the SLT will not be able to react to the remote commands from the exchange. This may lead to new resets, and in the worst case the exchange may even consider the SLT faulty. Reset also allows local operation to take precedence over remote operations, which is against the spirit of the specification. The solution in this case is to inform both controllers about the reset.

This is an example of a problem in the specification. Problems in the specification should be found in the analysis phase. However, this problem is related to the system as a whole and may pass through the analysis of the subsystems undiscovered. If you divide your system into subsystems before analysis, try to find out how the subsystems interact as a whole.

5

ANALYSIS PHASE

The analysis phase concentrates on the problem to be solved. The requirements specification and the application domain of the system are inspected and, based on the results, a model is built for the system and its environment. Even though the analysis model is neither formal nor complete, it is clearly more structured than the requirements specification. During the analysis phase, the requirements specification should be clarified, and different requirements validated. The questions are what to model and how to model it. Get acquainted with the requirements specification and other material describing the system and the problem domain. Also, investigate the designs of other systems in the same problem domain.

The goal of analysis is to understand the problem and to document that understanding. Do not try to construct a solution. Specify the system using the terms of the problem domain, not using the terms of the solution. Analysis models are descriptive models, and the notations used are declarative. Do not try to use analysis models to describe computations. All these models view the system as a composition of objects. Analysis objects are not very precise. They are specified only through their classes, and often there is no difference between a class and an object of that class.

The computation model used in analysis is very relaxed. Analysis objects are somehow able to satisfy the functional and dynamic requirements. The responsibilities of individual objects are not explicit, and there is no description of how different objects are notified, how objects communicate or how the desired concurrent behavior is achieved. However,

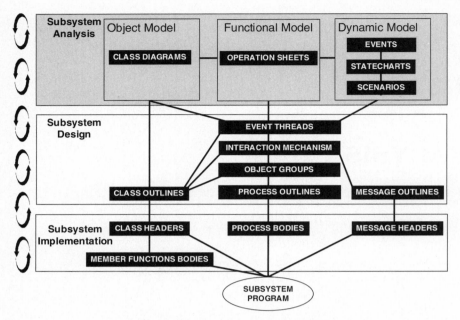

Figure 5-1. The viewpoints in analysis phase.

the requirements for the behavior of the system as a whole should be stated precisely, and all information relevant to the problem should be recorded.

In the analysis model, OCTOPUS uses the same high-level structure as OMT [Rumbaugh '91]. The system is modeled from three different viewpoints: structural, functional and dynamic (see Figure 5-1). Each view uses a set of appropriate notations. The structural model is also called the object model.

The *object model* shows the structure of the problem. It describes the objects of the domain and the relationships between them. It is central to the analysis, since it defines the terms that all the other models use. Classes are described in a class description table, and their relations are shown in a set of class diagrams. Class diagrams also show the boundary between the subsystem and its environment.

The *functional model* describes the operations and their effects. Operations are associated with the objects participating in their realization.

The *dynamic model* explains under what conditions the operations are performed and how long they are allowed to take. It captures the necessary order of interactions between the system and its users and shows what operations are possible in different states and how different operations affect each other.

At least two sets of analysis models are built, one for the application subsystem and one for the hardware wrapper. If the system is divided into more application subsystems, each is analyzed separately. The subsystems are not completely independent, and the relationships between subsystems affect the analysis. Some objects from other subsystems are visible as interface objects in the class diagram, and the application boundary separates different subsystems. The functional and dynamic models describe the operation of a subsystem across the application boundary; they define the interface.

The analysis phase is described model by model as a sequence of actions. In practice the order of actions is not fixed, and you can change attention from one model to another. The description in this chapter emphasizes the process of analysis. The notation is explained as needed. For a summary of notations, see the reference manual of this book.

5.1 Object Model

An object model describes objects and their relationships. Anything with an identity is a potential object, but in order for an object to warrant analysis, it must have a meaningful relationship to the problem. Analysis objects represent the concepts of the problem domain. As such, problem domain concepts are very complicated, and it is not possible to model them exactly. Every model is an abstraction of the reality, intended to capture the essential information needed to build the system.

It is very tempting to state that the reality consists of objects interacting with each other and object models simply capture this fact, but this is not true. Modeling is not merely recording the reality; it is a creative process. The abstractions have to be defined, and the structure of the model has to be created.

The object model consists of class diagrams, object diagrams and textual descriptions of the concepts involved. Class diagrams show generic descriptions of possible systems, and object diagrams show particular instantiations of systems [Rumbaugh '95a]. Often, the object model has only class diagrams, and this chapter focuses on them. Every designer tends to create a different model. At the end of this section, there is a description of how to validate the model.

Object modeling has been widely discussed in the literature. This chapter is only a concise introduction to object modeling. For a more detailed description, you can look at [Rumbaugh '95a, Coleman '93, Coad '91].

5.1.1 Objects and Classes

An object is an identifiable entity characterized with a set of applicable operations and a state. Since objects are often numerous, a set of abstraction techniques are used to hide the details. The most important abstraction is the notion of a class. A class describes a template for several objects and shows how these objects are structured internally. Objects of the same class have the same definition for both their operations and their information structure.

An object that is created according to a certain class is said to be an *instance* of that class. In the class diagram, classes are represented by boxes (Figure 5-2). For example, the SLT unit has 30 subscriber lines. Each line is unique and different, but since SLT treats

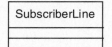

Figure 5-2. SubscriberLine class.

every line similarly, the details are hidden and all lines are represented by a single class, SubscriberLine. Each subscriber line is an instance of the SubscriberLine class.

The symbol representing a class has three areas. The upper area contains the class name, the middle area its attributes and the lower area its operations. Operations are not emphasized in the object model. A class can also be presented without operations and attributes.

Recognition of the right objects and their classes is the first, most important and perhaps most difficult task in the entire analysis phase. What makes it difficult is that there are no simple rules for finding the important objects. A successful search for objects requires a strong knowledge of the problem domain and experience in object-oriented analysis. Potential classes should be accepted without much criticism so that the "right" classes can be found. Useless classes can be eliminated later on.

Analysis begins most effectively with a brainstorming session, but before you can do that you need enough material. Read the requirements document. Study the use cases. Identify the purpose and critical success factors of the system or subsystem under consideration. Try to understand the interfaces with the other subsystems.

If you are building a system for a new area, you have to understand the problem domain before you start the analysis. Ask the customer for a concise summary of the problem domain. Talk to other experts. Ask others to explain what is interesting, what is important, what scenarios are most significant or most difficult. Check previous analysis results. Which classes can be directly reused? What lessons can be learned?

The brainstorming session should be carried out as a group exercise, and everyone should be familiar with the available material such as requirement specifications, use cases, a description of autonomous activities, the context diagram, functional overviews, subsystem division, the user's guide and other related documentation. The objective of the first session is to produce a list of potential classes and relationships.

Usually, classes appear as nouns in the requirements specification, and the *underlining of nouns* is one simple way to find potential objects. However, this method is also much criticized. Consider the following requirement from the SLT case study:

To increase the overall <u>reliability</u> of the <u>network</u> and to have a similar <u>quality</u> of <u>service</u> for the remote <u>subscriber lines</u> as the ones connected directly to the <u>exchange</u>, a new system called a <u>subscriber line tester unit</u> (SLT) is needed in the <u>DTS</u> to be responsible for the line <u>tests</u>. It must respond to the <u>line test commands</u> from the <u>exchange</u>, perform the <u>tests</u> and report the <u>results</u>. For that purpose a <u>test protocol</u> is specified. It is also required that a <u>local PC</u> can emulate the <u>exchange</u>. The <u>SLT</u> can also be configured to perform automatically the <u>line tests</u> and to report to the <u>exchange</u> when <u>faulty subscriber lines</u> are found.

This text contains underlined concepts. Most of these concepts are irrelevant for the problem of testing lines: *reliability, network, quality* and *service* can be ignored. The rest of the concepts are relevant, but not necessarily as objects of the system: *local PC* and *exchange* describe the context, *test protocol* is the interface, *line test commands* are operation requests, *faulty* is a property of another concept. Only *lines, tests* and *results* are essential parts of the problem.

As the example demonstrated, it is rather straightforward to find concrete objects. All subjects and objects of the domain are good candidates. However, the design of the system is based on the abstract objects, and it is important to find those abstract objects that best structure the solution (Chapter 6 and Chapter 8). These abstract objects do not reside in the domain as such, but in our mental model of the domain. Different designers tend to choose different abstract objects to structure the domain. Later in this chapter there is an explanation of how it is possible to evaluate different alternatives.

Class names should harmonize with the names used earlier in the specification of the problem domain. This facilitates the incorporation of different parts of the program and simplifies maintenance.

A good object model is an abstraction of the problem and avoids a direct coupling with the implementation hardware. An exception to this rule is the object model of the hardware wrapper, as explained later in Section 5.4.

5.1.2 Class Description Table

Class diagrams have limited expression capability. Consistent use of problem domain terminology helps with understanding, but the reader still has to rely on the common meaning of the terms. In order to avoid misinterpretations, each class should be described in a separate class description table. An example is given in Table 5-1.

Table 5-1. An extract from the class description table of SLT.

PeriodicTest	PeriodicTest initiates test regularly. It has start time, frequency, stop time and next test time. • PeriodicTest is related to one SubscriberLine.

Many other methods promote the use of a data dictionary. A data dictionary has the advantage of providing descriptions of all the terms in one place. The data dictionary works for class names reasonably well, because classes are often assumed to belong to a common name space, and therefore, conflicting definitions are illegal. Attributes and relationships, however, are defined in terms of their immediate context, and the meaning of the same term in different contexts may vary. OCTOPUS promotes only the use of a class description table.

5.1.3 Attributes

The lines in SLT are sufficiently similar to be described by one class, but they are not precisely the same: they have different numbers, they may be in different states, they have been tested at different times, and they may have different test permissions, some of which may be faulty. This variation is represented as attributes of the line. Attributes are common to all instances of a class, but they may have different values.

Attributes describe properties of the objects. They can be used in explaining the true nature of an object, and they hint at the responsibilities and capabilities of an object. Attributes could also be modeled as associated objects, but modeling them as attributes is simpler. An attribute does not have relationships or attributes.

In the requirements specification, attributes often appear as *adjectives* or *nouns associated to a genitive*, for example:

The requested subscriber line must be in the idle <u>state</u> and it must have a test <u>permission</u>.

Some of the attributes reflect the definitions given to classes. The SubscriberLine object has several attributes (see Figure 5-3).

It is inadvisable to model identity as an attribute, since a unique object identity is provided automatically in the implementation language. However, the SubscriberLine.number is essential in many use cases, and there must somehow be a way to provide it. Modeling something as an attribute in the analysis phase does not mean that the final implementation would have to do so. Sometimes, a value can be computed whenever needed.

Finding attributes may require a thorough understanding of the connections between concepts. It is not a mechanical process. The grammatical tips given above are only meant to make the finding of attributes easier.

5.1.4 Associations

Associations are used to model the relationships between objects. Each association represents a set of similar relationships. Associations are generic representations of relationships like classes are generic representations of objects.

Many associations are present in the text describing the system. They are often visible as verb phrases.

A periodic test <u>is performed</u> on a certain subscriber line.

SLT must <u>send</u> an alarm indication to the exchange.

Each of the 30 channels in a DTS <u>has</u> four signaling bits.

The local PC <u>can emulate</u> the exchange.

```
┌─────────────────────┐
│  SubscriberLine     │
├─────────────────────┤
│  number             │
│  test_permission    │
│  periodic_permission│
├─────────────────────┤
│                     │
└─────────────────────┘
```

Figure 5-3. SubscriberLine with attributes.

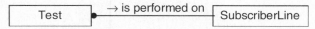

Figure 5-4. A test is performed on a subscriber line.

Some of the associations described in the requirements and use cases are relevant to the problem; most of them are not. Associations are represented as lines connecting classes, as in Figure 5-4.

Each association shows a potential relationship between corresponding objects. Cardinality constraints allow us to specify the relationship more precisely. Cardinality is expressed by modifying the joint between class and association using the symbols shown in Figure 5-5.

The example in Figure 5-4 shows that each Test is always performed on one and only one SubscriberLine, but the number of Tests performed on a SubscriberLine is not restricted.

Associations are bidirectional. This sometimes causes problems in selecting suitable names for the associations. It is always better to use the proper name, even if it is unidirectional, than to invent a bidirectional but unnatural term. The proper direction in which to read the name can be indicated by an arrow. The convention is to choose names that, together with the participating classes, can be read from left to right or top-down.

Class diagrams do not show the object identity. This is a common source of interpretation errors. Consider the class diagram in Figure 5-6. The association indicates that each ElementaryTest uses FaultLimits, but it does not say that each ElementaryTest uses the same FaultLimits.

This problem is so common that the object diagram notation has been extended. The 1 in the corner of FaultLimits shows that FaultLimits is a singular class. There is only one object of type FaultLimits, and therefore every elementary test will use same FaultLimits. Since the problem also occurs with nonsingular classes, this solution is not universal. In some cases the problem can be resolved by adding new associations. At least the text in class descriptions, as in Table 5-1, should resolve potential interpretation errors.

Associations may have attributes. Often, association attributes are combined with one of the participating objects, but sometimes this is not possible. In our example, each Test

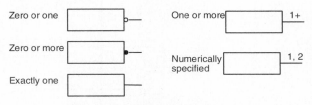

Figure 5-5. Cardinality symbols.

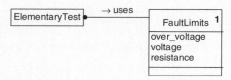

Figure 5-6. Elementary test uses fault limits.

is performed on several SubscriberLine objects, and each SubscriberLine can be tested several times. Thus, the result of the Test can be part of neither the Test nor the SubscriberLine; it is an attribute of the test association, as demonstrated in Figure 5-7.

5.1.5 Generalization

Often, classes have commonalities like similar attributes or associations. These commonalities can be placed into a generalized class. The generalization is often shown in descriptions as an "is-a" or "is-a-kind-of" relationship. A generalization forms a hierarchy. Theoretically the depth of the hierarchy is not limited, but in practice hierarchies should not be deeper than four levels.

Generalization hierarchy is used for typing. The general class represents the *supertype* and the special classes the *subtypes*. The properties of the supertype (the attributes and associations) are *inherited* by the subtypes. Inheritance allows subclasses to reuse the interface and even the implementation of the superclass.

The objects of a subtype cannot change the properties of the supertype, and therefore the objects of the subtype also belong to the supertype. The supertype may also have instances of its own. If it does not, it is an *abstract class*. In designing, abstract classes are used to represent common interfaces.

Analysis models often record common generalizations and use them to provide common interfaces for a set of objects. This type of generalization is declarative. The class diagram of the Cruise Control has many examples of this type of generalization. One example is given in Figure 5-8.

Sometimes the generalization represents a concept that is not commonly used in the problem domain. This type of generalization is constructive. The class diagram of SLT provides an example. The ElementaryTest in Figure 5-9 is constructed to provide a common interface for the different tests.

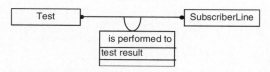

Figure 5-7. Modeling test result as an attribute of performing a test.

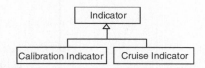

Figure 5-8. Declarative generalization.

Constructive generalizations are more difficult to use than declarative ones. For example, this ElementaryTest can be defined in two different ways. Each test consists of setting values, getting samples, analyzing samples and comparing results to the fault limits. However, RCTest needs two set of samples with different initializations. Thus, the alternatives are:

1. Include settings as attributes of each test and break the RCTest into two classes. Now analysis of the test result cannot be an operation of the ElementaryTest since the analysis of RCTest1 and RCTest2 cannot be separated.

2. Include analysis and comparison in each test. Now test setting and fault limits must be connected to individual tests since RCTest has two phases.

As Figure 5-9 shows, the SLT case study selected the first alternative. The reason is that setting and sampling are so similar that the implementation can also be generalized. The analysis of samples is always so different that only the interface can be generalized.

In complex models, objects may have several independent interfaces. Multiple generalizations allow a subtype to belong to more than one immediate supertype. The combination of generalizations often causes problems. An alternative to multiple generalization is to create an independent generalization, which represents the combination of original abstractions.

5.1.6 Aggregation

Aggregation is a special form of association with the connotation of a "whole-part" relationship. It is not always easy to distinguish between aggregation and an ordinary relationship. If the objects corresponding to classes are tightly bound, so that one is a part of the other, the relationship is an aggregation. If, on the other hand, objects are treated individually, the relationship is probably an ordinary association. Aggregation is illustrated by a

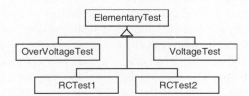

Figure 5-9. Constructive generalization.

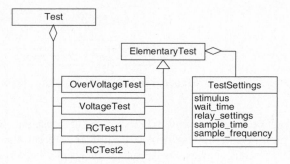

Figure 5-10. The composition of a Test.

specific diamond symbol. Cardinalities can be combined with aggregation, and aggregations can be named. Figure 5-10 shows how a Test is composed of different elementary tests. Each ElementaryTest has TestSettings.

Aggregation extends the semantics of a model, as the whole, made up of its parts, is often treated as one unit. It is created and deleted as a whole and often has only one interface. Like generalization, aggregation is often used to achieve reuse. The composite object delegates its tasks to the parts. However, aggregation is not generalization. The parts are not of the same type as the composite object, and the composite has total control over the interface.

Aggregation is inherently transitive and antisymmetric. A whole is made up of parts that can, in turn, be made up of smaller parts; these smaller parts are also parts of the largest whole. Aggregation is often assumed to be disjoint. A part of an object cannot be part of another independent object. However, it is typical to have other associations with the components. For example, the SLT has 30 subscriber lines. Many of the operations that SLT performs are partially delegated to one of the lines, but lines also have independent associations with other objects.

5.1.7 Dividing the Class Diagram

The correct use of generalization and aggregation makes class diagrams easier to understand. However, they may still grow too large to handle. Many modeling techniques are hierarchical. They provide leveling through hierarchical abstractions. Class diagrams are flat and do not naturally support hierarchy.

Generalization and aggregation provide local hierarchies, and if there is no relationship to the lower levels in the hierarchy, the superclass or composite object can represent the whole group. In Figure 5-11, Test represents the whole structure shown in Figure 5-10. These local hierarchies are typically too small to solve the problem.

Semantically, breaking class diagrams into subdiagrams is not a problem. The composition rule is simple. Classes with the same names are the same; associations with the same name connecting common classes are the same. Everything else is different, and composition is achieved by adding all different components into a single diagram.

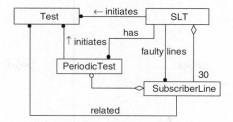

Figure 5-11. Collapsed test structure.

Since interpretation of each class is based on its environment, an arbitrary division of the object diagram will cause misunderstandings and mistakes. A reasonable approach is to restrict each subdiagram so that it represents a restricted view of the problem. Most of the classes in these subdiagrams will still appear in some other subdiagram too, but many classes and associations can be omitted.

Our case studies do not provide suitable examples of class diagram division. Let us instead consider a computer game of a Formula 1 car race. The class diagrams for the game can be built from several viewpoints:

- The structure of the race track: the signs, the buildings and the plants

- The structure of the car: the engine, the gear box, the tires and the wings

- The mechanism used to provide the three-dimensional view

- The simulation of the car's movement and the movement of other cars

- The structure of the competition: free practice, qualifying, pre-race practice and race

- The structure of the season

Each of these viewpoints will share objects, but they will still be reasonably independent. Modeling from these perspectives will be much easier than trying to capture the complexity into one diagram. Different viewpoints also make it possible to use precise names for the associations instead of general names.

5.1.8 Application Boundary and Relation to Other Subsystems

Different subsystems have different class diagrams. Associations crossing the application boundary connect the subsystems. Conceptually, subsystems communicate through these shared associations, and the interface between subsystems is the composite interface of the classes connected to these shared associations. The boundary between the subsystem and its environment is indicated by a line in the class diagram, as shown in Figure 5-12.

The classes left outside the boundary represent the objects communicating with the subsystem. Some of these objects reside in some other application subsystem, whereas others cannot be found inside any application subsystem. They are called *abstract envi-*

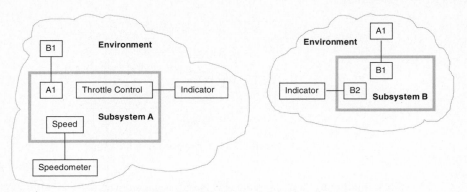

Figure 5-12. Two subsystems and the boundary.

ronment classes, and the hardware wrapper will take care of them. More about this subject is in Section 5.4.

Let us consider the example shown in Figure 5-12 and assume the subsystems shown, A and B, are the only ones. Subsystem A communicates with objects of classes B1, Speedometer and Indicator. B1 is part of subsystem B, but Speedometer and Indicator are abstract environment classes since they describe truly external concepts.

Often, information about an external object is essential to the operation of the system, and an abstract environment class representing this external object is used. The hardware wrapper implements the communication with the actual hardware, and in its own object model it maps the abstract environment class into a wrapper class. In the example, the abstract environment classes Speedometer and Indicator are replicated in the hardware wrapper object model.

Figure 5-13 shows the boundary between the SLT subsystem and its environment. Since there is no other subsystem, all the classes outside the border are abstract environment classes, and the hardware wrapper will cover them. The Line class represents the line in the real world, and the SubscriberLine class represents the line inside the subsystem. Most of the classes in the environment replicate concepts from the outside world. The only exception is the Clock class; it is internal to the hardware wrapper.

In Figure 5-13, the environment is considered from the application perspective. Many lines cross the boundary between the application and the environment, which is identical with the hardware wrapper in this case. These connections are logical and not necessarily implemented. A corresponding hardware wrapper class diagram would contain the mirror image of these connections. Of course, the hardware wrapper also has an interface to the external world.

Correct identification of the application boundary is very important. The functional and dynamic models describe the interfaces across that boundary.

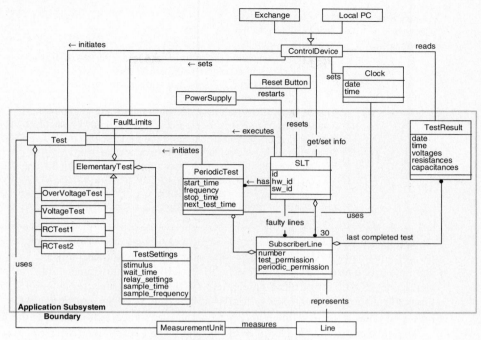

Figure 5-13. The class diagram for SLT.

5.1.9 Checking the Object Model

Object modeling is an iterative task. Discussions with other experts will help in discovering omissions and peculiarities. Cross-checking against the requirements specification is also useful. Check how concepts and their qualifications are represented. Check if all relevant relations mentioned in the requirements specification have representations.

A systematic way to check that there are no serious omissions is to go through each use case and imagine how the objects in the object model will cooperate in performing the given tasks. The following problems may appear:

- Difficulties in deciding how certain use cases are handled or what responsibilities each object should take. This is an indication of missing objects or misnamed abstractions.

- The participating objects have no relationship. This indicates missing associations.

- The object does not know how to respond. This indicates a lack of attributes or associations.

Let us take a look at the class diagram of the SLT application subsystem in Figure 5-13 and apply the above checks.

In order to save space, the Preconditions, Postconditions and Exceptions fields have been omitted from the use cases. Consider the Get information use case:

Use Case	(U1) Get information.
Actors	The exchange or the PC.
Description	Actor may request:
	identification of the hardware and software of the SLT.
	status of a selected subscriber line.
	test results of a selected subscriber line.
	list of faulty lines.
	The SLT sends all the requested parameters within 300 ms.
	The status of line is: the test result status (Normal | Faulty | Not Tested), the test permission (Allowed | Denied), the periodic test permission (Allowed | Denied) and its starting time and rate of occurrence.
	The test results include all the measured parameters of the line (VDCag, VACag, VDCbg, VACbg, VDCav, VACav, VDCbv, VACbv, VDCab, VACab, Rag, Rbg, Rav, Rbv, Rab, Cag, Cbg, Cav, Cbv and Cab) and an indication about what of these are inside the fault limits. Also the time and date of the test is reported.

Exchange and LocalPC will act as interfaces toward the hardware wrapper handling the communication. All the requests will be forwarded to the SLT object. Unit and software identity queries are handled by the SLT itself. The status request must be passed on to the correct SubscriberLine object, and the test result query through the Subscriber-Line object to the corresponding TestResult object. The SLT object has a list of faulty lines, but it has to request line numbers from the SubscriberLine objects in the list.

The most complicated activity of the system is the execution of a periodic test. A periodic test is initiated by the Set information use case:

Use Case	(U2) Set information.
Actors	The exchange or the PC.
Description	Actor may request the SLT to set certain parameters, one at a time:
	• The fault limits which are common to all lines:
	Over voltage limit (> 50 V and < 250 V, e.g., 150 V)
	Voltage limit (> 10 V and < 50 V, e.g., 20 V)
	Resistance limit (> 10 KΩ and < 100 KΩ, e.g., 50 KΩ)
	• For a selected subscriber line:
	the test permission right (Allowed | Denied),
	the periodic test permission (Allowed | Denied)
	the starting time of a periodic test (e.g., 01:00 AM)
	the rate of the periodic test (e.g., 6 times a day).
	The SLT checks that the given parameter is acceptable [Exception: the parameter is not acceptable], it then sets the parameter and sends a positive acknowledgment within 100 ms.
	Every setting parameter must persist in the system after reset. All the settings have default values.

The request arrives from Exchange or LocalPC object to the SLT object. The SLT object checks from the corresponding SubscriberLine object the permission to do periodic tests, initializes a new PeriodicTest object and sets this object into the queue of periodic tests. The new PeriodicTest object sends a request to the Clock to set the time of the first invocation of the test.

Use Case	(U6) Periodic Test.
Description	Periodic line tests are activated according to the starting time and rate settings for that subscriber line. A line test sequence is started as in U9.
Postconditions	The line is tested. Its results are updated in the memory. If a test result is inside the fault limits, then the SLT sends a fault indication to the exchange and PC, including the line number which was found faulty.

The Clock object activates the PeriodicTest object and checks if the Test object is free. Note that there is only one test object, because the equipment is only able to perform one test at a time. If the status of the Test object is free, the PeriodicTest object initializes it. The Test object starts to execute the test sequence and, at the end, sets a new TestResult object and assigns it to the corresponding SubscriberLine. If a fault is found, the Test object informs the SLT object, and the SLT object places the SubscriberLine object into the list of faulty lines and informs the Controller objects.

Note that it would have been possible to model the test results as characteristics of a line. This would be somewhat artificial, since all lines do not have test results. However, with the current choice, the update of the test result values is just a change of one reference.

This execution of the use cases shows that the object model of the SLT is sufficient.

5.2 Functional Model

The purpose of a functional model is to describe the functional interface of the subsystem. This interface consists of a set of named services provided by the subsystem to other subsystems and external agents. A service may require complex interactions between the user and the provider of the service.

Services are described using operation sheets similar to the ones in the Fusion method [Coleman '93]. Operation sheets are informal and may rely on natural language. They describe the operations declaratively. They do not try to explain how or when the service is provided. Each operation sheet has the fields shown in Figure 5-14.

Operation	Name of the operation.
Description	Short statement describing the operation.
Associations	Associations to the classes and objects and possibly also to the events and states to which it is related.
Preconditions	Conditions that need to be satisfied to start the operation; these do not guarantee that the operation will be successfully completed.
Inputs	Arguments that an operation needs to perform its desired function.
Modifies	What modifications the operation causes on its arguments or on common data in the subsystem.
Outputs	What information the operation needs to supply its client.
Postconditions	Conditions after the operation is successfully completed and the conditions that apply if the operation is terminated due to an error.

Figure 5-14. An operation sheet.

Services are easy to find since the requirements specification and especially the use cases concentrate on describing the services. The problem domain terms should be used to name the operations. Since services together form the interface, it is necessary to consider the collection of services as a whole. The collection should cover the functionality of the subsystem. Similar operations should be defined similarly.

Let us first consider the Cruise Control case study. The services selected are: calculate actual speed, maintain desired speed, calculate actual acceleration, auto-accelerate, recalibrate, generate 1 km pulse and generate 100m pulse. The operation calculate actual acceleration is not directly requested by the user, but it makes the interface to the acceleration control similar to the speed control. These operations naturally seem to follow the requirements, yet they have been designed to conform to the system boundary. Note, for example, that intermediate accelerating with the pedal is not included in the set of operations at all. Since this functionality is provided by the mechanics, it is not part of the software system interface.

Operation sheets describe the functions based on the attributes of the object model and the input values. The change in the state of the system is expressed in the Postconditions clause and in the Modifies expression (see Figure 5-15). Operation sheets can be built using only the Postcondition clause to express the state change. The Modifies expression can be used to keep the Postconditions clauses simpler. The syntax of the Modifies expression and Outputs expression is similar.

The formality of the operation sheets may vary considerably. The Modifies and Outputs expressions characterize values. A programming language variant or mathematical expressions can be used to express the values. Preconditions and Postconditions clauses are expressed as predicates over the input values and the objects of the system in the states before and after execution of the operation. Since these predicates are often used to indicate a state of the subsystem, it is also possible to replace the predicate with a reference to a state in a statechart diagram.

The following example describes the maintain desired speed operation from the Cruise Control case study:

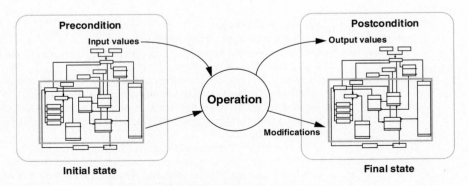

Figure 5-15. Operation as a change of state.

Operation	(O3) maintain desired speed
Description	Vary throttle opening from closed to fully open as speed varies from 0.84 m/sec above desired speed, to 0.84 m/sec below it. Restrict rate of opening to 10 sec for full range.
Associations	Class Speed, class Throttle Control
Preconditions	Cruise control has been activated, calibration not ongoing and neither brake depressed nor transmission out of top gear (see dynamic model).
Inputs	Desired speed (SD), actual speed (SA)
Modifies	Throttle actuator position (VTH) with
Outputs	

$$VTH = \begin{cases} 0 & \text{if} - 0.84 > SD - SA \\ \dfrac{0.84 + SD - SA}{2*0.84} * \max(VTH) & \text{if} - 0.84 \leq SD - SA \leq 0.84 \\ \max(VTH) & \text{if} - 0.84 < SD - SA \end{cases}$$

Postconditions	$\dfrac{dVTH}{dt} \leq \dfrac{\max(VTH)}{10}$

A postcondition is expressed as a predicate, but a precondition refers to a state in a statechart. This operation sheet describes the functionality in the Modifies expression. References are mainly in the input values, and there are only a few references to the object model. The SLT case study demonstrates a different style and makes many references to the object model, as shown in the next sheet and sheet 04 found in Chapter 9:

Operation	(O9) SetPeriodicTest
Description	Initiates a periodic test
Associations	SLT, SubscriberLine, PeriodicTest, ControlDevice
Preconditions	
Inputs	Number, start_time, frequency, stop_time
Modifies	PeriodicTest
Outputs	**if** start_time, frequency and stop_time are **not** valid **then** PeriodicTestError **elseif not** SubscriberLine.periodic_permission **then** NoPeriodicTestPermission(number) **else** PeriodicTestOK(number)
Postconditions	**if** start_time, frequency and stop_time are valid **and** SubscriberLine.periodic_permission **then** A PeriodicTest is created for the SubscriberLine and initiated using the given values Operation O13 is started periodically as requested

In these sheets, references to objects are made using the names of their classes. It is not possible to make precise references, since individual objects have not been identified yet. In this style:

- Attribute and object are separated by a point, for example: Subscriber-Line.periodic_permission

- References to relationships are made using the arrow notation, for example: (SubscriberLine->LastCompletedTest).result

- Relationships are used to limit objects, for example: **for each** SubscriberLine **in** the output list

It is also necessary to make sure that it is clear whether references in the Postconditions field are made to the model before or after the execution of the operation. The keywords *initial* and *final* can be used to avoid confusion.

Operation sheets are hierarchical. The SetPeriodicTest operation ends in a sentence: Operation O13 is started periodically as requested. This sentence refers to the TestLine operation, which is defined separately. The hierarchy should be made clear so that it does not obscure interface specification. In this case, the suboperation TestLine is not part of the interface.

Operation sheets can also build hierarchy using the dynamic model. The dynamic model describes the interactions required to perform an operation, and the functional model describes the effects of the operation. If a service is complex, functional and dynamic models can be layered. An abstract functional model describes what the services provide. The corresponding dynamic model describes the interactions required to perform them. A detailed functional model describes all the operations triggered by these interactions.

Operation sheets make it possible to capture complex functionality in a short form. The size of a real project may cause some problems; therefore, a project applying OCTOPUS should agree on certain policies regarding:

1. *Completeness of the description in terms of the preconditions*: Strong preconditions simplify the operation sheet and make it more readable by removing error cases from consideration. If the project tries to completely specify the functionality of the system, exceptions must be covered by additional operation sheets.

2. *Level of detail in terms of exceptional values*: At one extreme, all situations falling outside the scope of the precondition are considered to result in unpredictable behavior. At the other extreme, the response to every error case is described in detail.

3. *Precision*: Most of the operations simply access information, but some make nontrivial computations. Either the operation sheet specifies that the computed values are correct or it expresses the result. In the SLT case study, the results of voltage, resistance and capacitance computations are too complex to be expressed as a function of input values and system state.

4. *Level of formality*: It is possible to provide a naming convention within the operation sheets which, together with the use of predicate logic in expressing the conditions, gives formal semantics to the operation sheets. Formal specification has several benefits, but also severe drawbacks. In practice, an attempt to provide correct formal specifications

for real operations leads to very complex and almost unreadable specifications. The analyst must find a balance between formality and understandability.

Operational specifications are an essential part of subsystem interface specifications. The proper structure of the operational specification must be selected accordingly. Sometimes it is useful to structure the interface as a set of exported classes visible to the other subsystems. In this case, each public member function of the exported classes should be specified using operation sheets.

5.3 Dynamic Model

The dynamic model describes the operation of a subsystem across its application boundary and addresses the real-time, reactive aspects. It explains under what conditions the operations are performed and how long they are allowed to take. It captures the order of interactions between the subsystem and its environment needed to perform an operation, and shows what operations are possible in different states and how different operations affect each other.

In OCTOPUS, the dynamic model consists of the following phases; in each phase, a number of related components are produced:

- Analysis of events: event list, grouping of events and event sheets

- Analysis of states: concurrent statecharts and actions table

- Further analysis of events and states: significance table and compound events

- Validation of the dynamic model: scenarios for the complex operations

5.3.1 Analysis of Events

A real-time system simultaneously responds to random occurrences of events and gives the desired responses within the required time limits. Events that enter the subsystem are input events; events that leave it are output events. In the dynamic model, the focus is on the input events because they cause the activation, suspension, termination or abortion of operations in the subsystem. The output events are specified in the operation sheets of the functional model.

The emphasis is on the *logical* input events a subsystem receives from its environment, that is, from another subsystem or from the hardware wrapper subsystem, as demonstrated in Figure 5-16. For example, if a special key of a mobile telephone is pressed, the application subsystem is not interested in receiving the physical primitive event Special Key Pressed. It is interested in receiving a logical event such as Clear Display or Search for a Name in Memory. A logical event is based on what a primitive event means in the current state of the system. This is further explained in Section 5.4.

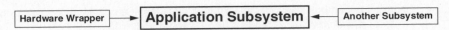

Figure 5-16. Input events.

In general, real-time systems have two different types of events, periodic and sporadic. Periodic events occur at a predetermined frequency, which may or may not be accurate. For example, requesting a memory check once every 10 seconds is a periodic event, although the intervals between successive occurrences need not be equal. Another example of a periodic event is the request to receive successive bits from a serial communication line at an exact rate of 1 Mbit/s. Periodic events can be used to monitor the environment and to signal when a particular condition arises. They are normally implemented using a clock or timer. A periodic event may occur at specified times, such as the request to generate a statistics report at 08:15 a.m. or 09:35 p.m.

Sporadic events occur randomly in response to a particular condition arising in the system or in the environment. Sporadic events are often handled using interrupts. The system has to respond within a particular time frame, called the *response time*. Sporadic events are often approximated by periodic ones in order to estimate the processor load, and hence to assess the temporal behavior of a system.

The analysis of events has the following steps, which are explained below:

1. Identify and describe the logical input events.

2. Find the commonalities between the events and group them.

3. Fill the event sheets.

Step 1: Identify and describe the logical input events

Dynamic modeling starts by identifying and understanding the events. This is best achieved by examining the class diagram and paying special attention to the associations that cross the application boundary, especially the ones directed towards the subsystem being analyzed. Some of these associations may indicate events:

• If the association indicates an autonomous interaction from the objects of the environment to the objects of the subsystem being analyzed regarding some changes in the system, then these interactions are considered to be events.

• If an object in the subsystem being analyzed (client object) issues a request to another object in another subsystem (server object), a closer look at the association between them may reveal that data flows from the server to the client in response to the request. The data flow from the server to the client as part of the request (e.g., a return value of a normal function call) is not an event. On the other hand, an independent response from the server to the client may be considered an event.

• If a class in the subsystem being analyzed inherits a class from another subsystem, including the hardware wrapper classes, then the objects instantiated from this class get the needed functionality directly by virtue of inheritance. This kind of association does not normally indicate an event.

The first two cases also apply if the association between objects is an aggregation. Remember that aggregation is only a special form of association with the connotation of a "whole-part" relationship.

Table 5-2 demonstrates some of the events extracted from the Cruise Control case study. Notice that the events are also numbered, E1, E2, and so on.

Table 5-2. Example of an event list.

Event	Description
(E1) rotation pulse	Senses rotation of the drive shaft.
(E2) activate cruising	Driver desires to be relieved from maintaining speed.
...	...

Step 2: Find the commonalities between the events and group them

Grouping of events helps to manage the complexity resulting from the possibly large number of different events. It is done bottom-up: examine the events in the event list, and identify the commonalities between them. Search for commonalities in relation to the source of events, data contents, the expected response and time requirements. The more things you find in common, the more beneficial it becomes to group them.

The class and inheritance notation of a class diagram can be used to represent the grouping of events graphically. An example is shown in Figure 5-17 from the Cruise Control case study. The leaf boxes represent the individual events, whereas other boxes represent superevents. Any event has a superevent to which it belongs and may have subevents belonging to it. For example, Command is a superevent for Operation Command and Calibration Command, and it is a subevent of Event.

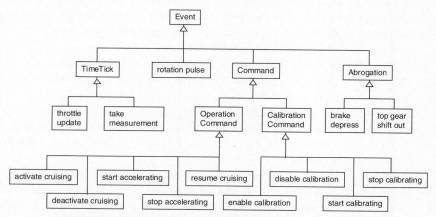

Figure 5-17. Graphical representation of event grouping.

Step 3: Fill the event sheets

An event sheet such as the one in Figure 5-18 is used to capture essential information about the event.

Event	Name of the event.
Response	The desired end-to-end response from the system.
Associations	Associations to the classes and objects and possibly also to the operations to which it is related.
Source	The originators of the event, for example, other subsystems or the hardware wrapper.
Contents	Data attributes that an event may hold.
Response Time	The maximum and minimum time limitations concerning the giving of the response.
Rate	The rate of occurrence that can be, for example, at startup, periodic every 10 minutes, timed at 8:00 AM and 2:00 PM, occasional, exceptional, and so forth.

Figure 5-18. An event sheet.

In step 1, a list of events and their descriptions was built, thus eliminating the need to have a description field in the event sheet. The *Associations* field is primarily intended to link the event with the classes and objects of the object model that are expected to manipulate the event. It can also be used to link the event with the operations to which it relates in the functional model. Although this association is vague, it reduces the effort needed in the design phase. The Response field lists the end-to-end subsystem response that the event activates. If this has already been described in an operation sheet in the functional model, a reference to the operation is enough. The source of the event is always explicitly stated in the Source field. An event from the hardware wrapper usually has only one source, but an event from another subsystem may have several sources. The destination of the event need not be mentioned, because it is always the subsystem being analyzed. The Contents field describes the data attributes carried with the event. For example, if we have an event Command, its contents would, at least, include a data attribute telling what the specific command is. Usually, there is a trade-off between having an event with contents or having a number of events instead. For example, the Command event could be replaced by Get Test Report, Enable Tracing, and so on.

The last two fields in the event sheet capture the time requirements. The Response Time field contains the maximum interval of time, during which the system is required to respond. Sometimes, it may also be necessary to specify the minimum response time before which the system must not respond. This case is not typical in soft real-time systems. The Rate field contains the rate of occurrence of the event which helps in estimating the load of the system. The event sheet in Figure 5-18 shows some examples of possible entries in the Rate field.

Events are grouped bottom-up, but the event sheets are built top-down. Traverse the hierarchy of events and fill an event sheet for each event if there are additions or differences compared to its superevent. This has the advantage of reducing the number of event sheets needed. In Figure 5-17, for example, if all subevents of Operation Command have only information similar to their superevents, Operation Command, Command and Event, then there is no need to fill out an event sheet for any of the subevents. The event sheet of a certain event refers to fields in the event sheets of its superevents if these fields are still applicable, and refers to other fields in the event sheets of its subevents when these fields cannot be collectively specified to cover all of its subevents. This fact is demonstrated, for example, in the event sheets Command and Operation Command from the Cruise Control case study. Notice the cross references between these sheets indicated by bold text.

Event	Command
Response	Subsystem performs some processing, **see subevents**
Associations	Event is represented by class Command
Source	Driver pressing buttons at physical command interface
Contents	Command identifier, equal to event number
Response Time	**See subevents**
Rate	**See subevents**

Event	Operation Command
Response	New position of throttle actuator
Associations	Class Throttle Control
Source	**See Command**
Contents	**See Command**
Response Time	Max 0.5 sec
Rate	Spontaneously, max. burst 1–2 Hz

5.3.2 Analysis of States

Harel's statechart notion is used to describe state-dependent behavior [Harel '87]. Statecharts extend conventional state-transition diagrams with essentially three elements: hierarchy, concurrency and communication. We introduce in brief the part of the notation that is used in this book and then describe the process of analysis.

Figure 5-19 shows two statecharts, ABC and DE. A state is represented by a rectangle with rounded edges. An arrow between states represents a transition. A transition is labeled with the event that triggers the transition and optionally with a parenthesized condition that guards against doing the transition unless the condition is true. An example is event g which causes a transition from C to B only if the condition P is true. The same event causes a transition from B to A if condition Q is true.

A state can nest other states, and is called a superstate; the nested states are called substates. A superstate is an abstraction of its substates. If the system is in a superstate, it is in exactly one of its substates. In Figure 5-19, the system is in the superstate ABC if it is either in A or in B or in C. State hierarchy or decomposition is visualized by nesting the state symbols within each other. An event received by a superstate is still valid in all of its substates. For example, when event a is received by superstate ABC, the system enters one of the substates A or B or C. In order to determine which one, a default substate within the superstate is defined. An arrow with a filled circle at its tail indicates the default state. Therefore, when a occurs, the system enters the default state C. When b occurs, the sys-

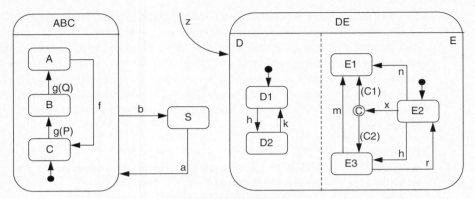

Figure 5-19. Statecharts.

tem leaves the superstate ABC no matter which substate it was in. Event b has priority over the events g and f inside the superstate.

Figure 5-19 also demonstrates state concurrency, visualized using a dashed line between the concurrent parts. If the system is in superstate DE, then it is simultaneously in D and E: it is in one of the substates which belong to side D (i.e., D1 or D2) and in one of the substates which belong to side E (i.e., E1, E2 or E3). If a transition occurs to superstate DE, the event causing the transition is broadcast to all the substates in DE. For example, assume events z, h and m occur one after the other. When z occurs, the system enters DE. It enters D1 in D and also E2 in E (these are the default states at each side). When h occurs, it results in a transition from D1 to D2 and synchronously in a transition from E2 to E3. When event m occurs, it results in a transition from E3 to E1 independent of D.

The term "concurrency" as used in this context does not mean concurrent execution, a term dealt with later in the design phase (Chapter 6).

The C-circle in Figure 5-19 means a *choice point*. An event causes a transition to a particular state based on different conditions. For example, event x causes a transition from E2 to E1 if the condition C1 is true, but to E3 if the condition C2 is true.

States that do not nest other states are called *elementary states,* although they can be at different hierarchy levels. For example, in Figure 5-20, Cruise.inactive and Cruise.suspend are at the first level of hierarchy, whereas Cruise.active.maintain and Cruise.active.accelerate are at the second level of hierarchy. On the other hand, state Cruise.active is a superstate.

The condition clause in a transition may refer to other statecharts that belong to the same or other subsystems. For example, the transition caused by the activate cruising event has a condition clause Abrogation.none and Calibration.disabled. This clause refers to states in statecharts Abrogation and Calibration, respectively. The Abrogation statechart even belongs to another subsystem, which is the hardware wrapper in this case.

Although the use of statecharts reduces the well-known state-blowup phenomenon attributed to flat and unstructured conventional finite-state models and their visual counterpart, state transition diagrams, modeling the system with only one fully detailed state-

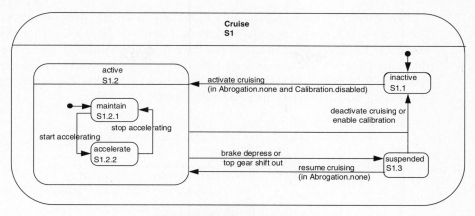

Figure 5-20. Cruise statechart.

chart continues to be very difficult. The analysis of states in OCTOPUS does not result in one complete statechart but in a number of them. These can be at varying levels of abstraction and detail: one statechart may describe the subsystem as a whole on a broad level, whereas another may describe the behavior of the objects of a particular class in the subsystem in detail. Statecharts improve our understanding of the dynamic behavior when there is some important, sufficiently complex state-dependent behavior. The information that is directly shown on the statecharts is limited to prevent them from becoming overwhelming. A statechart does not include:

- Events that cause no state transitions

- Entry and exit actions, actions accompanying an event and ongoing activities inside a state

The analysis of states has two steps that are elaborated on below:

1. Identifying and building the statecharts

2. Filling the actions table

Step 1: Identifying and building the statecharts

When considering major state behavior, the first step is to identify the important statecharts. This is done based on the knowledge already gained from analyzing the events, from the operation sheets and from examination of the physical environment. All of these may give an indication of the need to have a statechart. If a subsystem response to a particular event differs, this is because the handling of the event is based on the state of the (sub)system. Also, operations may have been described in terms of state. The state of the physical environment is often mirrored in the subsystems. For example, the state of a physical subscriber line in SLT can be FREE, BUSY, CONNECTED, and so on, and these are reflected in one of the statecharts of SLT.

After identifying the statecharts, investigate the concurrency or nesting between them. The outcome is several concurrent statecharts. There is no need to combine them in one statechart. The concurrent statecharts and their elementary states are entered in a list, as shown in Table 5-3, and are associated with the related classes in the object model. An additional field may be added to the table to describe each of the elementary states. Table 5-3 shows a partial list taken from the Cruise Control case study.

Table 5-3. Concurrent statecharts and associations to the object model.

Statechart	Elementary States	Associations
Cruise	(S1.1) inactive (S1.2) active (S1.2.1) maintain (S1.2.2) accelerate (S1.3) suspended	Command MGR, Throttle Controller, Cruise Indicator
Calibration	(S2.1) disabled...	...
Conversion	...	...

Step 2: Filling the actions table

Important information about events is already captured in the event sheets. State transitions and transition conditions are captured in the statecharts. The information omitted in statecharts are recorded in an *actions table*. It contains the elementary states of all concurrent statecharts and the associated actions with the reasons for taking the actions. For example, is the action always performed when entering or leaving an elementary state, or is it done only when a particular event occurs? The elementary states in which no actions occur need not be entered in the table. The table also includes those events that trigger actions but do not cause state transitions.

Table 5-4 is an example of an actions table. The first row in the table means that entering state Cruise.inactive, regardless of what event caused the entry, always triggers actions 1 and 2. It also shows that exiting from this state always triggers action 5. In state Cruise.active.accelerate, the third row in the table, event throttle update causes no state transition, but it triggers action 7 which is the performance of operation O4, described in its own operation sheet.

There is a difference between an action and an activity. An action is an operation that is atomic and typically accompanies the transition between states. An activity is an operation that consumes time and can be interrupted while the system is in a certain state. An activity can have associated start and stop events. It may also be an abstraction of those repeated actions triggered by a periodic event which causes no state transition. The actions table shows both actions and activities. An activity is identified by entering ongoing in the row of that activity, as in the fourth row in Table 5-4.

Table 5-4. Partial actions table.

Elementary State	Event	Actions/Activities
(S1.1) Cruise.inactive	\<enter\> \<exit\>	(1) cruise indicator off (2) nullify throttle actuator (5) set desired speed = actual speed
...	...	...
(S1.2.2) Cruise.active.accelerate	\<enter\> throttle update \<exit\>	(7) perform operation O4 (7) perform operation O4 (5) set desired speed = actual speed
...	\<ongoing\>	...
(Sx) collective other	rotation pulse take measurement	(17) perform operation O1 (18) perform operation O2

State Sx in the last row in Table 5-4 is called the *collective other state*. It is needed because the state model is not complete, that is, some statecharts and their states are missing. Sx stands for the rest of the states in the (sub)system being analyzed. The events that are not associated with any state can be associated with Sx. The actions they trigger can then be entered in the actions table in the Sx row. Shortly, the collective other state, Sx, is there to encounter the deficiency in the incomplete state model.

5.3.3 Further Analysis of Events and States

To further specify and understand dynamic behavior, an enhanced analysis of the events and states is done. This analysis includes two steps, which are discussed below:

1. Event significance analysis

2. Event laxity analysis

Step 1: Event significance analysis

How significant or important an event is depends on the *compound state* of the system, that is, the valid combination of the elementary states all concurrent statecharts are in. The response of the system to an event may differ depending on the compound state of the system. For example, if Cruise Control were in the compound state Cruise.active and Brake.released, the start accelerating event would be significant and would be handled (i.e., the car would accelerate). If the compound state were Cruise.active and Brake.depressed, the start accelerating event would be totally ignored (i.e., the car would not accelerate).

It is very important to know the event significance because it influences the object interaction threads and also the process priorities in the design phase. As the significance of the events is dependent on the compound state of the system, it can be entered neither in the event sheets nor in the state-event actions table. It is also unrealistic to enter the significance of the events in a table of the events against the compound states of the system because the number of compound states can grow very rapidly; in fact, it is the multiplication of the number of elementary states that each concurrent statechart has. Another, more effective, approach is to define the significance of events in the elementary states (i.e., the states that do not nest any other states inside them) and to calculate the significance of an event in any possible compound state from the significance values in the elementary states. A detailed explanation follows after the introduction of the different event significance values. These are:

- *Critical (c)*: If the subsystem must respond to the event in any compound state containing this particular elementary state and a failure is not acceptable. This significance is common for events with hard real-time requirements.

- *Essential (e)*: If the subsystem should respond to the event in any compound state containing this particular elementary state but occasional failure to do so may be acceptable.

- *Ignored (0)*: If the event can be ignored in all compound states containing this particular elementary state.

- *Neutral (1)*: If none of the previous significance values can be assigned to the event from the point of view of this particular elementary state. This implies that the significance of the event in all compound states containing this particular elementary state will be determined by some other elementary state.

A significance table records the significance values of all events in the elementary states. The default entries in all cells can be 1. Traverse the table cell by cell and modify the value to c, e or 0. Some entries will be left with the neutral significance 1.

Table 5-5 shows a partial significance table from the Cruise Control case study. All the elementary states, even at different levels of hierarchy, are entered, as well as all the events. The collective other state, Sx, is also entered.

If the significance table becomes large, it can be divided into a number of smaller tables, as necessary.

Table 5-5. Partial significance table.

State	Event				
	E1	E2	E3	E4	...
S1.1	1	e	0	0	...
S1.2.1	c	0	e	e	...
S1.2.2	c	0	e	0	...
S1.3	c	0	e	0	...
...	...	...	...	...	...
Sx	c	1	1	1	...

As already mentioned, the system is never in a single elementary state but in a compound state. The significance of an event in a compound state is simply calculated by multiplying all the significance values of the event in the elementary states that make the compound state. The multiplication rules are defined in Table 5-6. In Table 5-5, for example, if the system can be in the compound state S1.1 and Sx, then the significance of event E1 in this compound state is 1 multiplied by c, which is c, whereas the significance of event E4 is 0 multiplied by 1, which is 0.

Table 5-6. Significance multiplication calculus.

MUL	c	e	1	0
c	c	c	c	0
e	c	e	e	0
1	c	e	1	0
0	0	0	0	0

For any compound state, the calculated event significance must be c, e or 0. If it is 1, it means that the event significance is still unresolved. You have to change the values in the significance table until the calculated significance is not 1.

Notice that the significance properties of events reflect some relative importance between the events. If an event is critical in all states, it is considered more important than events that are essential or ignored in at least one state.

Step 2: Event laxity analysis

You may recognize that some events are independent of each other in such a way that they never occur simultaneously. In some cases it may be useful to replace such separate events by compound ones. A trivial example of this is switching a light on and off, as shown in the state diagrams in Figure 5-21. Instead of having two separate events, switch on and switch off, you could have a single compound event, toggle light, to replace the previous two events.

Replacing some events with compound ones has the advantage of reducing the number of events with which the system has to deal and eventually reducing the number of control lines in the actual hardware. Combining the events is not without disadvantages; for example, the meaning of a compound event cannot be determined unless the state in which it occurs is known.

The significance table helps you verify whether combining certain events into a compound one is possible or not, but it is left for you to determine if the combination is sensible (see examples in Chapter 10). The procedure to verify if two events, say E1 and E2,

Figure 5-21. Example of separate events versus compound events.

can be combined is simple: scan through the columns of events E1 and E2 and compare their significance values to each other in all elementary states and apply the following rules:

- If you find that both of them have either essential or critical significance in the same state, and E1 causes a transition to a new state which differs from the one caused by E2, then E1 and E2 cannot be combined.

- If you find that one of them is essential or critical and the other is neutral in the same state, and you find the opposite in another concurrent state, then E1 and E2 cannot be combined.

- In all other cases, they can be combined.

Combining events can be done with more than two events; the same procedure and rules are applied, but on all the separate events that are candidates for the combination.

Once you get a compound event, its significance needs to be determined. As demonstrated in Table 5-7, the significance of a compound event is the strongest significance of the individual events of which it is composed. Significance c is stronger than e, which is stronger than 1; the weakest is significance 0.

Table 5-7. Significance calculation for compound events.

MAX	c	e	1	0
c	c	c	c	c
e	c	e	e	e
1	c	e	1	1
0	c	e	1	0

An example of compound events is event **toggle cruising and calibration** from the Cruise Control case study which replaces events **activate cruising**, **deactivate cruising**, **start calibration** and **stop calibration**. These events obey the rules listed above, and their combination is sensible. In the actual hardware, only one control line is required to carry all of these events. At the user interface panel, only one pushbutton is provided which serves all the above functions.

5.3.4 Scenarios

Dynamic modeling includes enhanced scenarios between the subsystem and its environment. In contrast to OMT, a subsystem is treated as a black box, that is, the interactions are with the subsystem as a whole and not with its internals. However, in a scenario, several environment objects or complete subsystems may interact with the subsystem being analyzed. A scenario may represent a complete operation, a set of operations or only a part of an operation. It shows valid sequencing of events observable in a particular situation which may be an error situation. A scenario may show the time-outs between the events, the changes in the subsystem states and also the expected suboperations carried by the

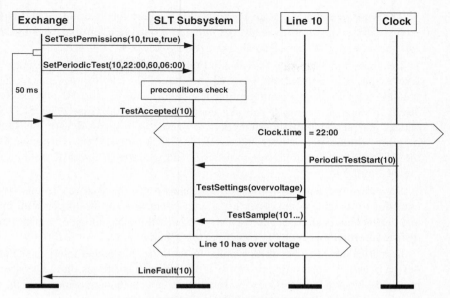

Figure 5-22. An example of a scenario.

subsystem between a sequence of events. The scenarios are built for all important and complex operations of the subsystem, including the error cases where the handling of errors is nontrivial.

The message sequence chart (MSC) notation specified in ITU standard Z.120 [Z120 '94] is used to present the scenarios. The standard also provides a textual notation, but the description here is restricted only to the part of the graphical notation used in this book and explained using the example in Figure 5-22.

Figure 5-22 shows a sample scenario. The vertical axis in an MSC represents the time increasing from top to bottom; hence, interactions are understood to follow each other in time. Communicating entities (the subsystem being analyzed, and objects and other subsystems from the environment) are represented by vertical lines concluded by small solid rectangles; their names are entered into boxes attached to the top of the lines. An interaction (event, message) between the entities is represented by a normal horizontal arrow and is labeled by a name. The time-out is represented by an arrow symbol and is labeled by the value of the time out. Suboperations are shown in normal boxes attached to the entity that performs them. The box with triangular sides is the condition symbol that can be used to describe a state of an entity or of a group of entities. In the latter case, the symbol is extended over the entities' symbols. If an entity is not involved with the condition, its symbol appears through the condition symbol. In Figure 5-22, for example, state Clock.time=22:00 concerns entities SLT Subsystem and Clock but not Line 10.

The MSC notation does not have specific support for iterations (i.e., loops). A commonly used technique is to repeat the interactions a couple of times and add dots to indicate the repetition. Other commentary text may be added.

Reading an MSC diagram is easy. In Figure 5-22 we have four communicating entities, Exchange, SLT Subsystem, Line 10 and Clock. The Exchange sends the SetTestPermissions(...) message to configure the test permissions of Line 10, and the SetPeriodicTest(...) message to start a periodic test on it at a certain time. The SLT Subsystem checks the preconditions for the operation and has to respond with the TestAccepted message within 50 ms. When the condition Clock.time=22:00 is true, the Clock sends the PeriodicTestStart message to the SLT Subsystem. The rest of the diagram is interpreted similarly.

Scenarios serve as a verification mechanism on the analysis results regarding the behavior of the subsystem. They are a convenient tool for discussion with the designers and the customers alike. Scenarios are often built at the beginning of dynamic modeling to deduce information needed elsewhere in the dynamic model.

Scenarios are also the starting point for building the object interaction threads in the design phase. A subsystem appears as a black box in scenarios. In the subsequent design phase, the black box is replaced by the specific objects that are responsible for the interactions. This issue is further elaborated in Chapter 6.

5.4 Analysis of the Hardware Wrapper

The object model, functional model and dynamic model are built for the hardware wrapper using the same notations and according to the same guidelines as for an application subsystem. However, the perspective is a little bit different.

By examining the environment of every application subsystem, we will detect classes that appear in one or more environments but do not belong to any of the application subsystems. Those classes represent concepts either internal in the system hardware or external to it. For example, in the Cruise Control case study a simple indicator LED exists internally, whereas a speedometer is externally connected to the system. We simply conceptualize each internal or external hardware item in the environment of the application subsystem as one class that, from the point of view of the application, provides all services. We say the class is wrapping the full chain of hardware, such as I/O ports, signals, transmission means, sensors, actuators, mechanics and whatever else is necessary to supply the required service. Such a class is called an *abstract environment class*. Of course, an indicator class, for example, cannot really wrap the LED or the driving transistor. Wrapping the hardware is just a mental image that makes the analysis of the application easier.

During analysis of the hardware wrapper, we explode this abstract view and recognize the inner structure of any abstract environment class in more concrete terms. This is done by mapping each abstract environment class into a class of the hardware wrapper, called the *wrapper class*, providing an interface to the services defined by the abstract environ-

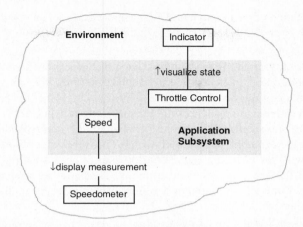

Figure 5-23. Example of two abstract environment classes.

ment class. Figures 5-23 and 5-24 illustrate this concept for the indicator and speedometer example.

In Figure 5-23, an extract of the class diagram of the Cruise Control case study, we take the perspective of the application subsystem. The application class Speed associates with the abstract environment class Speedometer, which is viewed here as a representation of a real speedometer, including everything needed for its purpose. The application class Throttle Control associates with the abstract environment class Indicator viewed as a

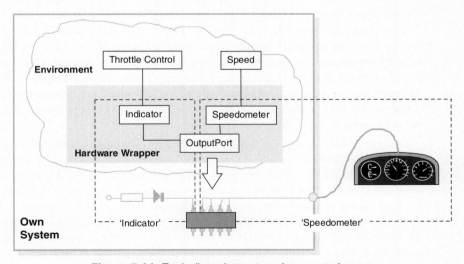

Figure 5-24. Exploding abstract environment classes.

representation of a real indicator LED, which can be set on or off or blink at a certain rate. Figure 5-24 shows the mirror image in the hardware wrapper.

As you can see in Figure 5-24, the two dashed boxes indicate the abstract environment classes Indicator and Speedometer. Each includes some hardware wrapper software, an output port, on-board electronics and, in the case of the speedometer, even the display unit in the car's console which is external to the system. Inside the hardware wrapper, a wrapper class with the same name as the abstract environment class is introduced to provide the concrete software interface to the services of the corresponding abstract environment class. In the example, further analysis has uncovered class OutputPort which is used by wrapper classes Indicator and Speedometer to access the physical output port. Notice that the LED hardware is not able to blink. The hardware wrapper software must provide this service in such a way that it becomes available for the application just like setting the LED on and off.

Generally speaking, in the class diagram of the hardware wrapper we gather the wrapper classes, each representing a corresponding abstract environment class defined in the environment of at least one application subsystem. The environment of the hardware wrapper mirrors the classes from all application subsystems that have been associated with an abstract environment class. However, now the association is between the application subsystem class and the wrapper class.

Inside the class diagram of the hardware wrapper we continue to identify classes until a reasonably sized hardware concept is reached, such as class OutputPort. This procedure typically results in discovering the important roles interrupt service routines and the time scheduler of the operating system play. To express this fact, we include them in the object model just like other classes and view them as part of the hardware wrapper. This way, the class diagram of the hardware wrapper shows special classes inside the boundary labeled by the name of the interrupt service routine or by the name Operating System. These special classes have associations with other classes too.

When analyzing a particular application subsystem, we recommend ignoring the details of the underlying hardware. We develop a dynamic model that is based on logical, high-level events about which we do not know how they are generated. This open issue is addressed in the dynamic model of the hardware wrapper: we map the events of the hardware wrapper, called primitive events, into the logical events. Sometimes this mapping is a simple one-to-one forwarding; in other cases, the logical event is computed based on a primitive event.

Any event has its roots in a hardware interrupt. If a primitive event is derived directly in the interrupt service routine of a particular interrupt, we classify it as a hard interrupt. An example might be a 1-ms timer interrupt from which we derive a poll input primitive event every 10 ms. This, in turn, may generate one or more logical events if the pressing of a certain button is detected by the polling. Besides those events classified as hard interrupts, the only other class of primitive events are soft interrupts derived from the time scheduler of the operating system. Both classes of primitive events have their source inside the hardware wrapper and not outside in the environment, whereas a logical event always enters the application subsystem from outside the boundary.

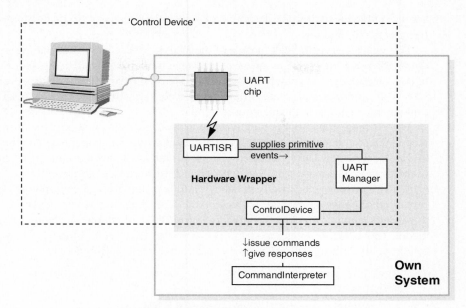

Figure 5-25. Partial wrapper class diagram.

Notice that the operating system itself has to be provided with a timer tick too. More-over, events emitted by one subsystem to another may also be based on soft interrupts.

An example illustrates the relationship between a primitive event and a logical event. Let's assume that an abstract environment class **ControlDevice** exists in the object model of an application subsystem. An association with the application class **CommandInter-preter** indicates the reception of command events. The corresponding hardware wrapper class diagram, Figure 5-25, mirrors this relationship and explodes the high-level view of the abstract environment class: a class **UARTmanager**, an interrupt service routine **UAR-TISR** and a PC connected to a UART chip is involved. By means of the interrupt service routine, the UART chip supplies, for example, a primitive event to the hardware wrapper when the UART reception buffer is full. The result of a sequence of these primitive events is a command event issued by the hardware wrapper to the application.

5.5 Summary

During the analysis phase, we are clearly oriented towards a practical analysis of the prob-lem, but not its solution, which is left to the design phase. The analysis is not formal, but it is systematic and verifiable. Being informal allows the models to have some degree of flexibility, which is an advantage. It results in simpler models, still with enough detail. This also reduces the effort needed to produce the models. Fully detailed analysis models are not a prerequisite for the design phase where the designer systematically decides and formalizes the solutions.

This chapter presented the models of the analysis phase and their relationships to each other. These are the object model, the functional model and the dynamic model. Because of the complex dynamic nature of real-time systems, the dynamic model is the most intensive. It has a number of related components which describe the dynamic behavior from different viewpoints complementing each other.

The process of analysis is iterative; the analyst may start with an approximate object model, then go to a piece of the functional model or the dynamic model and then go back to the object model. This is repeated until he is satisfied with the accuracy and correctness of the models. The models are verified, and inconsistencies are removed.

The chapter presented briefly the notation for each model, and concentrated on the process of building the model and linking it to the other models. The components of the functional and dynamic models are always associated with the components of the object model. This gives the object model a special role as the reference model, and for this reason the analyst must focus on getting a correct and stable object model.

6

DESIGN PHASE

This chapter introduces the design phase of the OCTOPUS method, which takes the middle ground between the analysis model and the implementation of executable code. Starting from the specifications produced during analysis, the goal is to systematically develop a description of how the system will work at a level of abstraction above that required by programming languages.

The common mistake made during design is to start programming. The better approach is to view design primarily as a body of work that makes our understanding of a solution to the problem explicit and explains the rationale for a chosen alternative while at the same time preserving the requirements, definitions and semantic relationships settled in the analysis phase. Paradoxically, the key to the success of the software system in areas like implementation, testing and maintenance rests on the insight that, during design, these areas are only side effects of the effort.

A major concern of design is the finite speed of, eventually, a single processor. Unlike other branches of software development, in real-time systems this is not just a performance issue. The nonzero time it takes to process any particular event permits other events to occur before this processing has been completed. This situation demands designing concurrency into the system, particularly if the second event is more urgent or important. However, any interleaved processing deserves special attention because missing or improper synchronization will potentially corrupt the results.

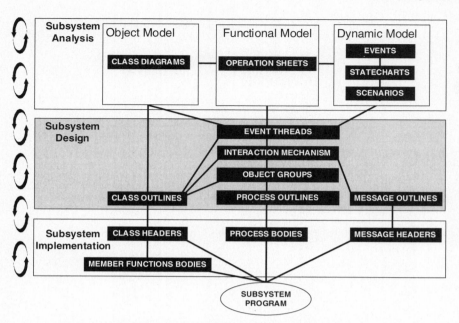

Figure 6-1. Overview of design phase components.

Taking these facts into account, the OCTOPUS design phase provides a controlled transition from the implicit concurrency model applied during analysis to the explicit model. This includes incorporation of a conventional real-time operating system that enables multiple, quasi-concurrent threads of execution. Figure 6-1 shows an overview of the components and their links in this transition process. Each of these components will be introduced, and we provide guidance in developing them. Rules are given to check for completeness and consistency at each stage, and to validate the quality of the design.

In contrast to the analysis phase, designing the system takes into account that an event will be directed toward an object, which in turn will interact with other objects until the response is generated. The designer explicitly describes these object interactions in terms of the event thread concept and uses the object interaction graph notation to visualize them.

Based on the event threads, the design proceeds with a decision on the interaction mechanism: synchronous or asynchronous. This decision yields object groups, which are associated with processes in terms of the underlying operating system. The process outlines describe these processes in more detail. The messages they exchange are described in optional interprocess message outlines.

In parallel with these activities the class outlines emerge, because the designer continuously records details about all design decisions in them.

As in the analysis phase, this design process is run at least two times, once for the application system and once for the hardware wrapper. If the system has been divided into subsystems, each one of them is designed separately according to its defined boundary and environment. From the point of view of a particular subsystem, some objects from other subsystems will appear in the environment as either originators of an event or objects with which the particular subsystem is interacting. If only one application subsystem exists, all its environment objects belong to the hardware wrapper.

Designing the hardware wrapper applies the same concepts, mechanisms and notations as for an application subsystem.

6.1 Design Objects

The object model produced in analysis mainly describes classes. The class diagram and the class description table are the standard ways to capture this information. The developer also had objects in mind during analysis, but the distinction between classes and objects was somewhat vague. The class diagram shows the classes and the associations between them. Behind the classes, analysis assumed the existence of objects that receive and react on the events broadcast in the subsystem.

In the design phase, the focus is on *design objects*. A design object is an extension of the object we had in mind during analysis which was not detailed further than describing it in terms of its class. Nonetheless, a design object may be an abstract, high-level design component that needs further decomposition in the implementation phase.

A design object is an instance of its corresponding class. The class describes each such instance. Design will keep object and class clearly distinct from each other. Design objects, even if they are instances of the same class, can be distinctly identified. In case data members are declared in the class, any design object instantiated from that class holds its own values of these data members. When evolving the design objects of a subsystem, their corresponding classes may undergo some refinements. In particular, we will extend the objects with an operational interface and declare it in the corresponding class outline.

If we are going to show design objects graphically, we draw a single object as a solid outlined box like the one shown in Figure 6-2. The box gets a label identifying the design object the box represents. The syntax for this label is ClassName::objectIdentifier.

Either the ClassName:: specifier, including the double colon, or objectIdentifier is optional. The object identifier may bear no class name specifier if it is obvious from which class this design object is instantiated. Frequently, embedded systems deal with single instances of classes. Those singularities are best labeled with an object identifier only. The class name can be derived from the object identifier by the convention that the object identifier is identical to the class name except that it starts with a small letter, whereas the class

```
SubscriberLine::
    subLine7
```

Figure 6-2. Sample of the notation of design objects.

name starts with a capital letter. As you can see in the Cruise Control case study, it consists of such singularities only. For example, the solely existing object of class ThrottleControl will be simply labeled throttleControl.

A box does not get an object identifier and bears only the class name, including the double colons, if it represents some unique part of the class shared by all instances of that class or classes derived from this class. Sometimes this is referred to as the static part of a class. For example, in the Cruise Control case study you might detect an object box labeled Rotationmeasure::. Notice the capital R and the double colons. Such a box denotes the static part of class Rotationmeasure.

Sometimes, in conjunction with aggregation, the structure of the object identifier will take the form masterIdentifier.memberIdentifier. An example from the SLT case study is SubscriberLine::subline7.testResult. Any instance of class SubscriberLine has a test result. Referring to the particular instance of class SubscriberLine and accessing its member identifies the test result of this subscriber line.

The purpose of any identification of a design object is only to understand the design. This does not anticipate any specific implementation means. Due to this limited purpose, formally ambiguous identifications are acceptable. Humans are well able to make proper use anyhow because they automatically apply context knowledge or common sense for clarification.

The graphical notation of a design object results in building object diagrams that extend and complement the class diagrams. Whereas a class diagram contains classes, an object diagram shows the individual design objects of a subsystem together with their associations to other design objects, but it is possible to mix classes and objects when necessary, so the separation is not rigid. Figure 6-3 shows an object diagram of the Cruise Control case study. Analysis focuses on class diagrams. Occasionally, it is worthwhile to add object diagrams to illustrate complicated data structures or basic interaction links. The remainder of this chapter simply refers to design objects as objects.

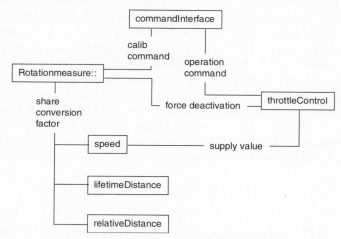

Figure 6-3. Example of an object diagram.

6.2 Interaction of Objects

6.2.1 Object Interaction Threads

Designing the system cannot be done adequately by looking at individual objects in isolation. Instead, it is necessary to take a more holistic view and to define how the pieces collaborate, making behavior happen that satisfies the specifications. In particular, the abstraction of the analysis phase in which an event simply broadcasts and just the involved objects react, must be changed into some more concrete design that shows how the proper set of objects will be notified about an occurrence of the event and how they produce the response. This requires following the flow of control and data from object to object, a design issue generally called *object interaction*. Because good analysis should not pay attention to this how issue, we know only a little about the interactions of objects at the beginning of design, but before implementation can start all object interactions must be settled.

Object interaction is directed and point-to-point. The object initiating a request for service is referred to as the *client*. The object receiving the request and providing the service is known as the *server*. Of course, the server object may become a client requesting subsequent services and so forth.

Unlike conventional design, object-oriented technology always binds the storage of data to an object. Upon request by a client, a server object shall perform, for example, a transformation of its data. The request may be accompanied by data flow either unidirectional from the client to the server, known as parameter passing, or from the server to the client, known as return value(s), or bidirectional between both. Processing the request may require access to data in other objects, but plain moving of data from object A to object B under control of object C violates the object-oriented principles and should be avoided. This rule forces data flow to play only a secondary role compared to control flow. In short, object interaction primarily means passing the thread of execution from the client to the server.

If a given object interaction can be traversed completely by only one thread of execution, the more specific term *object interaction thread* is assigned to such an object interaction. An object interaction thread always has an object at the top receiving the initial request and initiating the whole interaction. This top object is sometimes referred to as the *controller* [Coleman '93].

Object interaction threads are the most natural, basic form of object interaction. Other authors do not distinguish object interaction threads with exactly one path through all objects from the more general term *object interaction*. Fusion [Coleman '93], for example, restricts its graphical notation of object interaction by definition to object interaction threads. OCTOPUS starts with object interaction threads but goes further, as explained below.

6.2.2 Notation of Object Interaction Graphs

The *object interaction graph notation* has been introduced widely to visualize object interactions nicely [Coleman '93, Rumbaugh '95c]. OCTOPUS complies to the object interaction graph notation as defined by OMT [Rumbaugh '95c]. This notation, as well as others, allows visualization of object interaction threads. However, OCTOPUS lifts the restriction that the graph can have only one path of execution with only one controller object. This is a property of object interaction threads which can be observed when expressing an object interaction thread in the form of an object interaction graph. Relaxing the formal definition of the object interaction graph notation extends usage of the notation to the more general cases where multiple object interaction threads interfere with each other.

An object interaction graph presents an overview of the interaction of objects. To understand the meaning of an interaction shown in the graph, you should read the outlines of the classes from which the interacting objects are instantiated. Section 6.4 describes class outlines in more detail.

An object interaction graph is a figure that shows boxes linked by lines. The boxes represent design objects as introduced earlier. The lines indicate interactions between the objects that are detailed further by one or a few labels along the line. Each label denotes a request between the linked objects. A small arrow in front of the label shows the direction of the request from the client to the server. Note that the client and server roles may swap from label to label along the same link. The interaction sequence number is added after the small arrow. The initial request of an object interaction thread to its controller is shown by an arrow, optionally labeled. Figure 6-4 shows a very simple example that refers to the SLT case study.

The sequence numbers make the sequencing of requests explicit [Coleman '93]. They are Dewey Decimal numbers, for example, 1. 1.1 1.1.1 ... 1.2 ... 2. 2.1 and so forth. The sequence numbers 1.1 and 1.2 on requests from a client indicate that the client will issue the request with the number 1.1 before that with the number 1.2. A request from a client to a server with the sequence number 1.1 and requests from this server to other objects with the sequence numbers 1.1.1 through 1.1.n indicate that the requests 1.1.1 through 1.1.n are subsequent requests of request 1.1, and their results must be completed before control is returned to the original client. Always adding a new Dewey number level for a subsequent interaction will make these numbers cumbersome. In simple graphs with single subsequent interactions you may relax the numbering scheme by incrementing the given base number only.

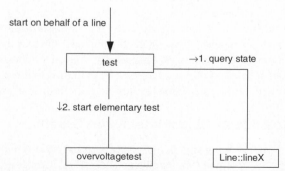

Figure 6-4. Simple example of object interaction graph notation.

The existence of a label along the line indicates that the client may issue this request, not that it must happen under all circumstances. Whether to issue a certain request or not may depend on the actual runtime evaluation of some data contained within the client. The object interaction graph shows all possible interaction links. For example, in Figure 6-4, interaction start elementary test will take place only if the evaluation of the state allows this at that instant. If an actual interaction is not performed, all its subsequent interactions are not performed either. When following a particular path in an object interaction graph, parallel examination of the class outline of the currently regarded objects will reveal the circumstances under which a request will be issued. Or, vice versa, when developing an object interaction graph, we should record these design decisions in the class outline.

Due to the nature of real-time systems, an object interacting with external physical entities may require an explicitly defined delay to synchronize its processing. Although it is basically always possible to define an event indicating that the associated delay has expired, we may prefer to design a so-called *internal delay* where the object interaction thread halts for the specified delay time.

A decision for an internal delay should be made explicitly. It should be documented, for example, in the object interaction graph of the object interaction thread. The notation for that is a circle with a capital **W** inside attached to the object performing the internal delay. Optionally, the delay time may be indicated. The W-bubble also gets an interaction sequence number assigned to it which specifies when, in the sequence of interactions, the delay is done. Figure 6-5 shows a small example from the SLT case study. In this example, the internal delay is required between the setting up of the stimulus and starting sampling in the measurement unit because the electrical signals need time to stabilize.

If the graph depicts a single object interaction thread, like Figure 6-4 does, the incoming request to the controller object does not need a number, and we start numbering with the requests from the controller to its servers. Should we draw a graph that involves more than one object interaction thread, a unique number is assigned to the initial request of each object interaction thread. All requests belonging to a particular object interaction thread start their sequence number with the number given to the initial request. This num-

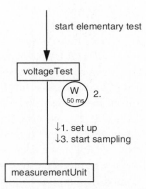

Figure 6-5. An internal delay example.

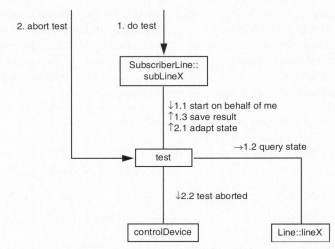

Figure 6-6. Object interaction graph with two object interaction threads.

bering system allows us to distinguish multiple object interaction threads in a single graph even if they cross each other in certain objects. Figure 6-6 shows an example. One object interaction thread starts with the **do test** request, whereas the second starts with an **abort test** request. The controller objects of the two object interaction threads are distinct here. In other cases, the same object may become the controller in multiple object interaction threads.

The numbers assigned to the initial requests of object interaction threads do not define any sequencing, however. Their sole purpose is the identification of the corresponding object interaction thread, and any association like 1 comes before 2 is not meant. In the example shown in Figure 6-6, we are still able to identify the object interaction thread from Figure 6-4 because the number 1 has been assigned to it and all interactions belonging to it start with a 1, whereas the other object interaction thread is marked by the starting number 2. In this way we recognize that, for example, request 2.2 is not subsequent to 1.1 as it belongs to another object interaction thread, although the graphical layout appears to suggest that a bit.

As was said earlier, any service request may also involve data flow. For the purpose of the object interaction graph in OCTOPUS, such details of a data flow that accompanies the control flow are of minor interest, or the request intuitively includes that anyway. For example, in Figure 6-6, request 1.2 has been labeled **query state**, a phrase indicating data flow (i.e., the state here) from the server to the client. Also, interaction 1.3, labeled **save result**, indicates that some result data is transmitted—in this case, from the client to the server. There is no need to express this fact formally because the graph is intended to give the human reader an overview, and this reader also recognizes the data flow informally. Therefore, OCTOPUS does not recommend showing such data flow explicitly in the object interaction graph unless it is really important. Instead, this issue fits much better into the class outlines (Section 6.3) where it can be recorded as is usually done for function invocation with parameters and return values. Should it become necessary to add data flow in an object interaction graph, please refer to OMT [Rumbaugh '95c] for details of the notation.

Note that return data flow occurs from the server to the client, which is in the reverse direction of the request causing production of the data. We should not confuse this with a subsequent request reverting to the direction of the original request. Such a subsequent request is naturally shown in the object interaction graph.

6.2.3 Integrating Statecharts

In the analysis phase, we also developed a few statecharts describing state-dependent behavior wherever it might clarify the situation. Although any strong or weak association with one or a few classes may be given during analysis, OCTOPUS introduces, unlike other authors, the statechart as a conceptual item in its own right. Together with other parts of the analysis, statecharts describe behavior directly in terms of state changes caused by events but leave open how this happens and which objects read or write the state information. Closing this issue is a major body of work in design.

OCTOPUS allows any number of statecharts. They are considered to be concurrent according to the statechart notation, although we neither stress this point nor show it formally. In the context of the statechart notation, the term "concurrent" has a specific meaning (see [Harel '87] or Chapter 5). This should be clearly distinguished from the usage of the term "concurrent" with respect to threads of execution.

As a matter of fact, the primary service a statechart provides is state information. Thus, the client/server model, as introduced for objects, fits for statecharts as well. In the simplest case, a statechart only represents a state variable that objects will read or write. This manipulation of state may be packed as a service that a statechart provides on request from an object. Designing a statechart this way applies the *passive statechart model*, because the statechart plays a mostly passive role here. On the other hand, the statechart may act as the client and request services from objects when making a state transition. Such a statechart will receive events and will act. Consequently, this design is referred to as applying the *active statechart model*.

Both statechart models push the statechart into a position similar to that of an object which participates in the object interaction thread. In OCTOPUS, any object interaction thread may include statecharts. In the object interaction graph, a statechart is represented by a box linked with other objects. The keyword **statechart** distinguishes statecharts from objects. A label follows the keyword. Analogous to the label of the object box, the syntax of the label of the statechart box is StatechartName::statechartIdentifier with the same options and similar naming conventions.

The statechart represented by a box in an object interaction graph may undergo some refinements compared to the one from analysis. More states or even new, additional statecharts may be necessary due to the particular way in which the object interactions or the internals of the related classes are designed.

If a statechart is designed according to the passive model, only interactions directed toward the statechart are feasible. Further, we know that only data flow (i.e., read and write of the state variable) is involved in the interactions. Because we are usually not inter-

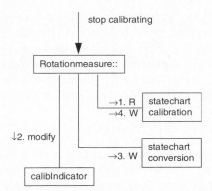

Figure 6-7. Example of statecharts in the object interaction graph.

ested in showing exact details of this data flow in the object interaction graph, we allow a label consisting of a simple R or W denoting read or write respectively. Figure 6-7 shows an example of an object interaction thread from the Cruise Control case study.

Good design of the passive statechart model avoids usage of the same statechart in many places. An ideal solution would be that any statechart is accessed by exactly one object only. However, real life forces us to make compromises. To find the optimum, we explicitly show the statecharts at the beginning just like other objects, except for cases where it is instantly apparent that the statechart belongs to a certain object. The latter is usually true if there are several instances of the same class, each having its own state. This approach allows us, when proceeding, to iterate on the design and balance it in such way that the use of statecharts becomes optimally local to certain objects. If we finally achieve the result that exactly one object uses a particular statechart, we treat this statechart as a local member of this object's class and drop its representation in any object interaction graph. An example of that kind is statechart conversion from the Cruise Control case study. During design of the Cruise Control application subsystem, we will discover the fact that statechart conversion is accessed only from the static part of class Rotation-measure. As a result, we do not show it in the final graphs found in Chapter 10.

6.2.4 Event Threads

Object interaction threads can be expanded downward and upward. Downward expansion simply means that a server object not yet considered is detected. However, an object interaction thread is normally designed only inside a particular subsystem. Thus, expansion stops whenever the subsystem boundary is crossed. Upward expansion of an object interaction thread stems from the fact that regardless of what level we are at, the controller cannot initiate the interaction spontaneously. It too requires a trigger. By examining this trigger, we iteratively build bigger and bigger nested object interaction threads until we reach the point where, instead of another object of the subsystem, a logical event from the environment across the subsystem boundary triggers the entire object interaction.

If downward and upward expansion have led to an object interaction thread that starts with a particular event and branches to all servers except where the client is outside the current subsystem, it is called an *event thread*. An event thread defines what objects are involved and what requests are exchanged between the objects of a subsystem, and across the boundary, in response to a particular event from a particular object in the environment.

A dashed arrow to the controller expresses the incoming event in the object interaction graph. The dashed arrow denotes that, from the viewpoint of the subsystem, the event occurs spontaneously at any time. Of course, there must exist an object in the environment from which the event originates, called the *originator*. A box added at the tail of the event arrow shows the originator of an event thread in the object interaction graph. During analysis we numbered the events. The event arrow is labeled with this event number. All subsequent interactions inside this event thread bear a sequence number starting with this event number. Optionally, the subsystem boundary can be marked in some way in the graph. Figure 6-8 shows an example of an event thread. It is an expansion of the object interaction thread from Figure 6-4 upward to the originator of the TestRequest event E10 and downward to the subsystem boundary. The objects controlDevice, measurementUnit and lineX are from the environment, in this case from the hardware wrapper. Notice the read or write accesses of statechart sltSystem by three objects and the internal delay at object test.

Sometimes, the designer might discover that the originator directs the same particular event to more than one controller in the subsystem. Hence, more than one interaction thread is triggered by the same particular event, each having its own distinct controller object at the top. Here, the event thread is defined as the union of all these object interaction threads together with the sole originator. Visualization of such an event thread in an object interaction graph overlays all the related object interaction threads and splits the event arrow from the originator to each controller. Each such arrow is labeled with a Dewey number with the event number as base followed by an identification number, just as introduced generally for overlaid object interaction threads. These two-level Dewey numbers become the base for the sequence numbers of all interaction links of the interaction thread triggered by the corresponding arrow.

By convention, the object interaction graph of an event thread shows the originator object on top and all other environment objects at the bottom. If the environment object that behaves as the originator becomes a server object in another interaction, the graph shows the same object in its role as server by a second box at the bottom. For example, in Figure 6-8, object controlDevice issues the event E10 and, via interaction 10.2 or 10.6, it receives a positive or negative acknowledgment or a report on no connection.

The analysis phase also grouped events. Instead of an elementary event, we may build an event thread for a superevent as well. This is a practical and efficient approach in situations where the event threads of the subevents of a particular superevent would not differ or would differ only slightly. Furthermore, we may build an event thread for any of the compound events from the laxity analysis.

Building the event threads is a major task in subsystem design. You have reached an important design milestone if the design describes a consistent set of event threads that cover any event, either individually or bound inside a superevent or bound by a compound

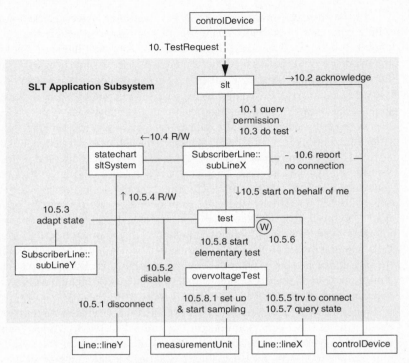

Figure 6-8. Example of an event thread.

event. Preferably, a few of those complete sets are developed. Looking at all event threads of each alternative set together, an assessment of the relative quality of the alternative designs is possible. Usually, the best design alternative is the one that achieves minimum distribution of objects across the event threads and minimum usage of statecharts by more than one object. You will notice that the two goals contradict each other in real life applications. Thus, you have to compromise.

Later, design will consider even multiple, overlaid event threads. Although it may become technically hard to produce and to read, the object interaction graph notation allows us to do this overlaying graphically in one graph.

6.2.5 Unqualified Interaction Model

When initially building the event threads, we replace the idealized event broadcast principle of the implicit concurrency model used in analysis by concrete object interactions. This is our first step in shifting from the implicit concurrency model to the explicit one. For a short while, however, we still keep the second principle of the implicit concurrency model, that is, we mentally view all processing as infinitely fast. This view allows us to defer the constraints on how the interaction will be implemented, and to concentrate exclusively on the required functionality first.

Therefore, as the event threads are built, OCTOPUS recommends having the so-called *unqualified interaction model* in mind, meaning that when a server object receives a request, it completes the processing before execution is returned to the client. If the processing at the server also issues requests to other objects, these nested requests must all be completed before the initial request is completed. Assuming infinitely fast processing, completion of any requested service will happen at once. Finally, the entire event thread completes execution of all its branches in zero time, regardless how many and how deeply they are nested.

Since any event thread completes instantly, our model allows execution of as many event threads as we want in a time window as close to zero as you like, and nonetheless they all run one after the other without any interleaving. You can think of everything as concurrent or everything as strictly sequential. It is both at the same time. This view defers all synchronization problems.

An internal delay, however, contradicts this infinitely fast assumption and deserves special attention. By definition, the internal delay expands the timing of the event thread in such way that the interaction with the next higher sequence number than the one of the internal delay will be started when a specified delay time has expired. Assuming there is no further internal delay nested somewhere within, this interaction and all subsequent interactions will complete instantly at the end of the delay. At the same point in time, all interactions wherein the internal delay is nested will complete. This, of course, affects the time when return values are available and can be evaluated, a fact that needs special consideration if an internal delay is designed in an event thread.

If a particular event thread halts in an internal delay, the system would not react on any further occurrence of the same event anymore. This is an unacceptable limitation in most cases, however inherent to our unqualified interaction model. We left this issue pending because the purpose of the unqualified interaction model is to gain an initial design that will be changed and enhanced immediately in the next steps. There, we will see why the appearance of this limitation is only deceptive.

Conversely to the model just introduced, we view the event-based interaction from the originator to the controller differently. By nature, the event is a trigger only. Completion of the event thread is not nested in the execution path of the originator, although it would be possible to conceptualize it this way too since we just postulated an immediate completion of the entire event thread. Due to this asynchronous model for the event, any control or data flow backward to the originator requires an extra interaction that must be shown separately in the object interaction graph. See, for example, interactions 10.2 and 10.6 in Figure 6-8.

Note that the unqualified interaction model allows nothing else except the internal delay to break the immediate completion assumption. An internal wait point for any condition does not make sense in the unqualified interaction model because the event thread setting the condition can run the related interactions as well. If, for example, an event thread E1 is required to continue at object a with the interactions 1.x.2, 1.x.3 and so forth only if another event thread E2 has occurred before, we design E1 and E2 as shown in Figure 6-9. In any solution, the two event threads share state information. Instead of waiting until E2 occurs, E1 returns via interaction 1.x. Later, E2 requests, via interaction

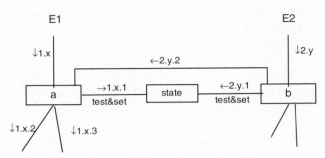

Figure 6-9. Interfering event threads.

2.y.2, the same service as interaction 1.x does if E2 has occurred before. The zero time assumption allows this arrangement without any problem. For now, this design looks a bit different from how it is usually done. Later, however, we will learn, that this appearance is deceptive.

After we have designed all event threads in this way, OCTOPUS approaches the second step in its shift to the explicit concurrency model, and at that time the interaction mechanism issue will arise again.

6.2.6 Building the Event Threads

This section gives guidelines on how the event threads of a particular subsystem can be built. The procedure involves the following seven main steps, which are explained below and then demonstrated in an example. Remember that an event thread can be built for an elementary event, a superevent or a compound event. In the following text, the term "event" refers to all three cases.

> *Step 1*: Select an event not yet considered.
> *Step 2*: Identify an object involved in the processing of the selected event.
> *Step 3*: Design and record subsequent interactions.
> *Step 4*: Merge the new object interaction thread with existing ones.
> *Step 5*: Repeat from step 3 as long as other involved objects can still be found.
> *Step 6*: Repeat from step 1 unless done for all events.
> *Step 7*: Iterate and balance the use of objects and statecharts.

The purpose of the first step of the procedure is to build the event threads incrementally for each event. The designer may select any of the events not yet covered by an already specified event thread. In principle, it does not matter with what event one starts, but it is good practice to build the simpler ones first because they may reveal useful information about the more complicated ones.

Second, the procedure seeks, based on the selected event, all objects for which this event is relevant. Although preferable, this is not limited to the objects directly receiving the event. Any object that performs a service related to the event is a candidate with which to start an object interaction thread. For the moment, it does not matter if it is still unclear from where and how the request comes in. An alternative, equally effective approach is to examine the scenarios from analysis and to develop the event thread in a top-down manner from there. Note, however, that the purpose of the message sequence chart is to show sequences of events with the subsystem as a black box. For any distinct event found there, the designer must build an event thread. Any association with a class documented in the corresponding entry of the event sheet is another way to start. Objects of a class mentioned there are obviously involved in processing this event. If the event sheets or the operation sheets document an association between an event and an operation, the event thread started by this event performs the operation.

Next, think about whether the service of the chosen object should be structured into further subservices. As a rule of thumb, each service an object provides should have only one purpose at either the elementary or composite level (i.e., nesting other subservices). In case the chosen service is a composite one, we identify the objects providing the subservices. For each, we design and record the interactions between the client and the server. Also, access of statecharts, either reading the actual state or writing a new state, is recorded. This process repeats iteratively until we reach elementary services of reasonable complexity.

The first time you come to step 4 for a particular event, it can be skipped. Later, when repeating from step 3, the situation is different because there is an object interaction thread already existing from the former cycles in addition to the one being built. Both inherently belong to the same event thread, each forming another branch. These branches must always merge into one. In most cases one is a side branch of the other, but sometimes they do not link immediately and we have to expand one or both branches upward to close the gap. It may also happen that both object interaction threads are triggered directly by the event, but the event is received by two distinct controller objects. In this case, we overlay the two object interaction threads and direct the event to both controllers.

After that, the procedure repeats from step 3 with the next object involved in processing the same particular event and not yet included in the already built object interaction thread, until no such object is found anymore. In the latter case, you should check if the result is really an event thread, meaning it starts with the event across the subsystem's boundary. In rare cases, it is necessary to expand the object interaction thread upward until the event triggers the interactions. Also examine whether a response to the event originator should be given, and express this fact by adding a final interaction.

When one event thread has been completed according to this procedure, the next can be built by repeating from step 1 with another event not yet considered. When finished with all event threads, examine them all together. Thoroughly investigate alternative arrangements and iterate the whole procedure. In particular, try to avoid distributed, shared statecharts. The goal is to balance the use of objects and statecharts in such way that the objects become optimally local to the event threads and the statecharts local to the objects.

To illustrate this procedure, we run an example from the Cruise Control case study. In this example, we postulate the existence of an analysis document like the one found in Chapter 10. This document is the basis for the various design decisions when following the steps of the procedure.

1. Select an event not yet considered (Step 1).

From the event list found in the analysis document, we pick the enable calibration event E7.

2. Identify an object in the processing of the selected event (Step 2).

The analysis document states that the enable calibration event will implicitly deactivate Cruise Control. This involves object throttleControl. Although we do not know yet how the enable calibration event forwards a deactivate request to object throttleControl, we start an object interaction thread with it.

3. Design and record the object interactions (Step 3).

The event thread of the **deactivate** event (imagine that we built it already!) becomes an object interaction thread of the event thread we are building now. Figure 6-10 shows this branch.

4. Merge the new object interaction thread with existing ones (Step 4).

We can skip this in the first cycle.

5. Repeat from step 3 as long as other involved objects can still be found (Step 5).

From the analysis document we get a hint that calibration commands are directed to the static part of class Rotationmeasure. The enable calibration event is also directed to it. The static part of class Rotationmeasure starts another object interaction thread.

6. Design and record subsequent interactions (Step 3).

The analysis document specifies that the enable calibration event triggers a state transition in statechart calibration to the enabled.ready state. Further, the actions table indicates that, when entering state enabled.ready, the calibration indicator will start blinking at 4 Hz. This leads to an object interaction thread, as shown in Figure 6-11.

7. Merge the new object interaction thread with existing ones (Step 4).

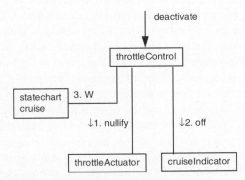

Figure 6-10. Object interaction thread E7a.

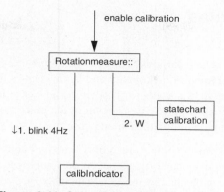

Figure 6-11. Object interaction thread E7b.

We have built two object interaction threads, E7a from the former cycle and E7b in this cycle. Each is another branch of the same event thread. Since only object interaction thread E7b receives the enable calibration event, we link object interaction thread E7a with E7b by designing an interaction from the static part of class Rotationmeasure to object throttleControl. This combination is shown in Figure 6-12.

8. Repeat from step 3 as long as other involved objects can still be found (Step 5).

Other involved objects are not found anymore. Adding a box for the event originator commandInterface and a dashed arrow for the event to the controller object completes the event thread.

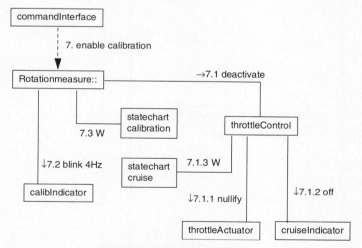

Figure 6-12. Event thread E7.

6.3 Class Outlines

In OCTOPUS, class outlines are used to record the details of design. A class outline describes the common functionality and behavior of any object that is an instance of this class. They evolve in parallel to all other design activities. At the end of design, the class outlines are the most precise description of the inner workings of the objects and serve as a starting point in the implementation phase.

Initially, the class outlines are simply a textual copy of each class from the class diagram developed in the analysis phase. As design progresses, the outlines gradually expand with details about the data members and member functions. In particular, outlines of member function bodies are added. By skipping over the function bodies, a class outline serves as an interface description as well. Since the class outline finally gives much more detail about how to implement the required functionality than inspecting the object interaction graphs, there is less margin for error when it is actually translated into code. Indeed, an OCTOPUS class outline resembles a C++ class in the sense that both specify data members and member functions. It differs in the more relaxed, but also more verbose, syntax.

The use of structured English inside the statements of the class outlines enables other engineers to understand the designer's intent and not to become overwhelmed by the level of exactness required by programming languages to satisfy the compiler. An OCTOPUS class outline combines the rigor of a simple syntax with the readability of short sentences. Listing 6-1 shows an example.

```
class  Speed inherits Rotationmeasure
    int lastCount;
    SpeedValue actualSpeed, actualAccel;
    function takeMeasurement()    //invoked by INT1 at 20 Hz
        if   lastCount > 0
        then calculate actualSpeed and actualAccel
             according to operations O1 and O2;  // . . . . . . . . . . . . *A*
             outputPort.speed(actualSpeed);  //. . . . . . . . . . . . . . . *B*
        endif;
        lastCount = count;
        count = 0;
    endfunction;
    function actualSpeed()
        disable interrupt;  //sync access
        auxiliarySpeedStore = actualSpeed;  // . . . . . . . . . . . . . . . *C*
        enable interrupt;
        return auxiliarySpeedStore;
    endfunction;
    function actualAccel()
        disable interrupt;
        auxiliaryAccelStore = actualAccel;
        enable interrupt;
        return auxiliaryAccelStore;
    endfunction;
endclass;
```

Listing 6-1. Example of class outline.

Another difference compared to C++ is that blocks are opened by a keyword like class, function or if and closed by the corresponding keyword like endclass, endfunction or endif. Curled parentheses are not used for that purpose. Also, at other places a keyword like inherits, is used instead of a single special character. Notice, in Listing 6-1, the flexible mixture of informal phrases like calculate actualSpeed and actualAccel according to operations O1 and O2 (marked *A*) with almost exact C++ statements like outputPort.speed(actualSpeed) (marked *B*). In Chapter 11, "Reference Manual," a syntax summary can be found.

Since the class outline is intended mainly for human readers, types and identifiers do not need to be declared formally before their appearances. Common sense bridges the gap, for example, with the identifier outputPort appearing in the class outline shown in Listing 6-1 (marked *B*). As said earlier, design objects can be distinctly identified in some way; and by using that identification mechanism, whatever it is, they can appear in the class outlines. This also allows things like the object of class X with number 77. The visibility problem of how to get a reference to an object is solved eventually (see Chapter 8); the design phase does not address this. The description given in the class outlines simply assumes that objects are freely visible to each other. This frequently holds in embedded systems due to their highly static nature.

Variables for local use inside a particular block can appear whenever needed. An example of this is the statement auxiliarySpeedStore = actualSpeed as found in Listing 6-1 (marked *C*). Also, the type of formal parameters in a function declaration can be omitted because often the reader is able to guess its type easily from the context or the name itself. In other situations the type of a parameter is still undecided, but nonetheless we want to indicate the existence of a parameter.

In case the class outline states another object as a plain data member of a class, any instance of this class possesses such an object locally bound, and this binding will never change. This does not anticipate any particular means of implementation for such an aggregation and how the fixed binding is achieved. It may be a real data member or a pointer or anything else. From the perspective of designing class outlines only the fixed, locally bound identification is relevant. For example, Listing 6-2 shows an outline of class **SubscriberLine** from the SLT case study that contains the statement Line line (marked *A*). It means that any instance of class SubscriberLine knows about one fixed, unique object of class **Line**. The local identifier line refers conceptually to this object. Later, during implementation, it may turn out that all line objects have to be placed sequentially at a specific memory address, and consequently we define all line objects together as a global array. In this way any usage of line becomes a global array subscript with the subscriber line number as index, and the member line of the class outline is just a concept with no implementation counterpart.

Conversely to the plain data member statement, the class outlines may declare a data member with the syntax ref(ClassName) identifier. This indicates a data member whose binding may change at runtime. Once more, such a statement does not anticipate specific tactics for its final implementation. The class outline of Listing 6-2 shows an example of this, as can be noted in the statement ref(TestResult) latestResult (marked *B*). This is necessary here because this reference will be changed to a new result when the test is completed. If this is implemented by a pointer assignment or by storing an index of an array, it is an issue deferred to implementation.

```
class SubscriberLine
    int number;
    Line line;  //identifies the correponding, physical line . . . . . . . . *A*
    ref(TestResult) latestResult;  //reference to . . . . . . . . . . . . *B*
    statechart SubscriberLine state;  //local, refer to its graph . . . . . *C*
    function doTest(requestPriority)
        if   line.state() != busy  //   . . . . . . . . . . . . . . . . *E*
        then state.Testing = Ongoing; // . . . . . . . . . . . . . . . *D*
            statechart sltSystem.Request = requestPriority;
            if   test.startOnBehalfOf(this) == connectionFailed
            then state.Testing = None.NoConnection;
                statechart sltSystem = Idle;  // . . . . . . . . . . . . *F*
                controlDevice.reportFault(noConnection);
            endif;
        endif;
    endfunction;
    function testFinished(resultUpdate)
        free = latestResult;
        la  stResult = resultUpdate;
        state.Testing = None.Tested;
        state.TestResults = Valid;
        return free;
    endfunction;
    ...
endclass;
```

Listing 6-2. Example of class outline with statecharts.

Listing 6-2 also shows how to use statecharts in the class outlines. Obviously, each subscriber line has its own independent state. Hence, the class outline declares an instance of statechart SubscriberLine locally in `class SubscriberLine` by a statement of the form `statechart StatechartName identifier` (marked *C*). The identifier, simply `state` in the example, can be used locally in the class to test the actual state or to assign a new state. Those statements refer naturally to the terms defined by the statechart. For example, as shown in Chapter 9, "SLT case study," statechart SubcriberLine consists of a concurrent component named Testing that may enter the state Ongoing, which is expressed in the class outline by the statement `state.Testing = Ongoing` (marked *D*).

Access to the local state of an object from the outside should be made only by a function call and not directly read or written. An example is the statement `line.state()` found in Listing 6-2, revealing the fact that each instance of class Line also has a state which is returned by calling the function `state()` (marked *E*).

Besides local statecharts like the ones above, statecharts may also be shared between a few objects. In the class outline of Listing 6-2, you will detect the statement `statechart sltSystem = Idle` (marked *F*). In this way the class outline states the assignment of a new state to the globally shared instance of statechart SLT Subsystem. The syntax uses the keyword `statechart` followed by an identifier for the instance of the statechart. This identifier is usually the name of the statechart starting with a small letter instead of the capital one, just like the convention applied for a class and its single object. In fact, implementation may later declare a class covering this statechart and define a single global instance of that class. Any read/write access will then be mapped into a member function call, which also takes care of the critical synchronization issue (see Chapter 8).

Of course, making a statechart local or shared is a design decision with pros and cons as explained earlier.

6.4 Design of Concurrency

Concurrency does not usually "fall out" as a by-product of design. It must be seriously thought out and planned for. OCTOPUS departs here from traditional object-oriented design and becomes unique in its approach.

6.4.1 Rationale of the Approach

In the implicit concurrency model, different objects perform their tasks infinitely fast, whenever requested. This simple principle has so far made it possible to keep the OCTO-PUS method largely independent of the implementation artifacts, such as operating systems, programming languages and so on. Although some alternative proposals have been made, such as Actor [Agha '86], ACT++ [Kafura '89] and ROOM [Selic '94], OCTOPUS presumes that a standard object-oriented programming language and a conventional real-time operating system are used.

Commonly used object-oriented languages, such as C++, are sequential by nature. They do not support implicit concurrency of the objects, as defined in the implicit concurrency model; nor do they provide any other concurrency construct. Because of this deficiency, the required feature is made available through the operating system, assuming that it provides quasi-concurrency via the conventional process concept and a facility for interprocess communication.

Unfortunately, this preselection requires a combination of two distinct concepts, processes and objects, which in itself is not without problems. The purpose of the following sections is to indicate the way toward a practical solution. The adopted approach trades academic merits in the exploration of new, immature ideas and concepts for usefulness and robustness. In practice, new real-time systems usually evolve from some existing products, and a solution with objects alone may still not be affordable or feasible for some time. Hence, the environment for which objects are being created may also comprise non-object-oriented parts. Typically, these parts are based on a real-time operating system. Even if the authors had selected an alternative "objects only" approach to describe the object concurrency, the same basic difficulty would remain, because it is caused by the fact that the existing software is running on some operating system anyway.

It may be that the relationship between processes and objects is only a difficulty for practitioners, because the existing literature does not give a clear answer to this question.

Some authors, such as [Jacobson '92 and Pesonen '93], recognize the problem and give a few guidelines, but these are not sufficient for practical use. For example, the statement "it is essential to consider how the target environment can be adapted to fit the object structure, so that the structure is minimally distorted" [Jacobson '92] indicates a difficulty without giving any solution to it. OCTOPUS systematically develops the mapping of objects to processes, which implies shifting from the implicit concurrency model to the explicit one.

The concept of object group plays a central role in this approach. This term is defined by giving formal rules on how the groups are formed. From the object groups, process outlines are derived in a straightforward manner. The object groups define which part of each object is covered by the execution thread of each process.

A definite prerequisite for proceeding with the design in the following sections is to have all event threads of the subsystem built as introduced earlier in this chapter. As recommended there, object-interaction graphs are a technique to visually specify the event threads. We illustrate our discussion with a small example that Figure 6-13 illustrates.

The example is abstract in the sense that its objects are simply called a, b, c and so on, the environment objects x1, x2 and so on, and the events are numbered E1, E2 and E3. The interactions are marked by an ordinal number only. The name of the requested service is omitted, since it is not essential from the viewpoint of the explanation. As seen in the figure, event thread E2 represents two combined object interaction threads. The Dewey decimal numbers associated with each interaction allow us to follow each object interaction thread individually. For example, a branch of object interaction thread 2.1 of event thread E2 ends in object f, with interaction 2.1.3 being from object d to object f. The second object interaction thread 2.2 is continued with interaction 2.2.2 after entering f.

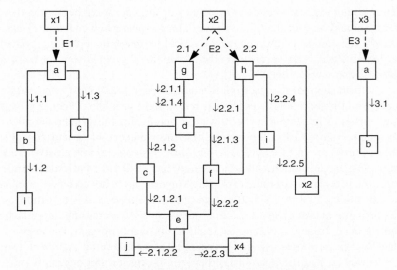

Figure 6-13. Abstract example of event threads.

6.4.2 Synchronous vs. Asynchronous Interaction

As a matter of fact, event threads describe the control flow each particular event will trigger upon occurrence. Because we are only halfway toward the explicit concurrency model, the event threads we have built so far assume neither sequential nor parallel processing. Each object in an event thread can be thought of as an independent and infinitely fast processor triggered by requests. This certainly does not represent a likely configuration for a real system. Now we consider the fact that the implementation will certainly require time for the processing and may have only one physical processor.

This brings up the question of the interaction mechanism. Basically, there are two alternative mechanisms to implement an interaction between objects:

1. *Synchronous interaction*: calling a member function or directly accessing data of another object.

2. *Asynchronous interaction*: the sender transmits a message to the receiver via an operating system facility and continues its execution (asynchronous communication).

As we build the event threads initially, we mentally view any interaction as synchronous. Considering processing time will make the effects of synchronous and asynchronous interaction quite different. We are therefore forced to decide on either synchronous invocation or asynchronous interaction for each interaction specified by the event threads. This can be visually described by an extended object interaction graph, in which asynchronous communications are indicated by a dashed arrow, and synchronous invocations by solid lines as before. If it happens that two dashed arrows are fully in parallel but one points in the reverse direction of the other, both can be combined into one.

Figure 6-14 shows the event threads of the example after selecting asynchronous interaction at a few places. Parallel to this graphical overview, we record the result of any decision concerning the interaction mechanism in the class outlines.

The decision about the interaction mechanism is made by focusing on each interacting pair of objects and inspecting the context of the interaction. The default is to specify a synchronous interaction everywhere. With respect to the flow of execution, this initial decision means that a nested member function call is used everywhere. However, for some interactions asynchronous communication may be preferable.

Specifying an interaction to be asynchronous enables the sender to continue its execution or terminate it, independent of the request sent. A good example is a request that initiates a time-consuming computation. During this computation, the system fails to react to lower-priority events within the given time interval. If the processing of the initial event is separated from the subsequent heavy computation by means of an asynchronous communication, the computation can be performed at a lower priority level, and the system is able to defer the computation when a more important event occurs. Similarly, it may be meaningful to break a long sequence of synchronous interactions by an asynchronous one.

However, when inserting asynchronous communication into an event thread, the significance table should be consulted. If the table specifies essential only for the event, it will not matter that you are going to break the event thread with asynchronous communication. On the other hand, be careful if the significance table specifies critical. An asynchronous

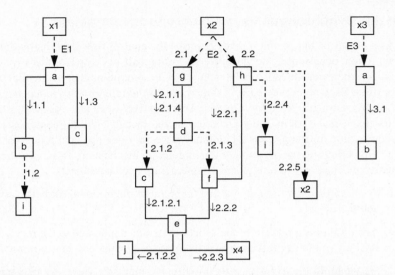

Figure 6-14. Selecting asynchronous interaction for the event threads of the example.

communication between two objects of the event thread may cause a failure to respond in the required time.

In the example, object i is a computational type of object. Since interactions 1.2 and 2.2.4 require a substantial amount of processing time, they are changed to an asynchronous request. In addition, the long event thread E2 is broken at object d by making the interactions 2.1.2 and 2.1.3 asynchronous. All processing that originally required completion of the now changed interaction gets a chance to run earlier and concurrently with the execution of the split-off asynchronous requests.

Any interaction with an environment object is also a good candidate to become asynchronous because low coupling between subsystems is preferred, and asynchronous communication achieves this effect. In some implementations, for example, with distinct address spaces, direct synchronous invocation between two subsystems may be unfeasible. Examining the interaction with an environment object from the target subsystem's point of view may reveal the fact that this has been defined anyway as an event there. In the example, object x2 belongs to subsystem 2 and, when inspecting subsystem 2, we discover that the interaction 2.2.5 from object h to x2 represents an event in subsystem 2. Thus, we change this interaction to asynchronous communication.

In certain situations, synchronous interaction is a necessity. For example, it makes no sense to check a state variable of another object via an asynchronous request and an asynchronous return, because the state may change before the requesting object makes its decision based on the value returned. Asynchronous communication is also less efficient than function invocation. All these aspects should be carefully studied before changing any interaction to asynchronous. Thus, you may stick with synchronous invocation, as we did for interaction 2.2.3 in the example, even if the interaction involves objects, like x4, from the environment.

6.4.3 The Return-Message Obstacle

The unqualified interaction model assumed that the server's processing is always nested in the client. Synchronous invocation just implements that. Asynchronous communication, however, behaves differently in this respect. Thus, it is necessary, wherever we apply asynchronous communication, to examine the original semantics of the control flow between the client and the server in the designed interaction.

The most simple situation is the one wherein the client sends a request to the server and is allowed to immediately continue processing at any pace up to its own end. The interaction is a trigger only. Both client and server can proceed in whatever way they like. Asynchronous communication serves this purpose without any further problems.

For all other cases, Figure 6-15 generally describes the semantics of the control flow between the client and server side of an asynchronous interaction. After the client side has sent the request to the server side, it is allowed to continue the processing specified in section C1 when, at the same time, the server side performs the processing specified in section S1. However, processing should not enter section C2 at the client side unless the server side has been entered at section S2. Such semantics require explicit means to achieve the proper order of processing.

One possible solution is to nest the client's processing of section C2 into the execution path of the server side somewhere in section S2 by simply calling synchronously a member function at the client's side that contains this processing. This solution looks simple and straightforward. However, it contradicts the decision, using asynchronous communication between the client and server. It will also most likely increase the number of objects shared between the independent execution threads.

If more than "trigger only" is required, only one further alternative remains. The decision to use asynchronous communication requires an additional asynchronous communication to maintain the inherent requirements in the control flow arrangements. The server

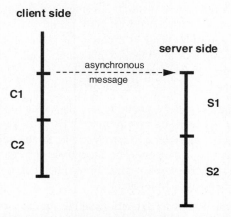

Figure 6-15. The client/server control flow semantics.

must send a message from within section S2, which the client awaits somewhere in section C1. Since this is obviously more complex than in the "trigger only" case, it is best to avoid asynchronous communication in any such situation and stick with synchronous invocation. However, sometimes this is not feasible or has other, even worse drawbacks, like shared objects.

The above general solution includes a degenerated "fully nested" case. Here, the client sends a request to the server and, immediately after that, waits until the server replies that it has completed its processing. Section C1 only contains this wait, and section S2 only contains the send of the reply. The server is fully nested in the client. This arrangement is sometimes referred to as *remote procedure call* (RPC).

Moreover, the above control flow considerations may be necessary to overlay with data flow if, in the unqualified event thread, the client requests a service that includes the production of a set of return values. In this case, the asynchronous request also requires asynchronous communication in the opposite direction for transmitting the return values. With synchronous invocation, this complication does not exist, and there must be strong reasons to justify the asynchronous solution in such a case. If asynchronous communication is definitely necessary, and control as well as data flow occurs from the server to the client, it is best, but not mandatory, to combine both into one return-message. The server side produces the return values in section S1 and sends them at the beginning of S2. The client side awaits the return values at the end of section C1 and makes use of them in section C2. Since the fully nested arrangement always fulfills these requirements safely, it is the recommended default for any return flow. However, it fully serializes the server and client.

Good design practice recommends further that the object receiving the asynchronous request sends the return-message back to the sender of the request. Occasionally, the designer may make other objects responsible for sending or receiving return-messages asynchronously.

There are, however, two basic design alternatives between which the designer must choose for the arrangement of the return-message reception point: *internal wait point* or *primary wait point*. The internal wait point means that we insert an operating system call to wait for the return-message at a particular place in a member function of an object. Hence, the class outlines must record this waiting call. The primary wait point means that we treat the return-message like an event. A waiting call is not inserted into the class outlines. Instead, the waiting occurs at the process level, as will be explained later.

Notice that an internal wait point blocks the execution thread. In particular, this execution thread will not serve its own primary wait point as long as it is in the internal wait point. If this is unacceptable, as it frequently is, the internal wait point cannot be selected. Even if acceptable, it is dangerous because an error or an exceptional situation may cause the message to never arrive. To avoid an infinite wait at the internal wait point, it should always be supplied with a time-out.

More about the design considerations of the alternatives internal wait point and primary wait point and how the client and server side is built will be discussed later in this chapter.

6.4.4 Qualified Event Threads

An event thread in which (a) synchronous invocation or asynchronous communication is specified for all object interactions, (b) asynchronous return-messages have been added where needed and (c) either an internal or primary wait point is defined for the reception of any return-messages is called a *qualified event thread*.

The object interaction graph of an event thread documents qualification in a convenient way. A dashed arrow denotes either an event or asynchronous communication. All remaining solid links are synchronous. An asynchronous return-message with an internal wait point is denoted by a dashed link to a wait bubble attached to the waiting object similar to the one for an internal delay. A sequence number is assigned to both the dashed link and the bubble. The notation of an asynchronous return-message received by a primary wait point is no different from any other asynchronous communication because the mechanism is the same. Only the fact that a so-far-unused Dewey root number is assigned to such an arrow indicates this decision. Furthermore, new subsequent synchronous interactions may be added, and the sequence numbers of others may change.

Figure 6-16 shows the event threads of the example in qualified form. Compared to the earlier Figure 6-14, asynchronous return-messages have been added. One appears in event thread **E1** from i to b. The new dashed arrow with the root number 4 indicates selection of the primary wait point. The additional synchronous interaction 4.1 passes execution back to object a after reception of the message. Since object a performs the former interaction 1.3 after 4.1, it has been renumbered to 4.2. This design requires us to restructure the class outlines. We cut the part of the member function of class B (the one describing object b) related to interaction 1.2, which has dealt with the return values before. The same applies

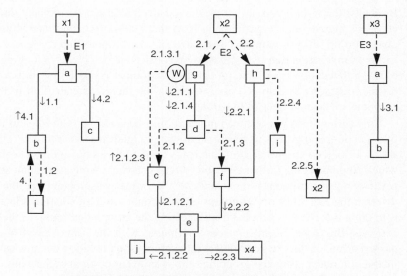

Figure 6-16. Qualified event threads of the example.

for class A. This cut code we paste as new, additional member functions into both classes. One becomes a member function in class B related to interaction 4, the other in class A related to interaction 4.1.

Considering event thread E2, you will recognize in Figure 6-16 the new dashed line 2.1.2.3 from object c to g with a W bubble. It expresses a return-message to the internal wait point with sequence number 2.1.3.1. The sequence number scheme specifies that object d, after sending the asynchronous message 2.1.2 to server c, still performs interaction 2.1.3 then returns execution to object g which starts waiting. The return-message link from server c to the wait point in g bears a sequence number that denotes its order in the sequence of interactions done by the server. Here, the return-message will be transmitted when the execution has been returned to object c. Upon reception of this message by object g, interaction 2.1.4 will be performed.

Qualification of the event threads defines the asynchronous communication between selected objects. Because a sequential programming language such as C++ does not provide such a mechanism, the implementation requires additional support. Some approaches enhance the objects themselves, either through a new or extended programming language or through inheritance from a class library. If you apply one of those approaches, then only the class outlines need to be updated according to the selected approach to complete design and start implementation. If such an implementation platform is not available or desirable or is not mature enough, OCTOPUS gives you another pragmatic solution at hand: usage of a conventional real-time operating system. It provides processes that are able to exchange asynchronous messages. The remainder of the design chapter describes how this is done.

6.4.5 Object Groups

Basically, the term *object group* means a conceptual union of objects together with synchronous interactions between them. Note that both objects and interactions belong to an object group. Any continuous sequence of synchronous interactions between objects forms an invocation tree. An object group consists of the objects belonging to one or more of these invocation trees. The property of the object group is that it associates with one distinct operating system process, providing the thread of execution to traverse all synchronous invocation trees of the group.

This definition is not of much practical use. Instead, we state rules to identify alternative sets of object groups in a subsystem with all qualified event threads given. One trivial set is: all objects in one group. This leads to an almost conventional sequential program which contradicts the former decisions of using asynchronous communication. Events and asynchronous communication related to the primary wait point are the key factors in determining any set of object groups. Asynchronous communication related to an internal wait point is formally excluded from affecting the grouping because, as the term "internal" suggests, this solution presupposes continuing with the same thread of execution. The dashed arrow of the extended object interaction graph notation denotes exactly any of the interaction relevant for the grouping: either an event or an asynchronous communication related to a primary wait point.

The maximum set of object groups can be determined by applying the following two rules:

1. If an object r of the subsystem under consideration receives an event E or an asynchronous message M related to a primary wait point, a group G can be formed that initially consists of object r and either event E or message M.

2. If object x is a member of group G, and there exists a synchronous interaction S from x to another object y, object y and interaction S belong to group G, if, and only if, the following condition is true: Interaction S must be a successor of interaction T to x, with T currently being a member of G.

These rules form the group using natural induction with rule 1 as the starting point. Object r is called the *root object* of group G. In the maximum set, each group has exactly one root object. However, the same object may be root object in several groups. There are as many root objects, and thus groups, as there are events or asynchronous messages to objects inside the subsystem; that is, every dashed arrow yields a group. Objects in the environment receiving an asynchronous message will define a group in the context of the subsystem to which they belong. The other members of any such group can be tracked by recursively applying rule 2. When applying rule 2 for the first time, object x is the root object r and interaction T equals either event E or message M of rule 1.

Let's illustrate this with the example based on the qualification specified in Figure 6-16. First we look at all controller objects of the qualified event threads E1, E2 and E3. We find four controllers since event thread E2 has two, namely object g and h. Those controller objects become root objects, and each starts its own group 1 through 4. Note that object a, which participates in E1 and E3, is the root object in group 1 as well as in 4. The other members of the groups are found by tracking all synchronous interactions from these root objects onwards. The object interaction graph notation enables a visual recording of this ongoing process by simply drawing a line around the objects that belong to the same group. Figure 6-17 shows the resulting final groups 1 through 4 by applying this circle technique. As you can see there, object j does not belong to group 3 because interaction 2.1.2.2 is not a successor of 2.2.2, whereas object x4 does because interaction 2.2.3 is a successor of 2.2.2.

Next we search for all objects that receive asynchronous requests. Each of them is a starting point for a new object group, even if it already belongs to some group. As usual, this object is called a root object. In the example, two additional root objects, b and i, are located as part of the event thread E1. These root objects are starting points for groups 5 and 6. The root objects c, f and i are located in event thread E2. These objects are starting points for groups 7 through 9, respectively. Groups 6 and 7 are distinct from each other, regardless of the fact that both of them originate from object i. Starting at the root object, other members of the group are found by tracking all the synchronous interactions that are successors of the asynchronous communication and the corresponding root object. The resulting collection of groups is the maximum set of object groups as shown in Figure 6-17.

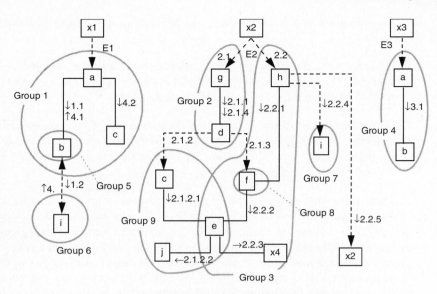

Figure 6-17. Maximum set of object groups.

It should be noted that the return value response 4 in event thread E1 is treated just as any other asynchronous communication. As can be seen in the graphs of the event threads, objects b and i have no successors. They are groups in their own right. The root object f is the only member of group 8, because the synchronous interaction 2.2.2 is not a successor of the asynchronous interaction 2.1.3. The root object c makes the synchronous interaction 2.1.2.1 to object e, and this connection, as well as 2.1.2.2 to object j, is a successor of the asynchronous interaction 2.1.2 from d to c. Thus, group 9 comprises object e and j in addition to the root object c.

For practical purposes, the maximum set of object groups is not a good alternative because it typically yields too many groups overlaying one another in too many objects. The maximum set has been introduced mainly to define the theoretical upper limit from which balancing may start. A better-balanced alternative to start with is the so-called *fair set of object groups*.

The rules for determining the fair set of object groups are:

1. If either (a) an object r of the subsystem under consideration receives an event E1 through Ex, or (b) the objects q1 through qy receive an event E, or (c) an object p receives only the asynchronous messages M1 through Mz, all related to a primary wait point, a group G can be formed that initially consists of either (a) object r and the events E1 through Ex, or (b) the objects q1 through qy and event E, or (c) object p and the messages M1 through Mz.

2. If object x is a member of group G, and there exists a synchronous interaction S from x to another object y, object y and interaction S belong to group G, if, and only if, the fol-

lowing condition is true: S must be a successor of an interaction T to x, with T currently being a member of G or T being an asynchronous communication.

As before, rule 1 is the starting point rule which identifies the root object(s) of the considered subsystem. However, we get fewer root objects, and thus less groups, compared to the maximum set because not every event or message creates a group, and not every object receiving the same event starts a separate group. The other members of any such group can be tracked by recursively applying rule 2. However, the groups of the fair set become bigger because we track all synchronous interactions regardless of which event thread they belong to.

Indeed, the rules of the fair set of object groups yield the result that parts of distinct event threads may belong to the same particular group. Therefore, the identification of the fair set of object groups implies that, at least mentally, the qualified event threads are merged. This merger can be accomplished graphically by overlaying object-interaction graphs as long as technically practicable. It would be best if a still readable graph of all event threads together can be produced, for example, by a specific tool. In this case, each object appears only once in the resulting overlay graph. Figure 6-18 shows this overlaying in the case of the example.

A search for the object groups of the fair set can be started at the controller object of every qualified event thread. If an event thread has more than one controller, like event E2 in the example, these objects will be considered as the root objects of the same group. In any case, the corresponding object group will be completed by including all objects that can be accessed along synchronous interactions from the chosen root object(s).

Once more, if visualization is preferred, you can draw a line in the object interaction graph around all objects that belong to the same group. Figure 6-19 describes those groups

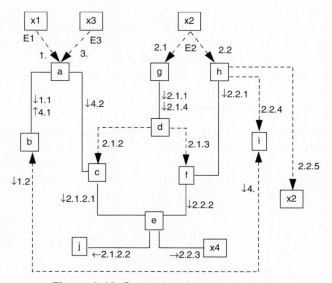

Figure 6-18. Overlaying the event threads.

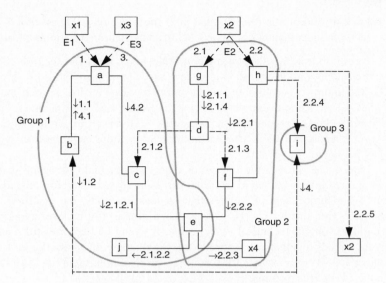

Figure 6-19. Fair set of object groups.

in the case of the example studied. Starting at the root, two object groups are found. The first group contains the objects a, b, c, e and j. The second group contains the objects g, h, d, f, e and x4, since the controller objects g and h of event thread E2 were assigned to the same group.

After the first grouping, there may be some objects which remain ungrouped. Some of these objects receive asynchronous requests. They can be used as starting points for additional new object groups. As before, these objects are called the root objects of the new groups, respectively. The rule of tracking all synchronous interactions is applied here too. In the example, object i constitutes a third object group. In the case of a real application, the search for object groups is continued until all objects belong to at least one group. The resulting collection of groups is the fair set of object groups.

6.4.6 Balancing the Grouping

You may have noticed already that the groups may overlap, and an object may belong to more than one group. Any such object we call a *shared object*. As can be seen in Figure 6-19, for the fair set of object groups of the example, object e belongs to two groups. It is the only shared object in the fair set, whereas there are many in the maximum set, as can be seen in Figure 6-17. Shared objects may cause synchronization problems. The more groups the solution has, the more concurrency is achieved; but, on the other side of the coin, the more shared objects will appear. The balancing problem of object groups is to find the smallest set of object groups that satisfies the inherent need for concurrency but not more and involves a minimum number of shared objects.

The fair set of object groups is intended as a starting point of the search for the optimum set of groups. If more concurrency is needed, you may consider a grouping closer to the maximum set. If objects are shared, you may consider merging the groups to get rid of the sharing. This is particularly recommended if one of the two groups is fully nested in the other.

Let's assume in the abstract example that the significance table specifies critical for event E3 in almost any state, and its event sheet specifies a rather short response time. Taking these facts into account, we recognize that event thread E3 represents a short and time-critical operation, and is required to run concurrently with other event threads (see also Chapter 7). Because the fair set, Figure 6-19, covers event thread E3 in group 1, which also covers E1, it is necessary to split group 1 into group 1A and group 1B, as shown in Figure 6-20. The drawback we have to accept for this design decision is that objects a and b are shared between groups 1A and 1B.

When balancing the grouping, you may also reconsider the decisions regarding the interaction mechanism. Obviously, the interaction mechanism affects the grouping of objects. If an asynchronous communication at a certain interaction would reduce the number of shared objects, it may be worth using it, although there are no real concurrency reasons. In the given fair set of object groups of the example, Figure 6-19, you recognize that changing interaction 2.2.2 to asynchronous will remove the sharing of object e. This is done in Figure 6-20.

If, on the other hand, your original decision for asynchronous communication does not cross any group border, you should examine this interaction once more. If even the corresponding asynchronous return-message occurs inside the same group, your design exhibits a deadlock, because the group's own execution thread will wait internally for the response it should produce at the same time. It may be necessary to define another group with a few shared objects, or changing the interaction back to synchronous might satisfy the concur-

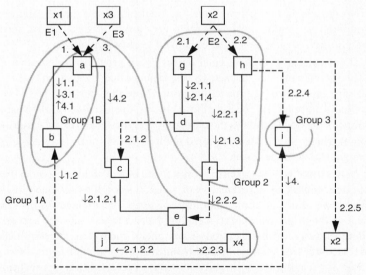

Figure 6-20. Balancing the fair set of object groups of the example.

rency requirement as well. In Figure 6-20, interaction 2.1.3 is changed back to synchronous and thus circumvents the problem.

In real systems, you will need either a big piece of paper or a dedicated computer tool. You are encouraged to do whatever it takes to have the entire grouping visible at the same time. For example, you can cut and paste or pin pages to a wall to get the groups all connected on one "page" so that they can be contemplated at once. This way, it is simpler to study alternative groupings.

6.5 Outlines of Processes and Messages

The system will be implemented using an operating system that provides processes for (quasi-) concurrent execution of code sequences. The process is the basic unit of activity the operating system manages. Each has its own thread of execution. Processes may be truly concurrent with each other if they run on different processors. In implementations with only one processor or more processes than there are processors, the operating system will simulate concurrency by switching between processes so that an external, macroscopic observer is unable to distinguish the system's behavior from truly concurrent execution. A process is strictly sequential in itself.

Because synchronous interaction does not require concurrent execution, each object group can be mapped to a single process, called the *object group process*. Either a call for a member function of the object is executed as a part of a given process, or a direct member data access is performed. The part of an event thread that is covered by an object group specifies the hierarchy of member function calls the execution thread of the object group process has to follow. Given all qualified event threads and a particularly selected grouping, the internal design of the object group process can be derived in a systematic, straightforward way, as will be explained later in this section.

If not currently running, each object group process awaits either an event or an asynchronous message, as defined by the objects that receive an event or an asynchronous message, and belong to the same group. Note that this also includes the objects with an internal wait point. By locating these objects, one can determine what the events and asynchronous messages are that the object group process has to await and which member function at which object must be called upon reception of the message. Typically, each group contains a few of these objects.

In the first cycle, we consider only those objects that receive an event or asynchronous message related to a primary wait point. Depending on how we balanced the object groups, we may find more than just one event or message. In this case the primary wait point is a multiple wait point, meaning that the process awaits several events or messages simultaneously. Upon reception of any one of them, the process awakes and starts execution with the first instruction following the primary wait point. First it must find out the reason for leaving the wait point in order to select the right execution branch within the process. Those branches always start with a call of the member function of the object that receives the event or asynchronous request, and follow the object interactions inside the object group. No process can simultaneously execute more than one of its branches. The branches of a process are mutually exclusive, alternative execution paths. If the process awaits exactly one event or message in its primary wait point, then only one branch exists, and a selection is unnecessary.

Note that the multiple wait point is a design abstraction that enables us to model the process at a level of detail that is sufficient at this point in time and defers other details. Depending on the features of the actual operating system, the multiple wait point may require further decomposition before coding, and you may select from a wide range of implementation tactics. One of the most frequently used tactics is the one where the multiple wait point denotes reception of a variety of messages all having the same structure, but distinguishable in a particular data tag. For a more detailed discussion, see Chapter 8.

The notation of *process outline* is used to capture the high-level design of a process. Its syntax is similar to the class outline except that it starts with the keyword `process function` followed by a function body outline. Because OCTOPUS processes have a common top-level structure, process outlines are built according to a standard pattern. Listing 6-3 shows this standard pattern from which you can start defining the specific outline of any process.

```
process function Name
    loop forever
       await any of some messages
       switch depending on reception
       message1: objectA.function1(...);
       ...
       messageN: objectZ.function7(...);
       endswitch,
    endloop;
endprocessfunction;
```

Listing 6-3. The process function pattern.

A process outline only describes the first layer of calls of a process in detail, but does not give any overview where the execution path continues. If you lack this overview, the structure of a process can be visualized optionally by means of a *process outline graph*. This graph always starts with the primary wait point on top. In case it is a multiple wait point, a flow chart selection box follows. From the selection box an arrow points to the object that the process's execution thread will call upon reception of a particular event or message. A label along this arrow denotes this event or message. The result of doing this for all events or messages that the process awaits in its primary wait point is just a graphical representation of the information already captured in the process outline. The process outline graph continues showing the complete synchronous interaction branch that follows the first object called by the process depending on the particular event or message received. The object interaction graph notation serves this purpose. You can cut and paste the branches from the object interaction graph showing your event threads. Figure 6-21 illustrates this by an example. The process outline graph shown there corresponds to the object groups as defined in Figure 6-20.

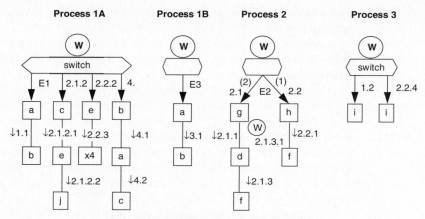

Figure 6-21. The process outline graph.

Sometimes an event, like E2 in the example, directs itself to more than one object. Earlier we learned that these objects are forced to belong to the same group of the fair set. Consequently, they are covered by a single process. Moreover, because each object interaction thread starting with such an object is triggered by the occurrence of the same event, those object interaction threads belong to the same branch of the object group process. The process outline graph expresses this by a split event arrow to all the objects receiving the same particular event. The designer can deliberately choose the order in which the process executes this set of object interaction threads upon occurrence of the event and mark this order in the graph.

The execution thread of a process will normally traverse the current branch completely and then return to the primary wait point. This arrangement has the advantage that the process is able to react on the occurrence of events or messages to it except when it is executing a particular branch. However, an event thread may also possess internal wait points at certain objects. This is either designed in as an internal delay or the result of an asynchronous return-message transmission. These internal wait points will force the process to wait whenever the execution thread of the process reaches such an object during execution of a particular branch. Therefore, a process may possess a number of secondary wait points in addition to the primary one. It is important to notice that a process, as long as it is waiting in a secondary wait point, does not react on the occurrence of events or messages in its primary wait point anymore. If this is even an internal wait for a message and the message fails to arrive, the entire process is dead. A time-out might take care of this exception.

Assuming the object groups have been balanced for the optimum automatically results in the optimum number of processes, although each one may have a few branches. Processes consume memory and runtime performance. If some other, more fine-grained grouping is used instead, the concurrency level of the system increases at the expense of processing overhead. The maximum set of object groups leads to the maximum number of processes with the maximum overhead. On the basis of the previous steps, it is clear that the number of asynchronous communications affects the number of object groups, which in turn is equal to the number of processes and thus determines some system overhead. Because of this correlation, the designer must look for a solution that has just enough concurrency to satisfy the requirements, but no more.

6.6 Design of the Hardware Wrapper

In Section 5.5, "Analysis of the Hardware Wrapper," we learned about the special characteristics of the primitive events of the hardware wrapper compared to the logical events of the application. This difference requires consideration when designing the hardware wrapper, although the procedure is basically the same as described for the application. We recommend a first iteration on the design of the hardware wrapper before designing the application. If the hardware wrapper is analyzed after analysis of all application subsystems has been done, both the analysis and the initial design of the hardware wrapper will be done in sequence. This is quite convenient. Typically, the design of the hardware wrapper needs to be updated several times when the design of the application clarifies further details.

An event thread triggered by a primitive event does not originate in another subsystem. If the primitive event is classified as hard interrupt, the originator of the corresponding event thread is an interrupt service routine. If it is classified as soft interrupt, its originator is the time scheduler of the operating system. Both originators belong to the hardware wrapper itself, and when drawing the object interaction graph of the event thread, we show them in the form of normal object boxes labeled by their class name specifier.

An interrupt service routine can be executed at almost any time. However, the primitive event originating from an interrupt service routine is unqualified at the beginning. We still have the choice of making this interaction a synchronous or an asynchronous one. Synchronous interaction is implemented by calling a member function of the controller object. For asynchronous interaction, some operating system functionality is used. As long as the event thread of a primitive event originating from an interrupt service routine is unqualified, we depict such a primitive event by a solid arrow in the object interaction graph. If qualification of the event thread explicitly selects asynchronous interaction for the primitive event, we change this arrow to a dashed one.

Figure 6-22 shows the unqualified event thread of the primitive event poll input from the Cruise Control case study. This event originates from the interrupt service routine ISRINT1 which is executed as a result of the periodic interrupt INT1 from the hardware timer.

In case analysis of the hardware wrapper indicates that a primitive event is simply forwarded as an event to the application, the event thread of this primitive event consists of nothing but the interrupt service routine as originator and a target object from one application subsystem across the boundary. Figure 6-22 shows this situation for the primitive

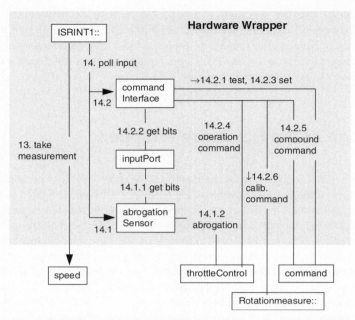

Figure 6-22. Example of unqualified event threads originating from
an interrupt service routine.

event **take measurement**. Nonetheless, a decision on the interaction mechanism is
required here too. When designing the application, we change our perspective and view
the same situation as an event of the application subsystem for which we build an event
thread with the interrupt service routine as originator. The selected mechanism of interaction remains the same. Hence, a solid arrow in the object interaction graph of a particular
event thread of an application subsystem indicates that the execution of this event thread is
nested in the interrupt service routine. If several qualified event threads start synchronously from the same interrupt service routine, we define an object group for each of these
events even though they all share the execution thread of this interrupt service routine.
Consequently, objects shared between these groups are never critical because they are
always executed mutually exclusively.

Figure 6-23 shows an example from the Cruise Control case study with the operating
system originating a few primitive events. By nature, each such primitive event is based
on some asynchronous mechanisms. This allows us to use a dashed arrow even at the
beginning, when the event threads are still unqualified.

Of course, the operating system can issue primitive events only if execution is passed
to it. In most systems, this is done by a periodically executed interrupt service routine that
invokes some piece of code in the operating system. Figure 6-23 denotes this by the interaction labeled **time tick**.

A primitive event issued by the operating system may be simply forwarded as a logical
event to the application subsystem too, as is, for example, the **throttle update** event in

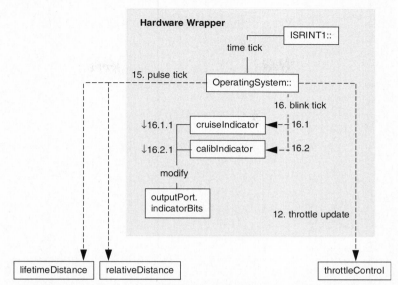

Figure 6-23. Event threads originating from the operating system.

Figure 6-23. In some cases it may even happen that the corresponding logical event of a forwarded primitive event has not been defined in the analysis of the application subsystem. An example of this case is the primitive event E15, pulse tick. The objects lifetimeDistance and relativeDistance are the single instances of application classes Lifetime Distance and Relative Distance. The class diagram shown in Chapter 10 reveals that both classes inherit wrapper class Output Pulser. Base class Output Pulser defines a member function that must be executed upon occurrence of event pulse tick. Consequently, the event must be forwarded to objects lifetimeDistance and relativeDistance, as shown in Figure 6-23.

6.7 Summary

Design transforms the abstract definition produced from analysis into a description that explains how we are going to implement the required features and functions. Constraints and problems specific to the implementation environment and decisions on alternative implementation tactics are still deferred.

The object interaction graph notation is used to identify and visualize the event threads. The class outlines document details not captured in the graph. When the interaction mechanism has been decided on, the object groups are obtained. Then an operating system process is assigned to each group, and its code is outlined. Shared objects are carefully examined regarding synchronization flaws, and a case-by-case solution is added.

7

PROCESS PRIORITIES
AND TIMING

This chapter describes a systematic approach for deriving the priorities of processes generated by the design procedure in Chapter 6. The concurrency behavior of the system is examined to ensure that it satisfies the specified time requirements. This chapter assumes a real-time operating system in which:

- Scheduling between the processes is priority-based, and first-in first-out scheduling is applied if the processes are at the same priority level.

- A process with higher priority can preempt one with lower priority.

7.1 Basic Concepts

A process managed by a real-time operating system can be in one of three distinct states (there are a number of different substates, which may vary between different operating systems):

- *Running*: The process is currently being executed by the CPU. In a single processor system, only one process at a time can be running.

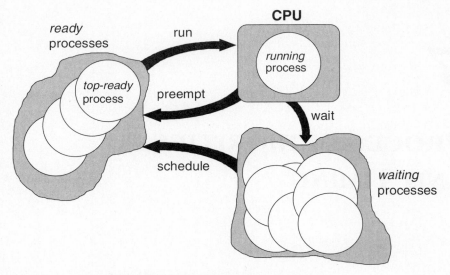

Figure 7-1. Basic process state changes.

- *Ready*: The process needs the CPU for execution, but it has not yet gained access to the CPU. Several processes can simultaneously be ready. At any given time, the ready processes are kept in a particular order. The foremost one is called the *top-ready* process. The top-ready process is the next one to run when the running process enters another process state (Figure 7-1).

- *Waiting*: The process is waiting for an event. It does not need the CPU. Several processes can simultaneously be waiting. They are not ordered in any way.

  Figure 7-1 shows basic process state changes.

  The running process can enter the waiting state if it calls an operating system service or terminates. In the latter case, an implicit call for an operating system service puts the process to sleep. A waiting process becomes ready when the event for which it was waiting occurs. The top-ready process enters the running state if the previously running process enters the waiting state, or if the operating system swaps the running process with the top-ready process (preemption).

  It is not essential to know what happens after preemption. The subsequent actions vary considerably between different operating systems.

7.2 Deriving Process Priorities

In the analysis phase, the significance table captured the significance of events in different system elementary states. Since events start event threads and trigger object group processes, there is some correlation between the significance of events and the priorities of processes.

Priorities of processes can be derived according to the following procedure:

1. Decide on preemption between process pairs.

2. Derive the pairwise priorities and use them to determine the priority order.

Step 1: Decide on preemption between process pairs

Inspect the processes pairwise. Assume that each process in turn is in the running state. Compare this process to every other process of the system, assuming that the other process is in the top-ready state. For each combination, decide whether the running process continues to run or whether the top-ready process preempts it. Record the results in a table showing the processes in the system paired against each other. Table 7-1 shows an example of the *preemption table* of a hypothetical system. The processes in the rows are the ones assumed to be running (Pr processes) and the ones in the columns are the ones assumed to be top-ready (Pt processes). Each cell in the table states yes (Y) or no (N) on preemption. For example, when process P1 is running and process P2 is top-ready, the Y in the table shows that preemption occurs: process P1 becomes ready, and the top-ready P2 becomes running.

Table 7-1. Preemption table of the assumed system.

Pr \ Pt	P1	P2	P3	P4	P5	P6
P1	X	Y	Y	N	Y	Y
P2	N	X	N	N	N	Y
P3	N	Y	X	N	Y	Y
P4	N	Y	Y	X	Y	Y
P5	N	Y	Y	N	X	Y
P6	N	N	N	N	N	X

Table 7-1 also contains X entries. An X is used wherever the combination of the top-ready and running processes is impossible. The table must always contain X entries in the diagonal cells because the same process can never be simultaneously in the running and ready states. Processes which run the same code are different processes, and each process requires a column and a row in the table.

Preemption between a process pair is decided based on the significance of the triggering events. For simplicity, let us assume that each process in Table 7-1 handles one event so that process P1 handles event E1, process P2 handles event E2 and so on. If the significance table states that event E1 is less significant than event E2 in all elementary states, then process P1 should not pre-empt process P2. On the other hand, P2 should preempt

P1. If we pick two other processes, **P3** and **P5**, from the table, we find that each of them preempts the other one which is running. This is because events **E3** and **E5** are of equal significance, and their threads need to be executed concurrently. Notice that if a process handles more than one event, the decision on preemption is based on the most significant one.

The decision on preemption indicates the pairwise priorities between processes, as shown in Table 7-2.

Table 7-2. Preemption combinations and their meaning on priority.

Preemption Combinations between Pn and Pm	Interpretation	Priority Order between Pn and Pm
N, Y	If Pn is running and Pm is top-ready then Pn continues to run. If Pm is running and Pn is top-ready then Pm is preempted and Pn runs.	Pn has a higher priority than Pm (Pn > Pm).
Y, N	If Pn is running and Pm is top-ready, then Pn is preempted and Pm runs. If Pm is running and Pn is top-ready, then Pm continues to run.	Pn has a lower priority than Pm (Pn < Pm).
N, N	Whichever is running, Pn or Pm, it continues to run when the other process is top-ready.	Pn and Pm have equal priorities (Pn = Pm).
Y, Y	Whichever is running, Pn or Pm, it is preempted, and the other top-ready process runs.	Pn and Pm have equal priorities (Pn = Pm).

The (Y, Y) combination in the table is the only case that may result in interleaving the two processes. This case occurs when the two processes should run quasi-concurrently. The operating systems may provide different mechanisms to handle interleaving processes. If time-slicing is applied, the operating system allows each currently running process to run for the length of its time slice. At the end of the time slice, it takes the top-ready process and allows it to run for the duration of its time slice. Assuming no third process with higher priority becomes top-ready, this scheduling is interchangeably repeated until one of the processes enters the waiting state.

Some operating systems rely on the fact that the running process will eventually call an operating system service, and this call will force it to sleep. This gives the top-ready process a chance to run. You can use this fact to control the scheduling behavior by inserting specific operating system calls to concurrently run the processes having equal priority.

After you are convinced that the entries in the preemption table are correct, you have actually achieved a solution for the concurrency requirements for any combination of the processes. If the operating system is able to look at the table to decide what process to run next, the scheduling of processes is readily solved. However, in many operating systems the basic scheduling mechanism is based on process priorities.

Step 2: Derive the pairwise priorities and use them to determine the priority order

Pick the results from the preemption table (Table 7-1) and enter them in the first column of a new table, as shown in Table 7-3. Determine which process in the process pair has higher, equal or lower priority based on the interpretations given in Table 7-2. Record the results in the second column. The table is divided into blocks. In each block, concentrate on one process. The priorities, obtained by pairwise inspections, are used to derive one priority rule, which is recorded in the third column. The same inspection and derivation is repeated for other processes, one at a time, but each time the derived priority rule from the previous block is taken into account. This procedure is repeated until there are no more blocks. The number of pairwise combinations is reduced by one in every block; thus, the number of blocks is one less than the number of processes in the system.

Table 7-3. Priority derivation.

Preemption between (Pr + Pt), (Pr + Pt)	Pairwise Priority Order	Derived Priority Rule
(P1 + P2), (P2 + P1) = Y, N	P1 < P2	({P2, P3, P5, P6} > (P1 = P4)
(P1 + P3), (P3 + P1) = Y, N	P1 < P3	
(P1 + P4), (P4 + P1) = N, N	P1 = P4	
(P1 + P5), (P5 + P1) = Y, N	P1 < P5	
(P1 + P6), (P6 + P1) = Y, N	P1 < P6	
(P2 + P3), (P3 + P2) = N, Y	P2 > P3	(P2 > {P3, P4, P5}) & (P2 < P6)
(P2 + P4), (P4 + P2) = N, Y	P2 > P4	using the result from the previous block:
(P2 + P5), (P5 + P2) = N, Y	P2 > P5	(P6 > P2 > {P1 = P4, P3, P5})
(P2 + P6), (P6 + P2) = Y, N	P2 < P6	
(P3 + P4), (P4 + P3) = N, Y	P3 > P4	(P3 > P4) & (P3 = P5) and (P3 < P6)
(P3 + P5), (P5 + P3) = Y, Y	P3 = P5	using the result from the previous block:
(P3 + P6), (P6 + P3) = Y, N	P3 < P6	(P6 > P2 > (P3 = P5) > (P1 = P4))
(P4 + P5), (P5 + P4) = Y, N	P4 < P5	(P4 < P5) & (P4 < P6)
(P4 + P6), (P6 + P4) = Y, N	P4 < P6	in line with the result in the previous block.
(P5 + P6), (P6 + P5) = Y, N	P5 < P6	(P5 < P6)
		in line with the result in the previous block.

In Table 7-3, the complete priority order is already reached in block 3:

P6 > P2 > (P3 = P5) > (P1 = P4).

Sometimes, one must proceed to the last block in order to determine the complete priority order. Even if the complete priority order has been reached in an earlier block, one should still proceed to the last block to check that there are no contradictions. Each contradiction must be solved before continuing the derivation of the priorities. A contradiction arises if the entries in the preemption table do not describe an order. Assume, for example, that a system contains processes Pa, Pb and Pc and has the preemption table shown in Table 7-4.

Table 7-4. Preemption table.

Pt Pr	Pa	Pb	Pc
Pa	X	N	N
Pb	Y	X	N
Pc	N	Y	X

Let us try to derive the priorities as shown in Table 7-5.

Table 7-5. Priority derivation results in a contradiction.

Preemption between (Pn + Pm), (Pm + Pn)	Pairwise Priority Order	Derived Priority Rule
(Pa + Pb), (Pb + Pa) = N, Y (Pa + Pc), (Pc + Pa) = N, N	Pa > Pb Pa = Pc	(Pa = Pc) > Pb
(Pb + Pc), (Pc + Pb) = N, Y	Pb > Pc	(Pb > Pc) *CONTRADICTS the result from the first block!*

The table shows that the priority rule derived in block 2 contradicts the rule derived in block 1. The first block indicates that (Pc > Pb), and the second block says the opposite. The behavior described in the preemption table of this system cannot be implemented by an operating system that is based on priority scheduling. Thus, the designer has to immediately remove the contradiction from the preemption table. It is necessary to decide which process is more important or if they are of equal importance. The corresponding entries in the table must be modified accordingly. After that, it is possible to continue the derivation of the priorities. If another contradiction is encountered, it must be resolved in the same manner. It should be noted that contradictions between process priorities should not appear often because the priorities of processes are the result of earlier analysis and design decisions.

7.3 Timing and Concurrency Behavior

Execution of a qualified event thread may involve more than one process to achieve the desired end-to-end response. Due to the one-to-one association between object groups and processes, you can see what objects are interacting with each other in every process and what services the objects request from each other to execute their part of the event thread (Figure 7-2). If you are able to estimate the duration of the requested services between the objects inside a process, then you can approximate the time needed to execute that process. If you sum the times of the involved processes, including the sending of messages between them and switching overhead, you will get the total time needed to fully execute the event thread. This assumes that the processes are executed one after the other immediately and are not interrupted by the processes of other event threads. For example, the full execution of the event thread shown in Figure 7-2 is the sum of the times needed to execute f1, f2, f3, f5 and f6, and the times to send the messages m4 and m7, including any switching overhead.

In practice, several event threads are executing concurrently, and their processes interrupt each other. It is possible to check if the system satisfies the timing requirements (specified in use cases and event sheets) based on the derived process priorities and the estimated duration of the processes of the event threads. It is important to check at least the most critical event sequence.

As an example, Figure 7-3 shows the most critical event sequence and how the system processes react in this situation. The processes of the system are given in Table 7-3. To simplify the example, we assumed that each process fully executes one event thread, so that process P1 fully handles event E1, process P2 fully handles event E2 and so on. We also estimated that each process needs three time units to execute all the object interactions of its event thread.

The figure demonstrates how the system behaves. For example, at time 4 the system has processes P1 and P4 in the ready state. It can be seen that P1 continues to run, because it has a higher priority than P4. After it is completed at time 6, process P4 starts running. At time 11, the system has two other processes, P5 and P3, in the ready state in addition to P4. Process P4 does not run because it has lower priority than both P5 and P3. These two processes have equal priorities and are assumed to interleave each other by switching at regular time intervals (e.g., through time slicing). This interleaving stops when process P6, which has higher priority, becomes top-ready at time 15 when event E6 occurs.

You can examine all critical event sequences by drawing a concurrency behavior diagram such as the one in Figure 7-3. If you are not satisfied with the behavior, it is possible

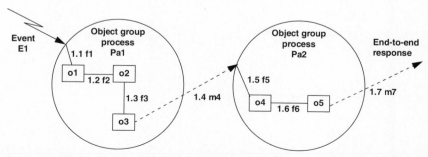

Figure 7-2. Object group processes and the objects involved in executing an event thread.

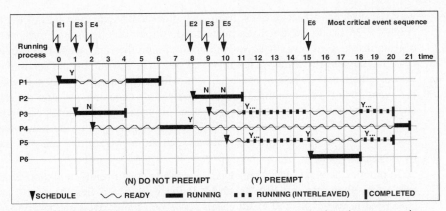

Figure 7-3. The concurrency behavior of the system in the given example.

to iteratively modify the process table entries, and thus the process priorities, in order to fine-tune the behavior. For example, from Figure 7-3 you can notice that process P4, which became ready at time 2, has completed the execution of its event thread at time 21, using the time units 6, 7 and 20. Execution of P4 started 4 time units after the occurrence of event E4 and completed after 19 time units. If this does not match the requirements, a change is required.

Scheduling is a limited mechanism to control the execution of processes. If a satisfactory concurrency behavior cannot be achieved, you must reconsider the design decisions made earlier. Sometimes a satisfactory behavior cannot be achieved without enhancing the system resources, for example, a more efficient CPU, increased amount of memory and so forth.

An introduction to real-time scheduling theorems and performance analysis can be found in [Gomaa '93].

8

TRANSITION FROM DESIGN TO IMPLEMENTATION

This chapter treats detailed design issues as well as implementation issues that are specific to embedded real-time systems. Throughout the chapter we use C++ programming language, but this chapter is not intended to be a reference on C++. For that purpose refer to [Lippman '91, Coplien '92, Stroustrup '91, Stroustrup '94]. The reader is assumed to be familiar with C++.

Implementation translates class outlines (including member function outlines), inter-process message outlines and process outlines into a programming language (Figure 8-1). The translation is relatively straightforward, as most important decisions have been made in the design phase and are recorded in the outlines.

Several object-oriented languages can be used to implement the design. C++ is currently the most popular object-oriented language used in embedded systems, and its use is increasing. C++ supports integration with earlier software development in C language, and many C++ cross-development tools are available for a large number of microprocessor families.

8.1 C++ and C Interoperability

This may be the one most important reason behind the wide usage of C++ in embedded systems. If some parts of the design are implemented using C language and other parts

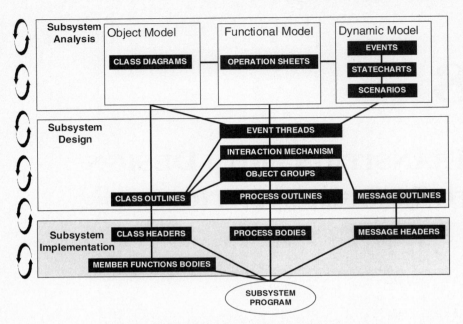

Figure 8-1. Subsystem implementation.

using C++, the integration of the C part of the program and the C++ part of the program is necessary. Since C++ is designed to integrate with C, it is possible to access functions and data between the two parts.

If the C++ part wants to call functions from the C part, the easiest way is to include the C header files containing the declarations of these functions inside a C++ `extern "C"` statement. The C functions can then be used in the C++ part exactly as in C. This case is typical when the C++ part uses standard C libraries:

```
// this is passed to the C++ compiler
extern "C"
{
    #include <math.h>
    #include "c_header.h"
//...
}
```

Another alternative is to encapsulate C functions and data structures in C++ class interfaces [Stroustrup '94].

If the C part wants to use C++ classes (including member functions and data), these classes must be presented to the C part as functions and data structures:

```
// this is passed to the C++ compiler
class D
{
public:
   void f1();
   int f2(char); //...
};
D objd;

// map class D into C callable functions
extern "C"// instructs C++ compiler to use the naming conventions of C language
{
   void D_f1(D* ptrd)
   {ptrd->f1();}

   int D_f2(D* ptrd, char c)
   {return ptrd->f2(c); }

   D* giveMeObjdPtr()// returns a pointer to a specific object,
   {return &objd;}
}
```

In the C part these functions are declared like this:

```
// this is passed to the C compiler
extern void D_f1(struct D*);
extern int D_f2(struct D*, char);
```

and are used in this way:

```
// this is passed to the C compiler
struct D* cptrObjd = giveMeObjdPtr();
D_f1(cptrObjd);
D_f2(cptrObjd, 'a');
```

The programmer must also be aware of other C++ and C language incompatibilities, for example, the different semantics of keywords such as `const`, `static`, and so on.

8.2 Member Access Control

Most of the member functions which were discovered in the design phase and recorded in the class outlines are intended for the users of the class (interface functions). These interface functions access data members and use other member functions which should not be directly accessible by the users of the class. The mechanism to control the access to data members and member functions in C++ is simple and is based on the use of `public`, `protected`, `private` and `friend` keywords inside class declarations. For more details see [Stroustrup '91].

It is a good practice to declare only interface functions in the public part. Other members are declared in the private and protected parts. However, the protected part should be used carefully because the members in the protected part of a certain class can be directly manipulated by the derived classes from this class.

8.3 Visibility

In the design phase objects interacted freely with each other synchronously and asynchronously. This freedom was based on the assumption that the objects somehow know each other. In practice, if the objects are in the same memory space, a client object interacts with a server object by using the runtime address of the server object. If the objects are distributed in different memory spaces, symbolic referencing has to be used. For different ways of implementing symbolic referencing you can see [CORBA '93].

8.3.1 Synchronous Invocation

Synchronous invocation means that a client object calls a function in the object server. The client continues execution only after the function in the server returns. The client can interact with the server in a number of ways. When selecting which to use, consider the scope of visibility, stability of the reference, the need to share the server object and the flexibility of the mechanism [Coleman '93].

- The client object uses a reference to a global server object.

- If the class from which the client object is instantiated aggregates the server object, the client object has a direct reference to the server object (case SC1 in Figure 8-2 and Listing 8-1).

- The reference to the server object can be passed to the client object as a parameter of a function (case SC2 in Figure 8-2 and Listing 8-1).

- The client object can have its own reference to the server object (case SC3 in Figure 8-2 and Listing 8-1). This reference must be set before using it, for example, by passing the reference to the server as a parameter to the constructor of the client object.

- If the client object creates the server object, then it gets a reference to it from the creation process (case SC4 in Figure 8-2 and Listing 8-1).

- The class from which the client object is instantiated may use a reference to a static member in the class of the server object.

- The client object may get the reference to the server object as a return value from a global function or from a member function.

- The client object may use an absolute physical address that is simply known, a mechanism typically used inside a subsystem. Sometimes it can be useful between subsystems because it reduces the coupling between them. At the absolute address, you could have a table of pointers to the objects of the other subsystem. Only the address of the table and the offsets of the pointers included in the table must be maintained. The pointers to the objects themselves could change. This enables one to build link-independent subsystems.

Always set the pointer to NULL after the deletion of the object (case **SC4** in Listing 8-1). This makes it possible to detect any accidental reference to the deleted object. Also, if a referenced object need not or must not change, you should use the C++ const keyword when defining the object.

```
// assuming classes X, Y, Z and S are declared and defined,
// also objects x and y are created

class D
{
public:
    D(Y&);                  // also in relation to case SC3
    Y& mry;                 // in relation to case SC3, if we would also declare it
                            // static, it becomes a reference shared by all objects
                            // of the class
    S s;                    // in relation to case SC1
    void f1(X&);            // in relation to case SC2
    Z* mpz;                 // in relation to case SC4
};

D::D(Y& y): mry(y)  {}      // in relation to case SC3, the reference to the server
                            // object is passed to the constructor of the client
                            // object and used to initialize mry

void D::f1(X& x)            // case SC2, the reference to the server object is
{                           // passed to the member function of the client object
    x.fx();                 // that needs it, the reference is used here

    mry.fy();               // case SC3, the already initialized reference to the
                            // server object (in the constructor) is used here

    Z* mpz = new Z;         // case SC4, reference to the server object is obtained
    mpz->fz();              // from object creation and is used here

    s.fs();                 // case SC1, the reference to server object is known
                            // because it is contained in the client object

    delete mpz;             // in relation to case SC4, server object is destructed
    mpz = NULL;             // and the pointer to it (reference) is nullified
}
```

Listing 8-1. Examples of referencing objects.

8.3.2 Asynchronous Communication

Asynchronous communication means that a client object communicates with a server object by sending a service request. The client object continues execution. Asynchronous communication is based on the services of the underlying operating system. However, the operating system cannot directly transfer asynchronous messages between objects. There-

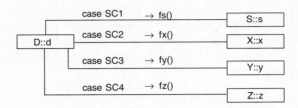

Figure 8-2. Synchronous communication examples.

fore, the client object has to request the operating system to send the message to the process associated with the object group to which the server object belongs in this context. In order to forward the message to the proper server object in the receiving target process, three basic implementation patterns are possible:

1. The target process has different message queues. Each queue leads to a member function call of one server object.

2. The target process has one message queue, but the message itself includes an identification tag that is used to select the server object and the member function to be called. Figure 8-3 and Listing 8-2 demonstrate this case.

3. The address of the server object and/or the address of a member function in the class of the server object is included in the message itself. Figure 8-4 and Listing 8-3 demonstrate this case. This way, the object group process associated with the server object becomes generic, and the client object has the ultimate control over what will happen because it sets these pointers (this is also a drawback because the client must know them). The pointer to the server object can be initialized to point to any instance of its class or to any instance of a class derived from this class. The member function pointer is declared to point to a member function with a certain signature. It can be initialized to point to any member function with a matching signature. The process associated with the server object has a simple structure that calls the function through the pointers from the received message. It does not need to know what the message was or where it came from.

A system typically uses a combination of these patterns. Notice that we can also represent asynchronous messages using classes. The actual messages are instances of these classes and can be defined statically or created dynamically at runtime.

A message needs a buffer (physical memory) to store its contents. Use the most effective and consistent message structure. Building and modifying messages should be easy and effective. Avoid combining multiple independent messages inside one message; it makes the program harder to understand.

Be prepared for failure in memory allocation for the message buffer if you use dynamic memory management for the message buffers. Always stick to one policy of message buffer ownership: typically, after a message is sent, the buffer is owned by the receiver.

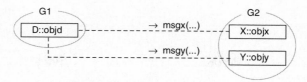

Figure 8-3. Asynchronous interactions.

```
// assuming classes X with function fx(Msg&), Y with function fy(Msg&) and D are
// declared and defined, and objects objx, objy and objd are created from these
// classes respectively

class Msg        // a class representing the data structure of an asynchronous
{                // message
public:
   enum MsgId{ToX, ToY};
   void send(MsgId toWho);
Private:
   MsgId id;// identification used to differentiate messages
// other content of the message structure
};

void Msg::send(MsgId toWho)
{
   id = toWho;
   // send the message using osSend(...) to process G2
}

Msg msgx, msgy;

void D::fd()// some function in class D defined
{
   msgx.send(Msg::ToX);
   msgy.send(Msg::ToY);
}

void G2()// process function
{
   for(;;)
   {
      // waiting to receive a message pointed to by a generic pointer msg of
      // type Msg& using OS service osReceive(...)
      switch(msg->id)    // notice that the more different messages are handled,
      {                  // the longer the switch statement becomes
      case Msg::ToX:
         objx.fx(msg);
         break;
      case Msg::ToY:
         objy.fy(msg);
         break;
      }
   }
}
```

Listing 8-2. Asynchronous messages example.

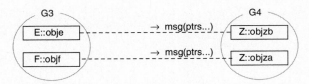

Figure 8-4. Pointers inside asynchronous messages.

```
// assuming classes E and F are declared
class Z
{
public:
   int fz1(Msg&);
   int fz2(Msg&);
};
// assuming the functions in Z are defined
Z objza, objzb;            // two objects from class Z are created

class Msg
{
public:
   Z *pz;                  // to be initialized to point to the desired server
                           // object of type Z*
   int (Z::*pmfz)(Msg&);   // a pointer to a member function that will be
                           // initialized to the relative position of the desired
                           // member function
//other contents of the message structure
};

Msg msg;                   // a message is statically created, to keep the example
                           // simple. In practice, different messages with
                           // different contents are created and filled dynamically
                           // and transferred using operating system services as in
                           // Listing 8-2.

void F::ff() // some function in class F defined
{
   msg.pz = &objza;        // initializing a pointer to the server object
   msg.pmfz = &Z::fz2;     // initializing offset to a member function in Z
   //...
}

void E::fe()               // some function in class E defined
{
   msg.pz = &objzb;        // initializing a pointer to a server object
   msg.pmfz = &Z::fz1;     // initializing offset to a member function in Z
   //...
}

void G4()                  // process function
{
// other contents
   int i = ((msg.pz)->*(msg.pmfz))(msg);        // calling through the pointers
      // contained in message, the desired functionality of the desired object:
      // objzb.fz1() is called if msg comes from obje.fe() and
      // objza.fz2() is called if msg comes from objf.ff().
}
```

Listing 8-3. Examples of object references inside asynchronous messages.

8.4 Memory and Performance Optimization

Embedded systems have limited memory and processor resources that need to be used efficiently. The objective is to use as little memory as possible and to achieve as high performance as possible. In practice, a balance between memory and performance needs to be achieved, because optimizing for one typically has the reverse effect on the other.

The following list points out some of the techniques that can be used to reduce memory consumption and improve performance:

- Use synchronous calls instead of asynchronous messages wherever possible.

- Instead of creating and deleting messages, reuse message buffers wherever possible. Often the buffer of a received message can be used to send a reply message and is then used for a new cycle.

- An asynchronous message used to control the execution may be substituted for by more effective operating system services, such as signals or semaphores.

- If you instantiate many objects from one class dynamically, consider writing a specific allocation mechanism (operators `new` and `delete` overloading) for that class to avoid memory fragmentation. Note that this may also increase the overall memory consumption in the system.

- Use references to objects as input parameters and as return values in functions wherever possible. Avoid copying objects and messages.

Dynamic objects and dynamic binding (implemented by virtual functions) increase memory consumption and may decrease performance, but they increase the flexibility of the program. When considering the use of these features, be careful not to compare single aspects with each other, but rather the whole solution using these aspects. It is well known that the time needed to call a virtual function is longer than the time needed to call a normal function, but if you compare a solution using virtual functions to another which does not use them, you may end up with the opposite result [Russo '88].

Also, be aware of padding inserted by the compiler inside structures, and avoid it by ordering data members and aggregated objects. You also need to know the hidden data members inserted by the compiler and their sizes; for example, each instance of a class which declares at least one virtual function has a hidden pointer to the virtual function table of that class. Each nonstatic member function has a hidden pointer to the object itself, called `this`, passed in its parameter list.

Many other techniques for effective C++ programming and their effects on memory and performance can be found in [Meyers '92] and [Gamma '94].

8.4.1 Classes with Singular Objects

Many of the classes in embedded systems have singular objects. The Singleton design pattern [Gamma '94] deals with this case in a very flexible way. However, if you have to minimize memory consumption and increase performance to the maximum levels possible, you may consider the alternative approach described here.

A class with all its member functions and data members declared as static can be used instead of its singular object. These static declarations need to be defined; after that, the class itself can be used instead of a single object instantiated from it, as shown in Listing 8-4. The designer of such a class must prevent instantiating objects from it. This can be achieved, for example, by declaring an empty constructor in the protected part of the class.

Concurrent access to static data members needs to be synchronized. This is discussed in Section 8.6.

```
class S
{
public:
   static void f1();
   static int d1;
//other static members
protected:
   S() {}              // an empty constructor in the protected part intended to prevent
                       // instantiating objects from this class
};
// definition and initialization of the static members in class S
void S::f1() {/* ... */}
int S::d1 = 5;

int main()
{
   S::d1 = 7;                    // the class identifier is used,
   S::f1();                      // no need for an object
   return 0;
}
```

Listing 8-4. A class with all members declared static.

8.4.2 Storage of Immutable Data Members and Objects

Many classes in embedded systems declare immutable data using the `const` keyword. However, many C++ compilers use the `const` keyword only to prevent direct assignment to these data members, but not to control the storage. In embedded systems with very limited RAM resources, it would be desirable to place the immutable part of objects in ROM or in other special memory. One solution to this problem is to partition the class into three parts:

• A part that contains data members and objects in RAM to be initialized via the constructor call.

• A part that contains the data members and objects in RAM to be initialized *not* via the constructor but from an initialization data image in ROM at startup.

• A part that contains the immutable data members and objects. This part is implemented using an aggregate class [Ellis '90]. The object of the aggregate class is declared constant and initialized using an initializer list, just as with C structures. This part can be placed in ROM or in other special memory.

It is also possible to store in EEPROM or FLASH those data members of objects that get immutable values after being calculated or after being read from the hardware when a program starts up.

8.5 Synchronization

One of the commonly accepted principles of object-oriented technology is that an object is in a consistent state provided that no member function of the object is currently executing. Execution of a member function may change the state of the object. The state of an object is represented by the actual values of all its data members.

The essence of object orientation is that objects encapsulate their own data. The data can be accessed by the clients only through member functions. These member functions are said to provide services to other clients. If clients request the service at the same time, which often happens in a real-time system, a concurrent access problem occurs. Synchronization is needed to control the access to shared resources. Synchronization must be properly designed and the solutions strictly applied in order to achieve reliable software.

8.5.1 Cases and Solutions

Figure 8-5 shows typical cases of *intra-object synchronization* and *interobject synchronization*. Intra-object synchronization is required when potentially two or more member functions of the same object concurrently request access to the same resource. Correspondingly, interobject synchronization means the same, but the involved member functions belong to different objects.

Figure 8-5 is also arranged to reflect the concurrent access cases based on the accessed resource:

- Case A, access of an external resource (e.g., a global variable).

- Case B, access of a local data member. In the case of interobject synchronization, the data member is owned by both objects only if it has been declared static. This is a typical case with a statechart shared between a number of different objects.

- Case C, access to a foreign data member which belongs to an object other than the one(s) trying to access it.

Synchronization problems may even occur in systems with only a single sequential thread of execution; for example, if an object objA calls a member function of another object objB, which in turn calls a member function of objA. This recursive calling can result in several layers of nested function calls between the two objects. Synchronization is needed only if the nested member functions access the same resource. In this case, a rearrangement of the calls is often enough to solve the problem.

At first glance, a mechanism resolving intra-object synchronization seems to be simpler than interobject synchronization since the participating member functions and the

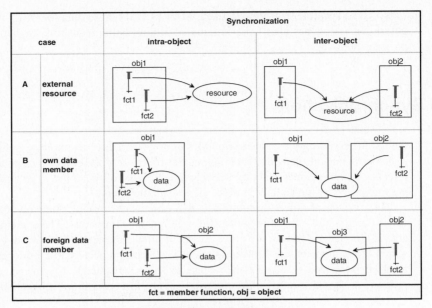

Figure 8-5. Synchronization.

accessed data members are bound to the same object. This may intuitively guide designers to introduce a new data member to guard against concurrent access of other data members. This approach works only if the access to the introduced new data member is synchronized, because it is itself a shared resource as well.

If a process shields the object from other objects outside the process, then from the viewpoint of the object, only a single sequential execution thread exists. With this solution, objects belonging to different processes do not share a resource. An object objX that wants to interact with an object objY shielded in another process must request that through the process of objY. The process in turn dispatches the request to objY (see also Section 8.4.2). Synchronization is needed now between the processes that share resources, not between the objects shielded in them. A shared resource can be protected by an operating system semaphore.

In small systems, where performance and memory consumption are most critical, a global disable and enable of context switching between the execution threads works as a synchronization mechanism.

Every synchronization mechanism finally requires a protected region. The whole protected region is guaranteed to be executed in one uninterrupted sequence (i.e., it is atomic). In a multithreaded program with preemption, this behavior can be achieved only if both hardware interrupts and context switching (software interrupts) are disabled while the protected region is executing. Try always to have as short protected regions as possible because as they get longer, the reactivity of the system decreases.

8.6 Implementing Statecharts

It was explained in Chapter 6 that there are basically two different kinds of statecharts:

1. If an object has its own state information, it can be declared as a data member in the class of the corresponding object, as in case **A** in Figure 8-6. Access to this state is through member functions.

2. If a number of objects use the same state information, it is declared as a static data member in a new class introduced to represent the statechart, case **B1** in Figure 8-6. Only a single object is instantiated from this class, or the class itself is used instead of its single object, as described in Section 8.4.1. However, if all the objects using the same state information are instantiated from the same class, the static data member representing the state and the member functions accessing it can be placed in the class of the objects, case **B2** in Figure 8-6.

Figure 8-7 shows an example of a statechart. It describes the operational mode of a certain system. Many objects in the system are using this statechart. This is an example of case **B1** in Figure 8-6.

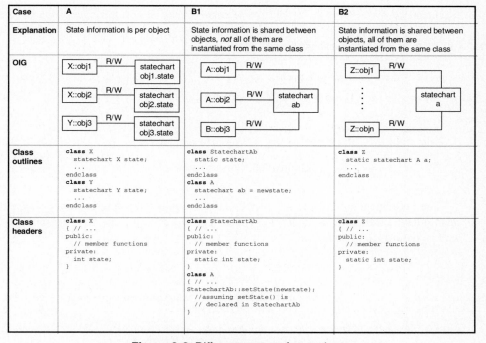

Figure 8-6. Different usage of statecharts.

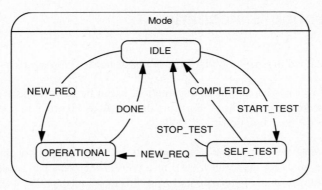

Figure 8-7. An example statechart.

A simple implementation of the statechart in Figure 8-6 follows in Listings 8-5 and 8-6. The class header declares two member functions in the public part: `transit()` to make a state transition and `report()` to supply the current state to a client. The data members are declared in the private part of the class, and `enum` type is used for the states and events. The statechart class may include other kinds of member functions, for example, to evaluate the state and then to issue a request to some other object.

```
class StatechartMode                    // represents the operational mode of a system
{
public:
   enum StateE {IDLE, OPERATIONAL, SELF_TEST};
   enum EventE {NEW_REQ, DONE, START_TEST, STOP_TEST, COMPLETED};

   bool transit(StatechartMode::EventE newEvent); // performs state transition if
                                                  // possible
   StateE report(); // reports the current state
   // ...
private:
   static StateE sys_state;
};
```

Listing 8-5. Class header.

The implementation of the member functions requires synchronization; because these manipulate a static data member, the concurrent access to it must be synchronized. This can be done as in Listing 8-6:

```
StatechartMode::StateE StatechartMode::report()
{
   StateE aux;              // a stack variable, see explanatory text below
   disableInterrupts();     // start of the protected region
   aux = sys_state;         // copying the state to the stack variable
   enableInterrupts();      // end of the protected region
```

Listing 8-6. Class implementation.

```
      return(aux);              // returning the stack variable
};

bool StatechartMode::transit(EventE newEvent)
{
   disableInterrupts(); // start of the protected region
   switch (newEvent)
   {
      case NEW_REQ:
         if ((sys_state == IDLE) || (sys_state == SELF_TEST))
         {
            sys_state = OPERATIONAL;
            enableInterrupts(); // end of the protected region
            return 1;
         }
         else
         {
            enableInterrupts(); // end of the protected region
            return 0;
         }
      case DONE:       // similarly
      case START_TEST:// similarly
      case STOP_TEST:  // similarly
      case COMPLETED:  // similarly
      default:
         enableInterrupts(); // end of the protected region
         return 0;
   } // end switch
} // end function
```

Listing 8-6. Class implementation.

Function `disableInterrupts()` disables context switching or hardware interrupts or both, depending on the synchronization need, whereas `enableInterrupts()` does the opposite. In case of nested `disableInterrupts()` and `enableInterrupts()` calls, only the last `enableInterrupts()` function call enables the interrupts. These functions are typically provided by the operating system.

Notice that `StatechartMode::report()` does not directly return the state data member becuase its value can change in the return statement as the interrupts are already enabled before that. Instead, a copy of the state data member is stored in an auxiliary stack variable, `aux`, which is returned instead of the state data member, `sys_state`.

Before the statechart can be used, the static data member is defined and initialized, and an object representing the statechart is created:

```
StatechartMode::StateE StatechartMode::sys_state = StatechartMode::IDLE;
StatechartMode stateLine;
```

Several clients can now call `stateLine.transit()` and `stateLine.report()` without problems, because they are synchronized against concurrent access.

8.7 Constructing Global Objects

In C++ local objects, that is, objects within the scope of the block where they are defined, are created on the stack and constructed correctly when execution enters this block. The construction of globally defined objects (i.e., objects with a file scope) is problematic. They are guaranteed to be constructed in the order in which they are defined only inside a single translation unit but not between different translation units. If you necessarily need global objects and want to control their construction, some workarounds may be employed:

• Define all of these objects in a single file, and arrange them according to the desired order of construction. Notice that this does not require that the declarations of the classes of these objects be grouped in a single header file.

• Define these objects inside a nonreturning function and use global pointers to access them instead. Make sure to initialize the pointers before they are used. One possibility is to define these objects and initialize the pointers to them in the first executed function which does not return, for example, inside a process. The process must be the one with the highest priority in the system so that it is guaranteed to run first; and thus, the pointers are initialized before they are used.

These workarounds have some penalties on performance and memory consumption. Other solutions are suggested, for example, in [Buroff '94].

Since the construction of global objects takes place before the execution of the `main()` program and before the initialization of the operating system, these objects cannot use any operating system service. If this is necessary, you must know what code your compiler generates to call the constructors of the global objects, and force it to execute after the operating system initialization routine is executed. This requires the manipulation of the compiler output.

8.8 Development Environment

The software of an embedded system is usually developed using at least two different compilers: a host compiler for simulation on the host and a cross-compiler to compile the code for the target system. In practice, several different C and C++ compilers and assemblers may be needed, for example:

• When using different hosts (e.g., PC, Sun, hp) or updating from one host to another

• If some of the debugging tools need or assume a specific compiler

• If the target system has different kinds of processors that are not supported by a single compiler

• If translators from C++ to C are used when there is no C++ cross-compiler available

The compilers developed by different vendors are definitely incompatible (no ANSI C++ standard yet; even if there were, each compiler has its own extensions and libraries). This causes additional difficulties to the programmer, such as:

• The program has to contain many environment-dependent variables (e.g., in the form of many `ifdef` statements) which make it difficult to read, test and maintain the program.

• Only the features supported by all compilers can be used.

• It is very difficult to suppress all the warnings of different compilers on the same code.

• Some libraries or object codes cannot be used.

The best solution is to use as integrated a development environment as possible; not just compilers, editors and simulation tools, but also real-time operating systems and libraries. An example of such a development environment is MasterWorks [MRI '93]. It is also desirable to acquire all components of the development environment from the same vendor.

There are situations where there is no C++ cross-compiler available for the target processor you are using. However, this should not prevent or discourage you from developing the program in an object-oriented way. Basically, there are two possibilities for handling this situation, which are discussed in the following subsections:

1. Using a C++ to C translator (e.g., AT&T C-Front)

2. Implementing the object-oriented design using C

8.8.1 C++ to C Translation

If you do not find a cross-compiler for your specific target microprocessor, you can use the front-end of any other C++ compiler (preferably a C++ cross-compiler) to translate C++ to C, or you can buy a separate C-Front product that does the translation. The output of the translation is a set of C files that you can pass to the C cross-compiler intended for your target processor.

However, there are some problems that need to be solved in the translated C code before passing it to the C cross-compiler. For example, C-Front version 2.1 drops away the `const` keyword in the generated C code and produces unnecessary zero initialization of global objects, thus wasting memory. The problems can be detected by compiling the translator's output from a small but full-featured C++ test program using the C cross-compiler. When the problems are known, it is relatively easy to write a script that operates on the output files of the translator to remove, substitute or add text to them to correct these problems. Also, commercial solutions are available for some targets, for example, Paradigm [PAR '94] for Intel 80x86 processors based on the output of Borland or Microsoft C++ compilers. Commercial solutions also support the use of different C++ libraries in the target system.

8.8.2 Implementing an Object-Oriented Design Using C

The other alternative when you do not find a C++ cross-compiler for your specific target microprocessor is to implement the object-oriented design using C instead of C++. This is not as odd as it may sound. In the previous section we pointed out that C++ to C translators are available, which means that every C++ construct can be expressed in C as well. We could therefore manually use the C representation of the desired C++ constructs. It is, however, better to use a standard and consistent method; for example, see the CORBA C mapping for classes and objects (creating, referencing, manipulating, inheritance, virtual functions, etc.) [CORBA '94]. Also, Bertrand Meyer discusses this issue [Meyer '88].

9

CASE STUDY:
SUBSCRIBER LINE TESTER

This case study is based on a real product in the telecommunications area. However, many of the details related to the product are ignored, and some information has been deliberately modified. Also, the names of the components do not match those of the existing product.

A remote digital transmission system (DTS) installed in the telecommunication network has 30 channels used for voice and data communication. Each channel is assigned to a unique subscriber line. A DTS is connected to a telephone exchange using a communication line at 2 Mbits per second and can be connected to a PC on a PC line (an RS 232 serial bus). A DTS has a multiplexer unit (MUX) and three channel units (CUs). Up to ten subscriber lines can be connected to a channel unit (see Figure 9-1).

9.1 System Requirements Specification

9.1.1 Problem Statement

The exchange performs a number of line tests on the subscriber lines that are directly connected to it. These tests require physical wire access to the subscriber lines that the exchange does not have with the remote subscriber lines of a DTS.

To increase the overall reliability of the network and to have a similar quality of service for the remote subscriber lines as the ones connected directly to the exchange, a new unit

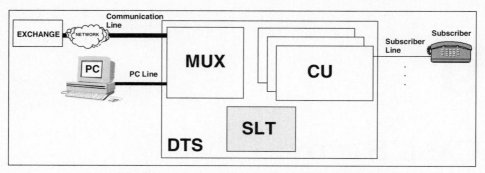

Figure 9-1. A remote digital transmission system (DTS).

called a subscriber line tester (SLT) is needed in the DTS to be responsible for the line tests. It must respond to the line test commands from the exchange, perform the tests and report the results. For that purpose a test protocol is specified. It is also necessary that a local PC be able to emulate the exchange. The SLT can also be configured to perform line tests automatically and to report to the exchange when faulty subscriber lines are found.

The exchange analyzes the results and can determine the location of the fault if there is any. The exchange blocks the faulty lines. Sometimes the test results do not indicate a fault but are not as good as expected. Preventative measures can be taken to fix the degrading subscriber lines before a complete failure.

The SLT, the subject of this case study, is therefore an add-on unit to an already existing and working DTS.

The Line Tests

The line tests on a subscriber line are a number of measurements that calculate the following parameters. Figure 9-2 demonstrates some of them.

- The foreign AC and DC voltages on both the **A** and **B** wires to the ground (**VDCag, VACag, VDCbg, VACbg**), to the supply voltage (**VDCav, VACav, VDCbv, VACbv**) and between the wires (**VDCab, VACab**). If any of the measured voltages is below –20 volts or above +20 volts, then the tested subscriber line is faulty. The system must be able to measure and withstand effective voltages between –250 volts and +250 volts.

- The leakage resistances of both the **A** and **B** wires to the ground (**Rag, Rbg**), to the supply voltage (**Rav, Rbv**) and between the wires (**Rab**). If any of the resistances is below 50 kohm, then the tested subscriber line is faulty. Normal values are usually above 500 kohm.

- The leakage capacitances of both the **A** and **B** wires to the ground (**Cag, Cbg**), to the supply voltage (**Cav, Cbv**) and between the wires (**Cab**). There are no fault limits for the capacitances, although their values range typically between 0,10 to 10,0 micro Farad depending on the type of the telephone set connected to the wires.

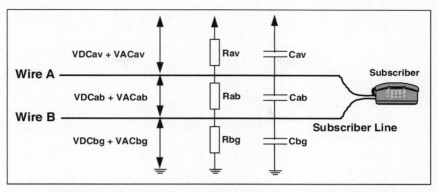

Figure 9-2. Some subscriber line parameters to be measured.

9.1.2 Use Cases

This section includes the use case diagram (Figure 9-3) and the use cases of the SLT system. The system has four primary use cases and three autonomous activities. U1, U2, U4 and U5 have an exception use case, U3. Activity U9 is part of both U4 and U6.

Use Case	(U1) Get information.
Actors	Exchange or PC.
Preconditions	SLT is running.
Description	Actor may request:
	identification of the hardware and software of the SLT.
	status of a selected subscriber line.
	test results of a selected subscriber line.
	list of faulty lines.
	The SLT sends all the requested parameters within 300 ms.
	The status of line is: the test result status (Normal I Faulty I Not Tested), the test permission (Allowed I Denied), the periodic test permission (Allowed I Denied) and its starting time and rate of occurrence.
	The test results include all the measured parameters of the line (VDCag, VACag, VDCbg, VACbg, VDCav, VACav, VDCbv, VACbv, VDCab, VACab, Rag, Rbg, Rav, Rbv, Rab, Cag, Cbg, Cav, Cbv and Cab) and an indication about what of these are inside the fault limits. Also the time and date of the test is reported.
Exceptions	Exception, no response within the time out: The actor waits another additional 300 ms, if still no response, the actor resets the SLT as in U3.
Postconditions	Requested parameters are sent.

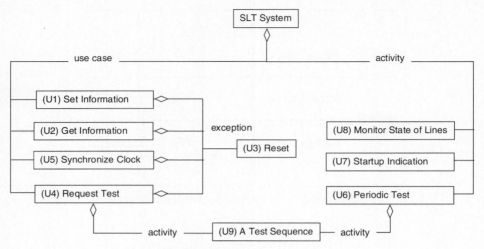

Figure 9-3. Use case diagram.

Use Case	(U2) Set information.
Actors	Exchange or PC.
Preconditions	SLT is running.
Description	Actor may request the SLT to set certain parameters, one at a time:
	• The fault limits which are common to all lines:
	Overvoltage limit (> 50 V and < 250 V, e.g. 150 V)
	Voltage limit (> 10 V and < 50 V, e.g. 20 V)
	Resistance limit (> 10 kohm and < 100 kohm, e.g. 50 kohm)
	• For a selected subscriber line:
	the test permission right (Allowed | Denied),
	the periodic test permission (Allowed | Denied)
	the starting time of a periodic test (e.g. 01:00 AM)
	the rate of the periodic test (e.g. 6 times a day).
	The SLT checks that the given parameter is acceptable [Exception: the parameter is not acceptable], it then sets the parameter and sends a positive acknowledgment within 100 ms.
	Every setting parameter must persist in the system after reset. All the settings have default values.
Exceptions	Exception: the parameter is not acceptable, the SLT sends a negative acknowledgment to the actor within 100 ms.
	Exception, no response within the time-out: The actor waits another additional 100 ms, if still no response, the actor resets the SLT as in (U3).
Postconditions	The parameter is set in the nonvolatile memory.

Use Case	(U3) Reset the SLT.
Actors	Exchange or PC in exception of U1, U2, U4 and U5.
Preconditions	SLT is running.
Description	SLT sends a positive acknowledgment to the actor within 50 ms indicating that it will reset itself and become once more available 1000 ms after sending the acknowledgment. The acknowledgment is sent to the other possible actor of the SLT system.
Exceptions	Exception 1, the SLT fails to send an acknowledgment within the time-out: The actor waits another additional 50 ms, if still no response, the actor tries to reset the SLT once more. If no change, the SLT is considered faulty.
	Exception 2, the SLT sends a negative acknowledgment: the SLT is considered faulty.
Postconditions	SLT is restarted.

Use Case	(U4) Request test of a selected subscriber line (voltages, resistance and capacitance).
Actors	Exchange or PC.
Preconditions	SLT is running and the requested subscriber line has a test permission.
Description	Actor requests the SLT to test a selected subscriber line.
	The SLT responds within 50 ms by an acknowledgment (Accepted I No Test Permission). The SLT then starts a test sequence on the line if it is idle, otherwise it will try later. If a test result is inside the fault limits, then the SLT sends a fault indication to the exchange and PC. Also, a failure to establish a connection to a line is reported as a fault as described in U9.
	The request from the exchange must be always serviced first. If a line is being tested because of a request from the PC or periodically, the ongoing test must be postponed and the exchange request is serviced.
Exceptions	Exception, no response within the time out: The actor waits another additional 50 ms, if still no response, the actor resets the SLT as in U3.
Activity	(U9) A line test sequence.
Postconditions	Requested lines are tested and the test results are updated in the memory of the SLT. Any fault found is indicated to the actors.

Use Case	(U5) Synchronize the clock in the SLT.
Actors	Exchange or PC.
Preconditions	SLT is running.
Description	Actor requests the SLT to synchronize its clock (date and time) to the ones given in the request.
	The SLT checks the validity of the clock and sends (Accepted I Not Valid) within 10 ms. It then resynchronizes its internal clock in case the date and time are accepted.
	The actor must do this use case always when the SLT gives a startup indication as described in U7.
Exceptions	Exception, no answer within the time outs: The actor waits another equivalent period. If there is still no answer, it resets the SLT as in U3.
Postconditions	The SLT clock is resynchronized.

Use Case	(U6) Periodic Test.
Actors	Autonomous activity of the SLT system.
Preconditions	SLT is running and no active test from the exchange or the PC. Periodic test is performed on a certain subscriber line if it has both test permission and periodic test permission.
Description	Periodic line tests are activated according to the starting time and rate settings for that subscriber line. A line test sequence is started as in U9.
Exceptions	Exception, a request from the exchange to test a line occurs while a periodic test is ongoing: the SLT suspends the periodic test and responds to the exchange request. If the request would have been from the PC, then the periodic test is allowed to complete and the PC request is postponed.
Activity	(U9) A line test sequence.
Postconditions	Line is tested. Its results are updated in the memory. If a test result is inside the fault limits, then the SLT sends a fault indication to the exchange and PC including the line number which was found faulty.

Use Case	(U7) Startup Indication.
Actors	Autonomous activity of the SLT system.
Preconditions	SLT is powered on or wakes from reset.
Description	SLT sends an indication to the exchange (SLT STARTED). As a result, the exchange must synchronize the clock in the SLT as described in U5.
Exceptions	
Postconditions	

Use Case	(U8) Monitor state of lines.
Actors	Autonomous activity of the SLT system.
Preconditions	SLT is running.
Description	The state (FREE I BUSY I CONNECTED_TO_TEST) of all lines is monitored.
Exceptions	
Postconditions	

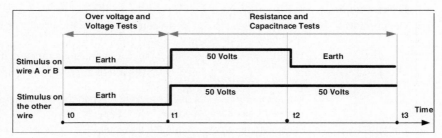

Figure 9-4. The stimuli on the wires.

Use Case	(U9) A line test sequence.
Actors	Autonomous activity of use cases U4 and U6.
Preconditions	A test request is approved from the exchange, the PC or periodically.
Description	SLT performs the line test in a certain order as following, see Figure 9-4:

- Establish a physical connection through the CU to the requested subscriber line.

  If no connection is established within 50 ms then disconnect the subscriber line and inform the requester with a fault (No Connection Established). The line tests for that particular subscriber line stop here.
- Before measuring the different voltage parameters, a protective overvoltage test is performed as following:

  > Earth both the A and B wires of the subscriber line.
  > Connect the test relays in the overvoltage test position.
  > Sample the response on both the wires for 10 ms at 8 kHz.
  > Analyze the result.

  If there is overvoltage (excessive transient voltages above effective 150 volts), then disconnect the subscriber line and inform the requester about this fault. The line tests for that particular subscriber line stop here.
- If there is no overvoltage, then the line tests continue as following (voltage test):

  > Keep both the A and B wires of the subscriber line earthed.
  > Connect the test relays in the voltage test position.
  > Wait 50 ms so that the response on the wires settles.
  > Sample the response on both the wires for 100 ms, at 8 kHz.
  > Analyze the result.

  If there is a foreign voltage inside the fault limits, then do similar actions as in the overvoltage test.
- If there is voltage inside the fault limits then the line tests, continue as following (leakage resistance and capacitance tests):

  > Connect 50 volts stimulus to both wires of the subscriber line.
  > Connect the test relays in the resistance and capacitance positions.
  > Wait 100 ms so that the response on the wires settles.
  > Sample the response on both the wires for 200 ms at 8 kHz.
  > Do analysis in which the results of the voltage tests are used.
  > Keep 50 volts connected to one of the wires and earth the other wire.
  > Wait 150 ms so that the response on the wires settles.
  > Sample the response on the wires for 200 ms each at 8 kHz.
  > Disconnect the relays.
  > Disconnect the subscriber line.
  > Analyze the result.

  If any of the parameters is inside the fault limits, then inform the requester.

Exceptions	
Postconditions	

9.1.3 The SLT Context Diagram

The SLT has a simple context diagram. It gets commands from an exchange or from a local PC. The PC is optional. The SLT performs the requested activities and sends the answers to the exchange or to the PC if needed. The activities performed by the SLT affect subscriber lines through the measurement unit (see Figure 9-5).

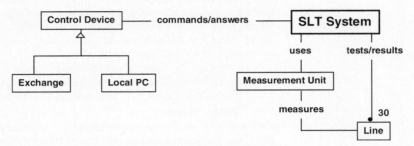

Figure 9-5. SLT context diagram.

9.2 SLT Application Subsystem Analysis

The architecture of the SLT system has one application subsystem in addition to the hardware wrapper. This is shown in Figure 9-6. This chapter contains the complete analysis and design of the application subsystem and leaves the hardware wrapper for the reader as an exercise. However, the necessary information about the hardware wrapper is given.

9.2.1 Object Model

The object model shows the system and its environment separated by the application border (Figure 9-7). The environment of the system has the same classes as the context diagram and some additional ones representing the interface to the hardware wrapper. The

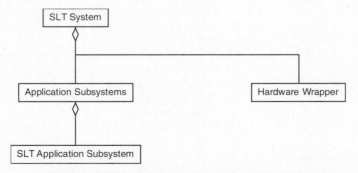

Figure 9-6. The decomposition of the SLT system.

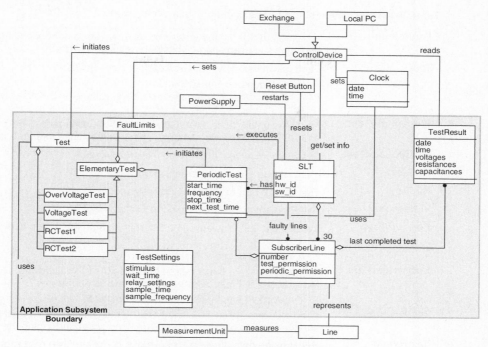

Figure 9-7. The object model of the SLT.

context diagram is reflected in the object model as is. The additional hardware wrapper classes are **Clock**, **ResetButton** and **PowerSupply**.

The system is built around the **SLT** object. The **SLT** has 30 subscriber lines and keeps track of faulty lines and test requests. Subscriber lines may have test results associated with them. The complex internal structure of **SubscriberLine** and **TestResult** reflects the requirements. We have decided to follow the physical structure and not the logical one. There is only one test. This test consists of three elementary tests. Three different kinds of elementary tests exist: **OverVoltageTest**, **VoltageTest** and **ResistanceCapacitanceTest** (abbreviated to **RCTest**). They all have different **TestSettings**.

Tables 9-1 and 9-2 explain the classes and their associations.

Table 9-1. The classes of the SLT application subsystem.

Class	Description
SLT	The line test unit having different identity codes. It • has 30 SubscriberLines • has PowerSupply • has ResetButton • has a list of faulty subscriber lines • has a list of periodic tests and executes the tests

Table 9-1. The classes of the SLT application subsystem. *(cont.)*

FaultLimits	A fault is indicated if the measured values exceed corresponding FaultLimits in overvoltage, voltage or resistance tests.
Test	Each test initiated by PC, Exchange or PeriodicTest • is related to one SubscriberLine • consists of four ElementaryTests: OverVoltageTest, VoltageTest, RCTest1 and RCTest2.
ElementaryTest	Four elementary tests exist: OverVoltageTest, VoltageTest, RCTest1 and RCTest2. Each elementary test has test settings and fault limits
OverVoltageTest	The ElementaryTest performing the overvoltage test
RCTest1	The first part of resistance capacitance test
RCTest2	The second part of resistance capacitance test
VoltageTest	The ElementaryTest performing the voltage test
PeriodicTest	Initiates the test regularly. It has start time, frequency, stop time and next test time. • It is related to one SubscriberLine.
SubscriberLine	Represents a line. It has number, status (FAULTY I NORMAL I NOT_TESTED), test permission and periodic permission. • It may have the TestResult of last completed test.
TestSettings	Each elementary test has its own test settings such as the fault limits and the position of relays. These are used when performing the test.
TestResult	Records the date, time and results of a completed test regarding each measured parameter. Each parameter also carries information showing if the measured value was out of fault limits. If measurement was interrupted due to excessive voltage, resistance and capacitance values will be zeros.

Table 9-2. Classes in the hardware wrapper.

Class	Description
Exchange	Represents the interface to the remote controller
Local PC	Represents the interface to the local controller
ControlDevice	Either Exchange or Local PC, it • initiates Test • sets FaultLimits • sets Clock • reads TestResult • reads SLT id
PowerSupply	The interface to the power supply hardware
ResetButton	The reset button
Clock	Controls the time settings consisting of date and time and provides timing services
MeasurementUnit	Represents the interface to the measurement unit
Line	Represents the interface to the line hardware and encapsulates information regarding the state of line (IDLE, BUSY, CONNECTED_TO_TEST)

9.2.2 Functional Model

The functional model is built by tracing all relevant use cases and deciding the names and the parameters of each operation. Each sheet is written so that the precondition is as general as possible. This saves some space, but makes the output and postcondition clauses more complicated. For each operation, the implicit precondition is that SLT is running. Only those changes that are explicitly mentioned take place; everything else is unchanged.

Operation	(O1) GetHardwareAndSoftwareId
Description	Provides the hardware and software identifications to the control device
Associations	SLT, ControlDevice
Preconditions	
Inputs	
Modifies	
Outputs	SLTId(SLT.id, SLT.hw_id, SLT.sw_id)
Postconditions	

Operation	(O2) GetLineStatus
Description	Sends the status of the line to the control device
Associations	SubscriberLine, SLT, ControlDevice
Preconditions	
Inputs	Number
Modifies	
Outputs	LineStatus (number, SubscriberLine.status, SubscriberLine.test_permission, SubscriberLine.periodic_permission)
Postconditions	SubscriberLine.number = number

Operation	(O3) GetTestResult
Description	Sends the test results to the control device
Associations	TestResults, SubscriberLine, SLT, ControlDevice
Preconditions	
Inputs	Number
Modifies	
Outputs	TestResult (number, TestResult.date, TestResult.time, TestResult.VDCag, TestResult.VACag, TestResult.VDCbg, TestResult.VACbg, TestResult.VDCav, TestResult.VACav, TestResult.VDCbv, TestResult.VACbv, TestResult.VDCab, TestResult.VACab, TestResult.Rag, TestResult.Rbg, TestResult.Rav, TestResult.Rbv, TestResult.Rab, TestResult.Cag, TestResult.Cbg, TestResult.Cav, TestResult.Cbv, TestResult.Cab) indicating with each value if it was within fault limits or not.
Postconditions	The reported test results are all from the latest fully completed test for the given line. If the test was aborted, all values are zeros.

Operation	(O4) GetListOfFaultyLines
Description	Provides the list of faulty lines to the control device
Associations	SLT, SubscriberLine, ControlDevice
Preconditions	
Inputs	
Modifies	
Outputs	FaultyLines (**list of** SubscriberLine.number)
Postconditions	**for each** SubscriberLine **in** the output list
	(SubscriberLine->LastCompletedTest).result **equals** FAULTY
	and for other SubscriberLines
	(SubscriberLine->LastCompletedTest).result **not equals** FAULTY

Operation	(O5) SetOvervoltageLimit
Description	Set the overvoltage limit to a new limit from the control device
Associations	FaultLimits, ControlDevice
Preconditions	
Inputs	The fault limit
Modifies	FaultLimits.over_voltage_limit
Outputs	**if not** (50 V < limit < 250 V) **then**
	LimitError
	else
	LimitOK
Postconditions	**if** (50 V < limit < 250 V) **then** FaultLimits.over_voltage_limit = limit

Operations (O6) SetVoltageLimit and (O7) SetResistanceLimit are similar to operation (O5).

Operation	(O8) SetTestPermissions
Description	Sets the permission to test a line
Associations	SLT, SubscriberLine, ControlDevice
Preconditions	
Inputs	Number, test_permission, periodic_test_permission
Modifies	SubscriberLine.test_permission, SubscriberLine.periodic_permission
Outputs	Acknowledgment
Postconditions	SubscriberLine.test_permission = test_permission and
	SubscriberLine.periodic_permission = periodic_permission
	if periodic_permission = FALSE **then** line has no PeriodicTest

Operation	(O9) SetPeriodicTest
Description	Initiates a periodic test
Associations	SLT, SubscriberLine, PeriodicTest, ControlDevice
Preconditions	
Inputs	Number, start_time, frequence, stop_time
Modifies	PeriodicTest
Outputs	**if** start_time, frequency **and** stop_time are **not** valid **then** PeriodicTestError
	elseif not SubscriberLine.periodic_permission **then** NoPeriodicTestPermission(number)
	else PeriodicTestOK(number)
Postconditions	**if** start_time, frequency and stop_time are valid **and** SubscriberLine.periodic_permission **then**
	A PeriodicTest is created for the SubscriberLine and initiated using the given values
	Operation O13 is started periodically as requested

The uses cases do not specify (O9) in detail. An alternative would be to create a periodic test even if the periodic test permission is not given.

Operation	(O10) Reset
Description	Resets the SLT within 1000 ms
Associations	SLT, ControlDevice
Preconditions	
Inputs	
Modifies	
Outputs	**if** SLT OK **then** ResetOK **else** ResetError
Postconditions	SLT is restarted

Operation	(O11) TestRequest
Description	Requests a test of a line
Associations	SLT, Test, SubscriberLine, ControlDevice
Preconditions	
Inputs	Number
Modifies	
Outputs	**if** Line is busy **then** LineNotIdle(number)
	elseif SubscriberLine.test_permission = false **then** NoTestPermission(number)
	else TestAccepted(number)
Postconditions	**if** test is accepted **then** start operation 013

Operation	(O12) AbortTest
Description	Interrupts tests on a line when Line becomes busy.
Associations	SubscriberLine, Line
Preconditions	Line is busy and was connected to test
Inputs	Number
Modifies	Test
Outputs	
Postconditions	Test hardware is disconnected from the line

Operation	(O13) TestLine
Description	Tests a line and stores the result. Not part of the interface.
Associations	SLT, Test, SubscriberLine
Preconditions	Test was requested by Exchange **or** Local PC **or** Periodic **or** A postponed test resumes
Inputs	
Modifies	TestResult, SubscriberLine
Outputs	**if** test result faulty **then** LineFault(number)
Postconditions	Disconnects Line from test hardware **and** updates test results for the line. Adds faulty line to SLT list of FaultyLines

9.2.3 Dynamic Model

A) Analysis of Events

A set of logical events enters the subsystem from the environment. The information requests and settings can arrive from either the local or the remote control device. Since Clock is part of the hardware wrapper, the clock synchronization event doesn't reach the SLT application subsystem. Line reports the change in its status and gives test samples during testing. Clock will cause the event PeriodicTestStart. The PowerSupply and ResetButton objects are able to generate the events PowerOn and Reset.

Table 9-3 describes these events, and Figure 9-8 shows the grouping of events.

Table 9-3. Event List.

Event	Description
(E1) GetLineStatus	Request for status of a line.
(E2) GetTestResult	Request for test results.
(E3) GetListOfFaultyLines	Request for the list of faulty lines.
(E4) GetHardwareAndSoftwareId	Request for identifications.
(E5) SetOverVoltageLimit	Request to set overvoltage limit to the given value.
(E6) SetVoltageLimit	Request to set voltage limit to the given value.
(E7) SetResistanceLimit	Request to set resistance limit to the given value.
(E8) SetTestPermissions	Request to set test permission settings of a line.

Table 9-3. Event List. *(cont.)*

(E9) SetPeriodicTest	Request to set to periodic test settings of a line.
(E10) TestRequest	Request to start a test on a given line.
(E11) PeriodicTestStart	Request to start a periodic test on a given line.
(E12) PowerOn	SLT was switched off and then on.
(E13) Reset	Request to reset SLT.
(E14) AbortTest	Request to abort an ongoing test of a certain line.
(E15) TestSample	A test sample arrived from the line connected to test.

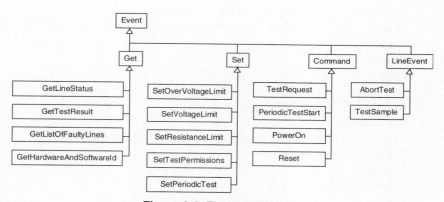

Figure 9-8. The event groups

The events are described in detail in the following event sheets:

Event	Get
Associations	SLT, SubscriberLine, TestResult
Response	Corresponding information record
Source	Local PC or Exchange
Contents	
Response Time	Max. 300 ms
Rate	Occasional

Event	Set
Associations	FaultLimits, SubscriberLine, PeriodicTest
Response	Acknowledgment
Source	Local PC or exchange
Contents	Data on the actual event
Response Time	Max. 500 ms
Rate	Occasional

Event	(E10) TestRequest
Associations	SLT, Test, SubscriberLine, FaultLimits
Response	LineBusy(number) **or** LineNoTestPermission(number) **or** TestAccepted(number)
Source	Local PC or exchange
Contents	Line number
Response Time	Max. 50 ms
Rate	Occasional, max. rate 200 Hz

Event	(E11) PeriodicTestStart
Associations	PeriodicTest, Test, SubscriberLine, FaultLimits
Response	Starts test on the given line if possible
Source	Clock in the hardware wrapper
Contents	Line number
Response Time	
Rate	According to the periodic test settings

Event	(E12) PowerOn
Associations	SLT
Response	Startup indication to the exchange and PC if connected
Source	Hardware wrapper
Contents	
Response Time	Max. 50 ms
Rate	Exceptional

Event	(E13) Reset
Associations	SLT
Response	Acknowledgment and within 1000 ms reset
Source	Local PC, Exchange, ResetButton
Contents	
Response Time	Max. 50 ms for the acknowledgment
Rate	Exceptional

Event	(E14) AbortTest
Associations	SLT, SubscriberLine, Test
Response	Interrupt test on the line
Source	Line
Contents	Line number
Response Time	Max. 100 ms
Rate	Occasional, max. rate 1 Hz

Event	(E15) TestSample
Associations	Test
Response	Analysis of samples to calculate line parameters
Source	Hardware wrapper
Contents	Buffer filled with sample values
Response Time	
Rate	After the setup of each elementary test

B) Interaction Scenarios between the Subsystem and Its Environment

Since the application subsystem is always able to respond to the Set and Get events, the scenarios are rather simple. However, the combination of different features is still rather interesting. The scenario in Figure 9-9 clarifies how a test is performed. It also demonstrates that the subsystem provides old test results until the test is finished.

The scenario in Figure 9-10 shows how a periodic test is initialized and how it later signals a fault.

Different events have different priorities. The scenario in Figure 9-11 shows how many times a test can be interrupted.

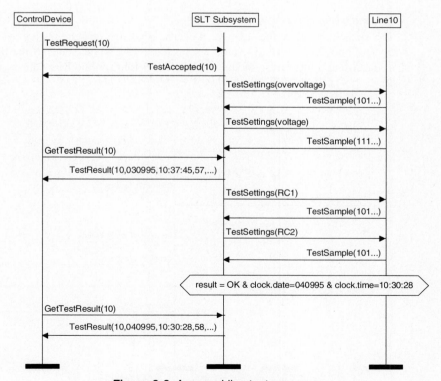

Figure 9-9. A normal line test sequence.

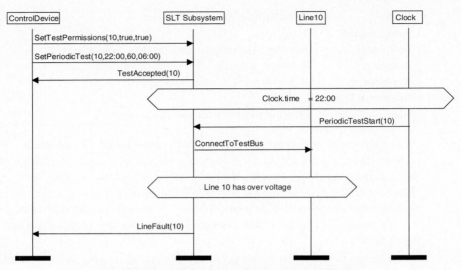

Figure 9-10. A fault is found during a periodic test.

C) Analysis of States

The statecharts show the states of the subscriber line and the testing system (Figures 9-13, 9-14 and Table 9-4). Since these statecharts refer to the states of the line, the statechart describing **Line** is also included, even if it belongs to the hardware wrapper (Figure 9-12).

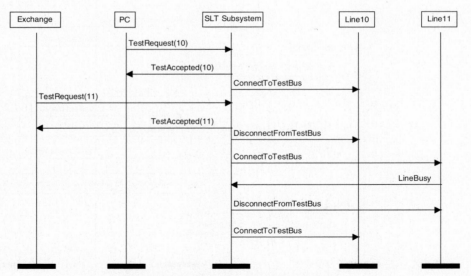

Figure 9-11. An interrupted test sequence.

Table 9-4. Application subsystem statechart list.

Statechart	Elementary States	Associations
Subscriber Line	1.1 TestResults side	Local to this object
	(S1.1.1) Not Valid	
	(S1.1.2) Valid	
	1.2 Testing side	
	(S1.2.1) None	
	(S1.2.1.1) Never Tested	
	(S1.2.1.2) Tested	
	(S1.2.1.3) No Connection	
	(S1.2.2) On going	
	(S1.2.3) Pending	
	(S1.2.3.1) Interrupted	
	(S1.2.3.2) Line in use	
SLT System	(S2.1) Idle	Line, SubscriberLine, Test
	(S2.2) Testing	
	2.2.1 Phase side	
	(S2.2.1.1) Connecting	
	(S2.2.1.2) OverVoltageTest	
	(S2.2.1.3) Voltage Test	
	(S2.2.1.4) RCfirst	
	(S2.2.1.5) RCsecond	
	2.2.2 Request side	
	(S2.2.2.1) Period	
	(S2.2.2.2) Exchange	
	(S2.2.2.3) PC	

Line has three states: Busy, Free and Connection to the test hardware (see Figure 9-12). When Line becomes busy while in the Connected state, it creates the AbortTest event.

The test behavior of SubscriberLine is modeled by two concurrent state automatons (Figure 9-13). The first one shows that test results may expire if they are too old. If the line has never been tested or the test results have expired, the line is in NotValid and Never-Tested state. Once a test is started, the test is either Ongoing or Pending. A test that is pending will be restarted when possible.

The testing system (Figure 9-14) is either in Testing or Idle. A Reset event will always put it back to Idle. Testing is started either by an external test request from control device or by a time out (Unattended). Testing is done in five phases (Table 9-5). A new test request starts testing of the requested line if it has higher priority. An AbortTest event always interrupts the test.

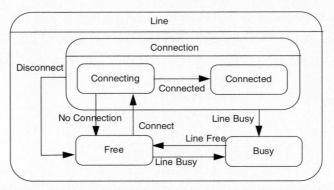

Figure 9-12. Line statechart (belongs to hardware wrapper).

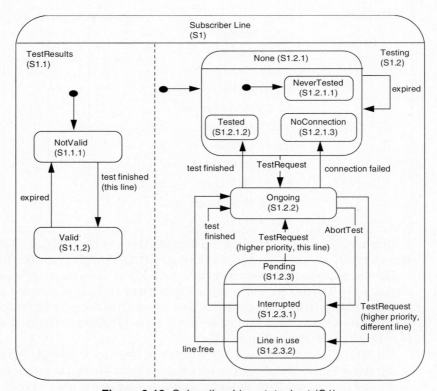

Figure 9-13. Subscriber Line statechart (S1).

The test phases are the connection phase, overvoltage test, voltage test and the two phases of resistance and capacitance test. Since the results of the overvoltage and voltage tests are needed before testing can proceed, it is possible to do the analysis and measurements in parallel only in the resistance and capacitance test.

Table 9-5. State-event actions table.

State	Event	Actions
(S2.1) Idle	Get	Provide the requested information
	Set	Set the requested parameter
(S2.2) Testing	\<enter\>	Start testing
	Get	Provide the requested information
	Set	Set the requested parameter
	Test finished	Update the test results for the line
	\<exit\>	Release the line, release the test hardware
(S2.2.1.1) Connecting	\<enter\>	Connect the line to the test bus, set up 50 ms timer
	TimeOut	Disconnect the line, inform fault
(S2.2.1.2) OverVoltageTest	\<enter\>	Set up an overvoltage test, sample 10 ms
	\<exit\>	Analyze the test sample
(S2.2.1.3) Voltage Test	\<enter\>	Set up a voltage test, wait, sample
	\<ongoing\>	Collect the test samples, set up a new sample
	\<exit\>	Analyze the samples
(S2.2.1.4) RC First	\<enter\>	Set up an RC test, wait, sample
	\<ongoing\>	Collect the test samples, set up a new sample
	\<exit\>	Analyze the samples
(S2.2.1.5) RC Second	\<enter\>	Set up the second RC test, wait, sample
	\<ongoing\>	Collect the test samples, set up a new sample
	\<exit\>	Analyze the samples. Analyze the results.
(S1.2.2) Ongoing	\<enter\>	Start test
	\<exit\>	Disconnect line from test hardware

Table 9-6 is the significance table of the subsystem.

Table 9-6. Significance table.

State \ Event	Get	Set	Test Request	Periodic Test Start	Reset	Abort Test	Test Sample
(S1) Subscriber Line	1	1	c	e	1	c	c
(S2.1) Idle	e	e	c	e	c	c	0
(S2.2) Testing	e	e	c	e	c	c	1

The significance table records some important decisions. It shows that the subsystem ignores some conditions that could have been considered errors, like the arrival of a test sample when the system is not expecting it. The **PowerOn** event is not listed in the table because it will not be handled by the SLT application subsystem.

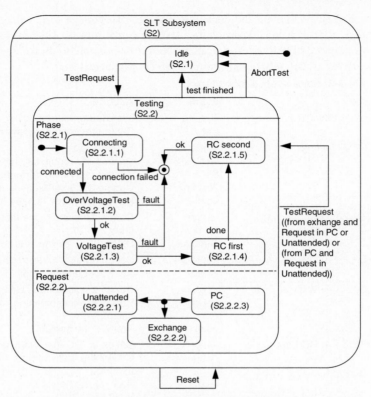

Figure 9-14. SLT subsystem statechart (S2).

9.3 SLT Application Subsystem Design

9.3.1 Event Threads and Object Groups

Figures 9-15 through 9-19 show the design of the event threads of the SLT application subsystem based on the given analysis. Environment objects appear outside the subsystem boundary, marked by a shaded rectangle. Here, all environment objects belong to the hardware wrapper subsystem. Their design is the subject of Section 9.4.

If only a singular object is instantiated from a class, the class name is not mentioned. Instead, the identifier of the object is the same as its class name except for a small initial letter. Most of the event threads are not overlaid, and objects appearing with the same identifier in different threads indicate the same object. The same applies for the object groups.

It is recommended to read the class outlines in Section 9.3.4 in parallel when examining the event threads.

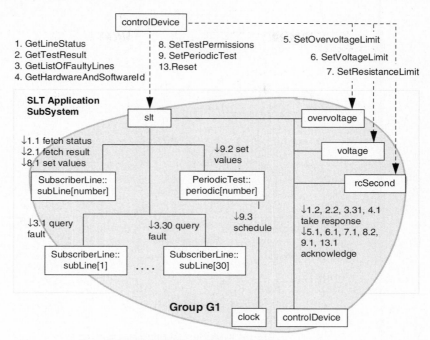

Figure 9-15. ControlDevice event threads.

Figure 9-15 shows the event threads of the event groups Get and Set. It also shows the event thread of the remote reset request that the control device issues via the Reset event. When object slt receives a Reset event, it first acknowledges the control device (interaction 13.1) and then performs a soft reset. All event threads of event group Get go through object slt which fetches data from a particular element of the object array subLine of class SubscriberLine. Remember that SLT has 30 different subscriber lines. The event thread of event GetListOfFaultyLines loops over all elements of array subLine. Object slt then requests environment object controlDevice to take the composed result.

The event thread of event SetTestPermissions is similar to the event threads of event group Get. The event thread of event SetPeriodicTest is a bit different, because it directs data to a particular element of the object array periodic of class PeriodicTest and from there to environment object clock. Each element of array periodic corresponds to an element of array subLine. Setting a fault limit is done directly with the corresponding object, which also acknowledges environment object controlDevice.

Figure 9-16 shows three event threads, each starting a test in a different way. First, the control device can issue a test request, as shown on the left. Second, object clock can start a test, as shown on the right, when the scheduled timeout elapses. Third, the system restarts pending tests whenever nothing else is actually requested. This is shown in the middle by the additional pseudo event anytime which occurs if the operating system has no other process to switch to. Notice that events E11 and E16 are directed to the static part of classes PeriodicTest and SubscriberLine, respectively.

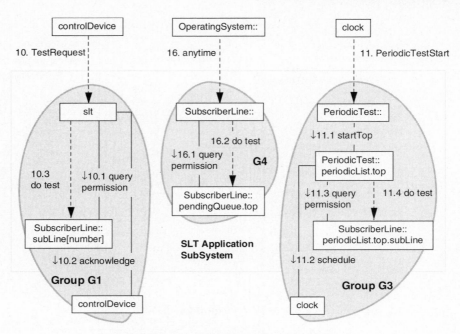

Figure 9-16. Test starting event threads.

All three event threads continue with the shared object interaction thread do test, as shown in Figure 9-17.

The object interaction thread shown in Figure 9-17 only starts the measurement of the first elementary test. If a test of lower priority is ongoing, it will be aborted by the event thread (interactions 17.1.1 through 17.1.3). Such a test request remains pending and will be restarted later. Internal delay 17.1.5 occurs within object interaction thread do test after connecting the line. Waiting inside the event thread is possible because it is rather short and nothing time-critical depends on it. Whenever the measurement unit finishes and the sample is ready, the TestSample event occurs. Figure 9-18 shows the corresponding event thread.

Each time event TestSample occurs, the event thread takes one of the alternative branches A15 through D15, depending on which phase the test is actually in (see class outlines). Internal delays A15.5.2, B15.5.2 and C15.5.2 occur within the event thread after connecting the stimulus to the lines.

If a line becomes busy and it is being tested at this time, then the ongoing test will be immediately aborted so that the user of the subscriber line can use it to make calls. In this situation, the corresponding object of class Line in the hardware wrapper immediately disconnects itself from the test bus and disables the measurement unit before it autonomously notifies object test in the application subsystem, as shown in Figure 9-19. The test of the line remains pending and will be restarted later.

Event PowerOn from environment object resetButton is not received by an object. It will execute some startup code. This code notifies the control device about the reset.

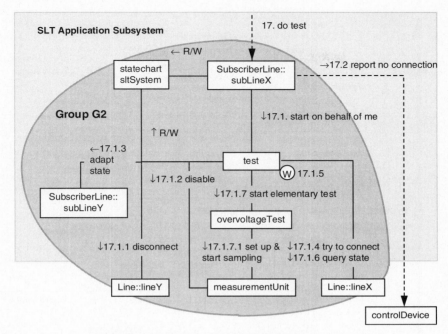

Figure 9-17. Object interaction thread for do test.

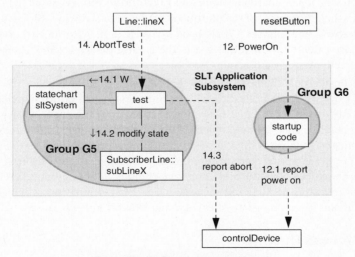

Figure 9-19. Special event threads.

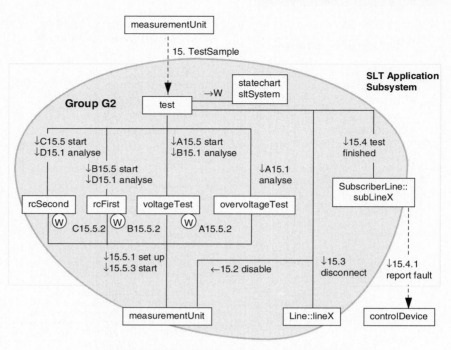

Figure 9-18. Event thread of event TestSample.

The event threads shown in Figures 9-15 through 9-19 are qualified. We selected asynchronous communication for interactions 10.3, 11.4 and 16.2, all covering the do test interaction with a particular object of class SubscriberLine, as shown in Figure 9-16. Due to this decision, the trigger of the do test object interaction thread, Figure 9-17, appears as a dashed arrow, and number 17 has been assigned to it. Also, reporting any fault or no connection, power on or abort test to the control device is done asynchronously. All other interactions are synchronous.

Based on the qualification, Figures 9-15 through 9-19 also show the object groups. Group G1 covers all event threads with environment object controlDevice as originator because only one of these requests is allowed at any time. Each event thread performs the required operation and replies to object controlDevice inside G1 after a short time, negligible compared to the specified maximum of 50 ms. Performing a test is covered by the separate group G2 which starts with either asynchronous request do test or event TestSample. Event PeriodicTestStart from object clock defines group G3. Group G4 takes care about restarting pending test requests when the system becomes actually idle. Group G5 and G6 are based on events AbortTest and PowerOn, respectively.

9.3.2 Process Outlines

The outlines of processes are rather simple and are directly based on the event threads. Processes RequestG1 and TestG2 have a single primary waiting point for messages, and depending on the input message, the correct functions of the proper objects are called upon reception. Please refer to the class outlines in Section 9.3.4 for the outlines of these functions.

Process `PeriodicG3` is time scheduled for the next periodic test. Process `AnyTimeG4` awaits nothing. Since its priority is lower than all others, it always runs when none of the others is running. Processes `TestG2` and `PeriodicG3` run at a lower priority than process `RequestG1`. This enables the system to respond to all kinds of requests from the control device, even when it is busy testing.

```
process function RequestG1 //associates with G1
   loop forever
      await message from controlDevice;
      switch message.id
         ResetMsg:
            slt.reset();
         GetHardwareAndSoftwareIdMsg:
            slt.getHardwareAndSoftwareId();
         GetListOfFaultyLinesMsg:
            slt.getListOfFaultyLines();
         GetLineStatusMsg:
            slt.getLineStatus(message.number);
         GetTestResultMsg:
            slt.getTestResult(message.number);
         SetTestPermissionMsg:
            slt.setTestPermissionS(message.number, message.testPermission,
                                        message.periodicPermission);
         SetPeriodicTestMsg:
            slt.setPeriodicTest(message.number, message.values);
         TestRequestMsg:
            slt.testRequest(message.number);
         SetOverVoltageLimitMsg:
            test.over voltage.setLimit(message.limit);
         SetVoltageLimitMsg:
            test.voltage.setLimit(message.limit);
         SetResistanceLimitMsg:
            test.rcSecond.setLimit(message.limit);
      endswitch;
   endloop;
endprocessfunction;


process function TestG2 //associates with G2
   loop forever
      await message
      switch message.id
         DoTestMsg:
            message.subLine.doTest(message.requestor);
         TestSampleMsg:
            test.testSample(message.sample);
      endswitch;
   endloop;
endprocessfunction;


process function PeriodicG3 //associates with G3
   loop forever
      wait for schedule by clock
      PeriodicTest::periodicTest();
```

```
    endloop;
endprocessfunction;


process function AnyTimeG4 //associates with G4, defines background processing
    loop forever
        SubscriberLine::restartTest();
    endloop;
endprocessfunction;
```

A process cannot be associated with groups **G5** and **G6**, and process outlines are omitted because both groups are of a special nature. The design of the hardware wrapper must elaborate on this issue, and an interrupt service routine is supposed to run each of these two groups.

9.3.3 Shared Objects

The above-defined object groups yield a few shared objects. Table 9-7 lists them all and indicates a solution to the potential synchronization problem. Where necessary, a more detailed discussion follows; also, see the class outlines. Design of the hardware wrapper will potentially add shared objects between the groups of the SLT application subsystem and the groups of the hardware wrapper.

Table 9-7. Shared objects.

Object	shared between		Solution
subLine[l]	(1)	G1 - G2	Disable interrupt
	(2)	G1 - G3	Atomic
	(3)	G1 - G4	Atomic
	(4)	G1 - G5	Atomic
	(5)	G2 - G3	Uncritical
	(6)	G2 - G4	Disable interrupt
	(7)	G2 - G5	Atomic
	(8)	G3 - G4	Uncritical
	(9)	G3 - G5	Uncritical
	(10)	G4 - G5	Uncritical
overvoltage	(11)	G1 - G2	Disable interrupt
voltage	(12)	G1 - G2	Disable interrupt
rcSecond	(13)	G1 - G2	Disable interrupt
periodic[l]	(14)	G1 - G3	Disable interrupt
test	(15)	G2 - G5	Uncritical
statechart sltSystem	(16)	G2 - G5	Disable interrupt

(1) Only the process associated with G1 can interleave with that one of G2 because the first has higher priority. G1 reads the local statechart `SubscriberLine::state` that G2 modifies. Any such statechart read/write is assumed to be an atomic processor instruction. When a test finishes, a short sequence of assignments in function `testFinished` forms a critical region. This is protected by an explicit disable/enable interrupt.

(2) Only G1 can interleave G3 due to higher priority. G3 reads the permission data that G1 modifies. Any read/write of this permission data is assumed to be an atomic processor instruction.

(4) G5 modifies the state of an object of class `SubscriberLine`. This is assumed to be an atomic processor instruction.

(6) Only G2 can interleave G4 due to higher priority. G4 contains a critical region regarding `pendingQueue`. This is protected by disable/enable interrupts.

(11) (12) (13) Only G1 can interleave G2 due to higher priority. G2 makes use of the limit that G1 sets up. This is made noninterruptable in G2.

(14) Only G1 can interleave G3 due to higher priority. Both manipulate the same data in rather long sequences. For G3, this happens in function `startTop`. This region is made noninterruptable.

(16) G2 evaluates, in function `doTest`, a compound logical expression using statechart `sltSystem` several times. This forms a critical region. The assumed atomicity of any read/write of the statechart is not enough here. The expression evaluation is protected by disable/enable interrupt.

9.3.4 Class Outlines

In the following class outlines, `send` is an operating system call that asynchronously transfers a message from the sender to the receiver. The parameters of the call are the message to be sent and the destination process.

Class `TestResult` is omitted because it only contains declarations of data members. Statechart `SltSystem` exists globally and is referred to by the identifier `sltSystem`.

Critical regions are marked by a disable/enable interrupt statement. This is commented by the case number from Table 9-7.

```
class SLT
    SubscriberLine subLine[1:30];
    PeriodicTest periodic[1:30];
    function setTestPermissions(number, testPermission, periodicPermission)
        subLine[number].testPermission = testPermission;
        subLine[number].periodicPermission = periodicPermission;
        controlDevice.acknowledge(ack);
    endfunction;
    function setPeriodicTest(number, values)
        if    values are ok
        then periodic[number].set(values);
            controlDevice.acknowledge(ack);
        else controlDevice.acknowledge(nac&badValues);
    endfunction;
    function getLineStatus(number)
        controlDevice.takeResponse(subLine[number].state ...);
    endfunction;
    function getTestResult(number)
```

```
        controlDevice.takeResponse(subLine[number].latestResult ...);
    endfunction;
    function getListOfFaultyLines()
        controlDevice.takeResponse(subLine[for each].latestResult.fault);
    endfunction;
    function getHardwareAndSoftwareId()
        controlDevice.takeResponse(id);
    endfunction;
    function reset()
        controlDevice.acknowledge(ack);
        reset system;
    endfunction;
    function testRequest(number, requestor) //E10 entry
        if   subLine[number].testPermission == Yes
        then controlDevice.acknowledge(ack);
            // subLine[number].doTest(requestor); changed to async
            doTestMsg = new DoTestMsg(subLine[number], requestor);
            send(process testG2, doTestMsg);
        else controlDevice.acknowledge(nac&noPermission);
    endfunction;
endclass;


class SubscriberLine
    inherits QueueElement //from a library, objects queued in pendingQueue
    static Queue(SubscriberLine) pendingQueue; //shared by all instances
    int number;
    bool testPermission, periodicPermission;
    Line line;  //identifies the correponding, physical line
    ref(TestResult) latestResult;  //reference to
    statechart SubscriberLine state;  //local, refer to its graph
    static function restartTest() //done when no other processing
        disable interrupt; //see (6)
        if   pendingQueue is not empty
        then pendingQueue.top.restartTop();
        enable interrupt;
    endfunction;
    function restartTop()
        if   testPermission == Yes and state.Testing == Pending
        then // pendingQueue.top.doTest(unattended); changed to async
            doTestMsg = new DoTestMsg(pendingQueue.top, unattended);
            send(process testG2, doTestMsg);
        else pendingQueue.top.dequeue();
    endfunction;
    function doTest(requestPriority)
        if   state.Testing != Ongoing
        then inqueue(pendingQueue);
            disable interrupt; //see (16)
            yes = statechart sltSystem == idle
                or statechart sltSystem.Request == Unattended
                    and (requestPriority == PC or requestPriority == Exchange)
                or statechart sltSystem.Request == PC
                    and requestPriority == Exchange;
            enable interrupt;
            if   yes and line.state() != busy
            then state.Testing = Ongoing;
                statechart sltSystem.Request = requestPriority
                if   test.startOnBehalfOf(this) == connectionFailed
                then state.Testing = None.NoConnection;
                    dequeue();
                    // controlDevice.report(noConnection); changed to async
                    reportMsg = new ReportMsg(noConnection);
                    send(process controlDevice, reportMsg);
```

```
                endif;
            endif;
        endif;
    endfunction;
    function testFinished(resultUpdate)
        disable interrupt; //see (1)
        state.Testing = None.Tested;
        state.TestResults = Valid;
        free = latestResult;
        latestResult = resultUpdate;
        enable interrupt;
        dequeue();
        if   latestResult.fault
        then // controlDevice.report(fault); changed to async
            reportMsg = ReportMsg(fault);
            send(process controlDevice, reportMsg);
        endif;
        return free;
    endfunction;
endclass;



class PeriodicTest
    inherits ListElement //from a library, objects linked in periodicList
    static List(PeriodicTest) periodicList; //shared by all instances
    int startTime;;
    int period;
    int stopTime;
    int nextTestTime;
    SubscriberLine subLine;
    static function periodicTestStart()  //invoked by E11 from clock
        disable interrupt; //see (14)
        if   periodicList is not empty
        then periodicList.top.startTop();
        enable interrupt;
    endfunction;
    function startTop()
            nextTestTime = nextTestTime + period;
            if   nextTestTime <= stopTime
            then search for matching position in periodicList
                and insert there
            else remove from peridicList;
            if   periodicList is not empty
            then clock.schedule(process periodicG3,
                periodicList.top.nextTestTime);
            if   subLine.periodicPermission == Yes
            and testPermission == Yes
            then // subLine.doTest(unattended); changed to async
                doTestMsg = new DoTestMsg(subline, unattended);
                send(process testG2, doTestMsg);
        endif;
    endfunction;
    function set(startTime, period, stopTime)
            set startTime, period, stopTime;
            nextTestTime = startTime;
            search for matching position in periodicList and insert there;
            if   periodicList.top == this
            then clock.schedule(process periodicG3, nextTestTime);
    endfunction;
endclass;
```

```
class Test
    ref(ElementaryTest) actualTest;   //captures statechart sltSystem.Testing.Phase
    ref(SubscriberLine) subLineUnderTest;
    ref(TestResult) resultBuffer;
    Over voltageTest over voltage;
    VoltageTest voltage;
    RCtest1 rcFirst;
    RCtest2 rcSecond;
    function startOnBehalfOf(subscriberLine)
        if   statechart sltSystem == testing   //lower priority will be canceled
        then measurementUnit.disable();            //by higher priority request
            subLineUnderTest.state.Testing = Pending;
            subLineUnderTest.line.disconnect();
        endif;
        statechart sltSystem = Testing;
        actualTest = Connecting; //set state
        subLineUnderTest = subscriberLine;
        subLineUnderTest.line.tryToConnect();
        delay(connectTime);
        if   subLineUnderTest.line.state() == Connected
        then clear resultBuffer;
            actualTest = over voltage; //save state via ref
            actualTest.startElementaryTest();
            return ok;
        else statechart sltSystem = idle;
            return connectionFailed;
        endif;
    endfunction;
    function testSample(sample)   //invoked by E15 from measurementUnit
        if   actualTest.analyse(sample, resultBuffer) == fault
        or actualTest.next == none
        then measurementUnit.disable();
            subLineUnderTest.line.disconnect();
            statechart sltSystem = idle;
            resultBuffer = subLineUnderTest.testFinished(resultBuffer);
        else actualTest = actualTest.next;
            actualTest.startElementaryTest()
        endif;
    endfunction;
    function abortOngoing()            //invoked by E14 busy from a line
        statechart sltSystem = idle;
        subLineUnderTest.state.Testing = Pending;
        //controlDevice.report(abortTest); changed to async
        reportMsg = new ReportMsg(abortTest);
        send(process controlDevice, reportMsg);
    endfunction;
endclass;



class ElementaryTest
    ElementaryTest next;   //used to switch when one done
    TestSettings settings;
    virtual function startElementaryTest() //subclasses may overwrite
        setup measurementUnit with settings;
        delay(setting.settleTime);
        if   statechart sltSystem == Testing
        then measurementUnit.startSampling();
    endfunction;
    virtual function analyse(sample, result);
endclass;
```

```
class OvervoltageTest inherits ElementaryTest
   FaultLimit over voltageLimit;
   function analyse(sample, resultBuffer)
      resultBuffer = compute sample;
      disable interrupt; //see (11)
      violation = over voltageLimit is violated;
      enable interrupt;
      if   violation
      then mark fault in resultBuffer;
           return fault
      else return ok;
   endfunction;
   function setLimit(limit)
      if   limit is ok
      then over voltageLimit = limit;
           controlDevice.acknowledge(ack);
      else controlDevice.acknowledge(nac);
   endfunction;
endclass;


class VoltageTest inherits ElementaryTest
   FaultLimit voltageLimit;
   function analyse(sample, resultBuffer)
      resultBuffer = compute sample;
      disable interrupt; //see (12)
      violation = voltageLimit is violated;
      enable interrupt;
      if   violation
      then mark fault in resultBuffer;
           return fault
      else return ok;
   endfunction;
   function setLimit(limit)
      if   limit is ok
      then voltageLimit = limit;
           controlDevice.acknowledge(ack);
      else controlDevice.acknowledge(nac);
   endfunction;
endclass;


class RCtest1 inherits ElementaryTest
   function analyse(sample, resultBuffer)
      resultBuffer = compute sample;
      return ok; //no fault checking done in this phase
   endfunction;
endclass;


class RCtest2 inherits ElementaryTest
   FaultLimit resistanceLimit;
   function analyse(sample, resultBuffer)
      resultBuffer = compute sample;
      disable interrupt; //see (13)
      violation = resistanceLimit is violated;
      enable interrupt;
      if   violation
      then mark fault in resultBuffer;
           return fault
      else return ok;
```

```
   endfunction;
   function setLimit(limit)
      if   limit is ok
      then resistanceLimit = limit;
           controlDevice.acknowledge(ack);
      else controlDevice.acknowledge(nac);
   endfunction;
endclass;
```

9.4 Exercise: Hardware Wrapper

Study the previous sections in this chapter, and then analyze and design the hardware wrapper of this case study. The rest of this section gives essential information regarding the implementation resources needed to accomplish that. You can make assumptions about missing details wherever necessary.

9.4.1 Implementation Resources

System Buses

The SLT is connected to the other units in the DTS using a number of buses, shown in Figure 9-20. Only the buses necessary for the operation of the SLT are shown.

- *The PC Bus:* The PC line connects transparently through the MUX to the SLT. The SLT picks up the commands from the PC bus and responds to it. It is a normal RS 232 serial bus. The UART block is responsible for this bus.

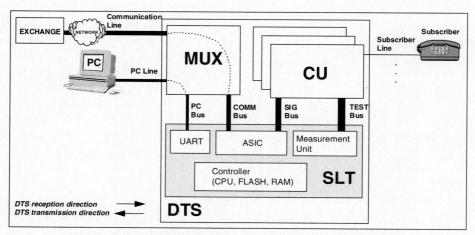

Figure 9-20. The system buses to which the SLT is connected.

- *The COMM Bus:* The communication line connects transparently through the MUX to the SLT. The SLT picks up the signals coming from the exchange and transmits signals to the exchange on this bus, for which the ASIC block is responsible.

- *The TEST Bus:* The subscriber line to be tested is physically connected to the test bus by the SLT and a CU. Only one line can be connected at a time. The Measurement Unit block is responsible for this bus and also for the actual measurement of the line parameters.

- *The SIG Bus:* The SLT picks up the signal from the COMM bus and connects it, possibly after modification, on the SIG bus to the CUs. It gets the signal from the CUs and connects it, possibly after modification, to the COMM bus to the exchange. On this bus, internal communication with the channel units is achieved. The ASIC block is responsible for this bus.

The Test Protocol between the Exchange and the SLT

Each of the 30 channels in a DTS has four signaling bits, ABCD, in both the transmission and reception directions (see Figure 9-1). Their idle value in both directions is 1000. The signaling bits for all the 30 channels are available in one multiframe, the duration of which is 2 milliseconds. The A and B bits are used to control normal traffic, for example, calling, ringing and metering. These bits must not be affected by the line tests under any circumstances.

On the other hand, the C and D bits are used in the test protocol. These bits are used by the exchange to send test requests and all other commands. The exchange keeps a request for the duration of only three multiframes. The request in at least two of them must be the same for a request to be valid. The exchange also expects answers from the SLT in the C and D bits. The SLT keeps the answer until a new request is received from the exchange. The exact coding for the requests and the answers is very complicated and is omitted for the case study.

The Test Protocol between the SLT and the CUs

If the SLT approves the test request of a certain subscriber line, no matter who the requester is—the exchange, the PC or periodically—it forces the C bit going to the CU on the SIG bus of the channel assigned to the requested subscriber line to 1. The CU is expected to connect the desired line to the TEST bus and to send the SLT a C bit on the SIG bus with a value of 1 as an acknowledgment in less than 30 milliseconds. When the test is over, the SLT forces the C bit back to 0 and the CU disconnects the line from the test bus and sends a C bit with a value of 0 in less than 20 milliseconds.

The controller block contains the CPU and the memories (FLASH and RAM). An area in the FLASH is reserved to store the settings values.

SLT Hardware

Figure 9-21 demonstrates the major hardware of the SLT. The signals with arrowheads are control signals coming from an output register in the CPU unless otherwise shown. The signals with broken arrows are interrupt signals.

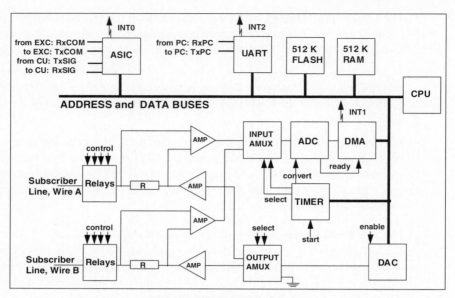

Figure 9-21. SLT hardware.

The Operation of the Measurement Unit

The measurement principle is based on feeding the wires of a selected subscriber line by a voltage stimulus and then measuring the response. See Figures 9-4 and 9-21.

A digital stimulus is written by the CPU to the DAC, which converts it to an analog signal. The OUTPUT AMUX is controlled to pass the stimulus and the earth to both or one of the wires. The stimulus is amplified, and through a field of relays it connects to the physical wires of the selected subscriber line.

The stimulus causes a response on the wires. After some waiting time, the response from both the wires is alternately sampled using the INPUT AMUX. The timer determines the sampling rate, and a signal from the timer determines from which wire to sample. The ADC starts converting the sample into digital, triggered by a signal from the timer. When a conversion is completed, the DMA transfers the sample to a memory buffer and interrupts the CPU (INT1) when the buffer is full. The samples are then digitally filtered, and a number of calculation algorithms are applied to calculate the different line parameters. The CPU initializes registers in the DMA for the address and size of the memory buffers it can use. The CPU also initializes the timer register to affect the sampling rate.

The Operation of the ASIC

The ASIC handles the signaling on the COMM and SIG buses in both the transmission and reception directions. See Figures 9-20 and 9-21.

The ASIC collects the signaling bits from the COMM bus into a memory buffer, RxBuf, that has 30 bytes. It gives an interrupt INT0 when the signaling bits of half of the channels have been written, one half for channels 1–15 and the other half for channels 16–30. After the interrupt, the ASIC starts overwriting the signaling bits of the other half in RxBuf. The interrupt rate is 1 ms.

The signal is transmitted to the channel units on the SIG bus from the memory buffers RxBuf and RxDataBuf. The RxDataBuf contains alternative signaling bits that the SLT may want to send to the CUs instead of the signaling received from the exchange in RxBuf. The selection is achieved based on the control bits stored in the memory buffer RxContBuf.

If a control bit Ac, Bc, Cc or Dc (see Figure 9-22) in the RxContBuf is zero, then the corresponding signaling bit of that channel transmits as it was received by the SLT from the RxBuf (i.e., from the byte containing the Ax, Bx, Cx and Dx bits). Otherwise, it transmits from the alternative signaling written by the SLT from the RxDataBuf (i.e., from the byte containing the Ad, Bd, Cd and Dd bits).

In the transmission direction, the operation is similar to that in the reception direction. The signaling received from the channel units is written in a memory buffer TxBuf, the alternative signal that the SLT may want to transmit to the exchange is written in a memory buffer TxDataBuf, and the control bits are written in the memory buffer TxContBuf.

The Operation of the UART

The UART (Figure 9-20) picks up the received characters coming from RxPC and puts them in its own memory buffer, RxBufPC. It interrupts the CPU with INT2 when the RxBufPC buffer is full or when a control character is received. The CPU reads a status register in the UART to know the reason of the interrupt. If it was because of reception, it reads the RxBufPC buffer. This causes the buffer to become empty and once again available for reception.

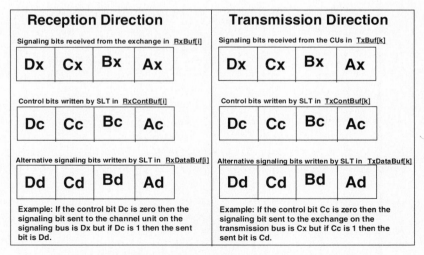

Figure 9-22. The signaling and its control in the ASIC.

In the transmission direction, the CPU writes to another memory buffer in the UART TxBufPC when it wants to transfer information to the PC; it then commands the UART to transfer it. When the UART transfers the TxBufPC buffer, it interrupts the CPU with INT2. The TxBufPC becomes empty. The CPU reads a status register in order to discover the reason for the interrupt. If it was because of transmission, it knows that the TxBufPC buffer is again empty and available.

In the hardware, INT0 has higher priority than INT1, which in turn has higher priority than INT2.

10

CASE STUDY: CRUISE CONTROL

A standard example of an embedded, real-time system is a cruise control system for a car. The cruise control description below partly takes the same view as the one used by Paul Ward [Ward '85] and the one used by Derek J. Hatley and Imtiaz A. Pirbhai [Hatley '87].

The case study takes the point of view of a hypothetical software subproject which applies the OCTOPUS method. Descriptive text is kept to the bare minimum and does not include explanations or annotations regarding the method itself. This software subproject is bound by a hypothetical master project that is already ongoing. Consequently, you will find the material on the software subproject only. Please imagine that a reader in the real project would be able to examine other documents whenever a question about a broader issue arose.

10.1 Recapped System Requirements Specification

10.1.1 Recapped Problem Statement

The embracing system project originally defined the problem in broad terms as follows:

The ordinary household thermostat performs "closed loop control"—given a desired temperature setting, it monitors the actual room temperature and turns the heat on and off to keep actual temperature close to the desired temperature. In maintaining a desired speed, the driver of an automobile does something quite similar: he or she monitors the actual speed by watching the speedometer, and depresses or releases the accelerator pedal to keep the actual speed close to the desired speed. A system, called Cruise Control, will be built for cars with automatic transmission, which relieves the driver of the responsibility of maintaining speed by taking over the closed loop control when commanded to do so by the driver (see Figure 1-14 in Chapter 1).

Cruise Control is to be implemented on a single microprocessor which shall be connected to a few sensors, to an actuator that affects the engine's throttle and to the control signals that come from the driver's console representing driver commands.

10.1.2 Use Cases

The use case diagram shown in Figure 10-1 defines the structure and roles of the use cases of Cruise Control. At the system level there are three use cases, U1 through U3, and two autonomously ongoing activities, U4 and U5. Use case U1 nests one further use case, U6. The use cases U10, U11 and U12 are autonomous activities related to use cases U1, U2 and U6, respectively. The use cases U7 through U9 describe complex exceptions of either U1 or U6.

Use Case	(U1) activate cruise control
Actors	Driver
Preconditions	Engine is running. Transmission is in top gear. The car's speed is at least 40 kilometers per hour. Brake is not pressed.
Description	When the driver gives an activate command, the speed at which the car is traveling at that instant is maintained.
	The driver may deactivate the cruise control at any time by a deactivate command. This returns control of the car's speed to the driver regardless of what has been done before.
Sub Use Case	(U6) auto-accelerate to new cruise speed
Exceptions	(U7) intermediate accelerating with pedal
	(U8) intermediate reducing of speed with brake
	(U9) suspension of cruise control by transmission
Activities	(U10) maintain selected speed
Postconditions	Cruise control is active. Throttle is positioned unattended, pedal can be released.

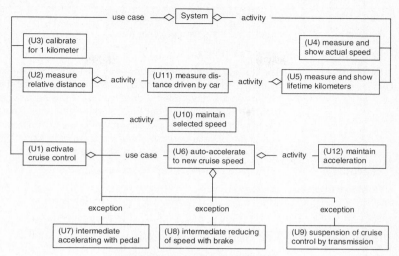

Figure 10-1. Use case diagram.

Use Case	(U2) measure relative distance
Actors	Driver
Preconditions	Engine is running.
Description	The driver's console includes a counter for hundreds of meters driven with the car. The driver can reset this counter to zero at a start point and look for the distance value when arriving at the destination point.
Exceptions	See U11.
Activities	(U11) measure distance driven by car
Postconditions	Know distance in hundreds of meters.

Use Case	(U3) calibrate for 1 kilometer
Actors	Maintenance person
Preconditions	Cruise control is inactive and calibration enabled.
Description	Since speed and distance per drive shaft rotation are affected by tire size and wear, the system is to have a calibration capability. The maintenance person drives the car and gives the start calibration command at the start of a measured kilometer, drives the kilometer, and then gives the stop calibration command. The system resets its internal conversion factor to correspond to the number of wheel rotations sensed within the time period of the start and stop command.
Exceptions	(1) Maintenance person does not drive for a kilometer: reject new values if out of a reasonable range, otherwise the device is miscalibrated.
	(2) Stop calibration command does not occur: calibration is canceled unattended after exceeding a reasonable upper limit.
	(3) Calibration is disabled: rotation sensing stops, old conversion factors remain valid.
Postconditions	New conversion factor obtained. Calibration is disabled.

Use Case	(U4) measure and show actual speed
Actors	Autonomous activity of system
Preconditions	Engine is running.
Description	The normal speedometers on many cars are inaccurate, and so the system is to measure speed by counting pulses it receives from its own sensor on the drive shaft. Count-rate from this sensor corresponds to vehicle kilometers per hour through a proportionality constant. Based on the resulting value, the system continuously drives a speed displaying unit at the driver's console either via an analog signal proportional to the speed or a digital output in 8 parallel lines.
Exceptions	(1) Engine is switched off: stops measurement.
Postconditions	Engine is running.

Use Case	(U5) measure and show lifetime kilometers
Actors	Autonomous activity of system
Preconditions	Engine is running.
Description	The driver's console includes a counter that counts and displays the lifetime kilometers driven by the car.
Exceptions	See U11.
Activities	(U11) measure distance driven by car
Postconditions	Engine is running.

Use Case	(U6) auto-accelerate to new cruise speed
Actors	Driver in use case U1
Preconditions	Use case U1 is ongoing.
Description	The driver may desire to cruise at a higher speed. The start accelerate command causes the cruise control system to accelerate the car at a comfortable rate. When the new desired speed is reached, the driver gives the stop accelerate command and the cruise control system maintains the new desired speed.
Exceptions	Same as U1.
Postconditions	Cruise control is active and maintains higher speed.

Use Case	(U7) intermediate accelerating with the pedal
Actors	Driver in exception of U1 or U6.
Preconditions	Use case U1 or sub use case U6 of U1 is ongoing.
Description	At any time, the driver may go faster than the cruise control is doing simply by pressing the accelerator pedal far enough. When the pedal is released, the system regains control and returns the car to the previously selected speed or continues auto-accelerating, depending on what was ongoing before.
Exceptions	(1) Start accelerate command occurs during manual acceleration: system auto-accelerates (U3) and attempts to position throttle; however, pedal may be pressed much further.
	(2) Stop accelerate command given during auto-accelerating and pedal pressed far enough: when pedal is released later, system is to maintain the speed the car had at time of stop accelerate command.
Postconditions	Cruise control is active, i.e., maintain desired speed or if auto-accelerating was ongoing before and no stop has occurred, continue auto-accelerating.

Use Case	(U8) intermediate reducing of speed with brake
Actors	Driver in exception of U1 or U6.
Preconditions	Use case U1 or sub use case U6 of U1 is ongoing.
Description	Any time the driver depresses the brake pedal, cruise control must suspend maintaining speed. Following this, when the brake is released and a resume command is given, the system returns the car to the previously selected speed or the speed it had reached during auto-accelerating. However, if a deactivate command has occurred in the intervening time, the resume command does nothing.
Exceptions	(1) Resume command not given: no return to previous speed.
Postconditions	Cruise control is active and maintains the car's speed.

Use Case	(U9) suspension of cruise control by transmission
Actors	Transmission in exception of U1 or U6.
Preconditions	Use case U1 or sub use case U6 of U1 is ongoing.
Description	If the transmission shifts out of top gear, cruise control must suspend maintaining speed or stop auto-accelerating. When the transmission is back in top gear, cruise control remains suspended until the driver, similar to U8, gives a resume command that returns the car to the previously selected speed or the speed it had reached during auto-accelerating. However, if a deactivate command has occurred in the intervening time, the resume command does nothing.
Exceptions	(1) Resume command not given: no return to previous speed.
Postconditions	Cruise control is active.

Use Case	(U10) maintain selected speed
Actors	Activity of U1.
Preconditions	U1 has been entered.
Description	The system serves as the feedback part of a servo loop, in which the engine is the feed-forward part. For smooth and stable servo operation, the system must update its outputs at least once per second. When the system senses that the actual speed is below the selected speed, it is to drive the throttle to a deflection proportional to the speed error until, at 0.84 m/sec below the selected speed, the throttle is fully open (the steep uphill situation). When the actual speed is more than 0.84 m/sec above the selected speed, it is to completely release the throttle (this situation would occur when driving downhill).
Postconditions	U1 has been finished.

Use Case	(U11) measure distance driven by car
Actors	Activity of U2 and U5.
Preconditions	Engine is running.
Description	Moving the car is continuously measured by sensing the rotation of the drive shaft.
Exceptions	(1) Engine is switched off: measurement stops.
Postconditions	Engine is running.

Use Case	(U12) maintain acceleration
Actors	Activity of U6.
Preconditions	U1 is ongoing and U6 has been entered.
Description	The system serves as a servo loop in the same way as for U10 except that a comfortable acceleration is maintained. When the system senses that the actual acceleration is below 0.4 m/sec^2, it is to drive the throttle to a deflection proportional to the error until, at 0.25 m/sec^2, the throttle is fully open (the steep uphill situation). When the actual acceleration is more than 0.4 m/sec^2, it is to completely release the throttle (this situation would occur when driving downhill).
Exceptions	
Postconditions	U6 has been finished and U1 remains ongoing.

10.1.3 System Context Model

The context of Cruise Control is modeled in Figure 10-2 using the object diagram notation. All relevant entities from the environment are arranged around the target system, and their association with the target system is shown.

As you can see in Figure 10-2, Cruise Control can be associated with many external entities. The fact that some are physically arranged on the console of the car is conceptual-

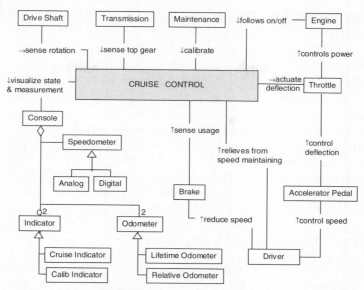

Figure 10-2. System context diagram.

ized by the aggregation in class **Console**. The odometers (i.e., distance meters) come in two versions: one counts the kilometers over the full lifetime of the car; the other can be reset by the driver and counts hundreds of meters. The car's console includes either a conventional analog meter for speed or a digital speed display instead. The two indicators are optional. They are of any simple binary kind (e.g., an LED) and give some feedback about the state of the system.

The engine is affected only indirectly by the throttle. However, if the driver switches the engine off, Cruise Control shuts down too (i.e., throttle actuator nullified, no reaction or activity). Whenever the driver starts up the engine, Cruise Control becomes operable, but maintaining speed is still inactive.

Note that the accelerator pedal does not affect Cruise Control. The rationale for this surprising fact is found in the next section.

10.1.4 Other Requirements

The system controls the car through an actuator attached to the throttle. This actuator is mechanically in parallel with the accelerator pedal mechanism, such that whichever one demands greater speed controls the throttle. The system drives the actuator by means of an electrical signal which has a linear relationship with the throttle deflection in that zero voltage sets the throttle at closed, and maximum voltage fully opens it.

To avoid rapid increases in acceleration, the throttle actuator must never open faster than to traverse its full range in 10 seconds. It may close at any rate, however, since the car just coasts when the throttle is closed. The automotive engineers have determined that, with these characteristics, the system will hold the car within ±1.5 km/h of the selected speed on normal gradients and will give a smooth, comfortable ride.

Rotation of the drive shaft will be sensed by pulses, each representing a certain angular unit of rotation. However, this unit shall be arbitrary, and consequently, the system can be connected to various types of rotation sensors.

The driver enters the commands via a physical command interface consisting of a few buttons. Besides the physical location, arrangement and look of these buttons, car designers also like to make different car models behave slightly differently concerning the usage of these buttons. For example, in one model calibration may be enabled by a special button, whereas in another model no such special button exists. Instead, the driver has to press the resume button, hold it, and then press the activate button too. The development of system variants for different command interfaces, which make use of the same hardware and software which can be easily configured, is requested.

10.1.5 Implementation Resources

Cruise Control is to be implemented on a single microprocessor system. It is connected to a rotation sensor at the drive shaft, a sensor for pressing and releasing the brake, and a sensor for the top gear. The maximum frequency of the rotation pulses is 1500 Hz. The system receives control signals representing the commands that the driver has entered at the physical command interface. Optionally, external indicators are connected. The system has an analog output driving the throttle's actuator. It provides the console with either analog or digital output representing the actual speed. Typically, only one of those is used. The system outputs pulses for the lifetime and distance odometers in the console. The hardware context diagram shown in Figure 10-3 illustrates this.

Internally, the microprocessor system of Cruise Control includes maximal 63-kByte ROM and 1-kByte RAM. The CPU can execute one million instructions per second; that is, one instruction takes 1 microsecond on the average. All input lines, except the rotation

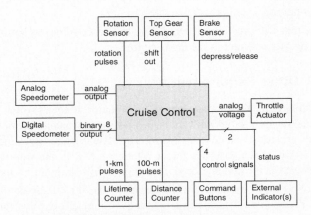

Figure 10-3. Hardware context diagram.

pulse line, are received by an input port. A maximum of four lines is reserved for the control signals from the physical command interface. The final assignment of this input is up to the configuration of the software system. All output is given via an output port. Two interrupts exist. Interrupt line INT0 is driven by the rotation pulses. A 10-ms timer uses interrupt line INT1. See the hardware block diagram shown in Figure 10-4 for more details.

Some systems may not be equipped with the D/A for an analog speedometer display; others may or may not have on-board indicators.

The RAM is supplied with standby power. This maintains the data of the RAM, even when the system's main power is switched off by shutting down the engine. Turning the engine on powers the system and resets the microprocessor. In case standby power has been lost, all bits in the RAM are set to zero.

A real-time operating system is available for the chosen microprocessor and permits a number of processes to run (quasi) simultaneously. A running process may be preempted by another process with higher priority. The operating system is capable of scheduling processes based on a timer to a resolution of 10 milliseconds. The operating system occupies 8 kBytes of the ROM space. Each process needs at least 48 bytes in RAM and some space for its own stack. The code of a context switch between processes is 400 instructions long.

The operating system provides the following functionality:

- Schedule a process

- Schedule a process with delay

- Disable and enable interrupt

- Disable and enable context switching

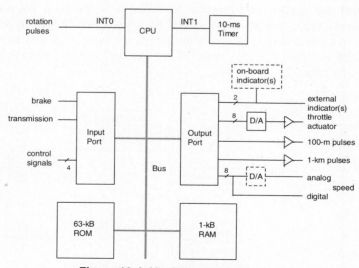

Figure 10-4. Hardware block diagram.

The disable and enable features can be nested in such way that only the outer enable of a nested sequence really performs the enabling. The feature disable/enable interrupt affects only the process that has demanded it. After a process switch, the interrupt reception is always in the state specified by the currently running process.

10.2 Application Subsystem Analysis

System architecture decomposes Cruise Control into only one application subsystem, called the Cruise Control application subsystem, and the hardware wrapper subsystem. The subsystems diagram, Figure 10-5, shows this breakdown.

The existence of only one application subsystem degenerates the subsystem structure. Here, the sole existing application subsystem becomes identical with the entire system of the system context diagram shown earlier in Figure 10-2. Because system requirements specification has covered this already, the system architecture phase misses a subject matter. Consequently, we immediately proceed with the analysis of the sole Cruise Control application subsystem, hereafter simply called the application subsystem.

10.2.1 Object Model

Figure 10-6 shows the class diagram of the object model of the Cruise Control application subsystem. This section focuses on the inner details of the application subsystem. The environment of the application subsystem abstracts the original environment manifested in Figure 10-2 from the point of view of the application. It consists of the entities shown outside the application subsystem boundary in Figure 10-6. For now, nobody cares at which layer and how these entities will be implemented. We simply define them in a manner best suited to the analysis of the application subsystem. Due to the degenerated subsystem structure, later discussion of the hardware wrapper will completely uncover this environment.

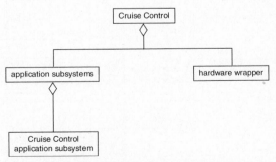

Figure 10-5. Cruise Control subsystems diagram.

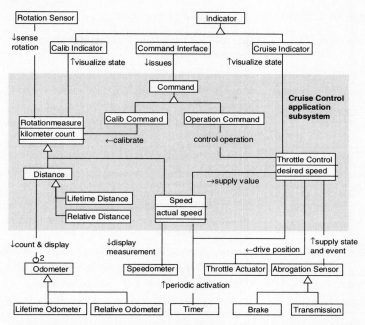

Figure 10-6. Cruise Control application subsystem class diagram.

As you can see in the class diagram, we dropped some of the classes from the context diagram, like classes **Console, Driver, Accelerator Pedal** and **Engine**, because they are of secondary relevance for the application subsystem. The class **Drive Shaft** has been replaced by the more specific class **Rotation Sensor**, as well as class **Throttle** by class **Throttle Actuator**. The former classes **Brake** and **Transmission** are embraced by the new class **Abrogation Sensor**. The class **Timer** has been added to the environment, although no such item exists in the system context diagram.

Tables 10-1 and 10-2 correspond to the class diagram shown in Figure 10-6. They give a more detailed description of all environment classes and all application subsystem classes, respectively.

Table 10-1. Environment class descriptions.

Environment Class	Description
Rotation Sensor	Senses rotation of the drive shaft in arbitrary angular units. It produces a rotation pulse for each rotation unit.
Speedometer	Allows the driver to read the actual speed of the car.
Timer	Generates abstract, time-based events that activate some defined processing.
Throttle Actuator	Performs the mechanical positioning of throttle in parallel to pedal based on a position value given to it.

Table 10-1. Environment class descriptions. *(cont.)*

Odometer	Generalizes the two distinct kinds of odometers (distance measurement device).
Lifetime Odometer	Counts 1-kilometer units and displays the value.
Distance Odometer	Counts 100-meter units and displays the value. It can be reset to zero by the driver.
Indicator	Generalizes all indicators. Physically, an indicator may exist or not (e.g., LED).
Calib Indicator	Indicates the state of calibration (see dynamic model).
Cruise Indicator	Indicates the state of cruising (see dynamic model).
Command Interface	Commands enter the application subsystem from here. Each command is a distinguished logical unit. It shields all details of the real physical interface and how the commands are entered by depressing buttons.
Abrogation Sensor	Senses physical brake and transmission. It provides the application subsystem with the state of these items and generates an event.
Brake	The driver can depress or release the brake.
Transmission	The transmission can be shifted into or out of top gear.

Table 10-2. Application subsystem class descriptions.

Application Class	Description
Rotationmeasure	Base class for anything that associates with class Rotation Sensor. All its derived classes will sense rotation by counting the pulses, but each for a different purpose.
Distance	Node in class hierarchy that generalizes the concept of distance. Two distinct kinds exist.
Lifetime Distance	A car measures the kilometers driven over its lifetime. It detects a driven kilometer and takes care of updating the corresponding odometer.
Relative Distance	The driver can measure relative distances. It detects a 100-m driven unit and takes care of updating the corresponding odometer.
Speed	Measures the car's speed by sensing rotation. The actual speed can be read from here. The actual speed value is also delivered to the speedometer for visualizing it.
Throttle Control	Positions the throttle actuator if maintaining speed or auto-accelerating has been activated.
Command	Via the command interface, the driver issues commands. In response to a command the subsystem performs some specific processing.
Calib Command	Any command of this kind requests processing related to the calibration of the subsystem.
Operation Command	Any command of this kind requests processing related to the operation of the subsystem, i.e., maintaining speed or auto-accelerating.

10.2.2 Functional Model

Taking the functional view identifies the following operations from the requirement specifications.

Operation	(O1) calculate actual speed
Description	The subsystem senses rotation pulses. Counting them in a known time interval allows calculation of the car's speed, which is required for O3.
Associations	Class Speed
Preconditions	Measurement rate = 20 Hz;
	> 2 measurement periods since start-up;
	kilometer count (KC) set, either default or from calibration (see O5);
Inputs	Rotation pulses;
	rotation pulse count (RC1) of last measurement period;
Modifies	Increment rotation pulse count (RC0) of this period;
Outputs	Actual speed (SA), when measurement period elapses;
	with $SA = \dfrac{100000*(RC0+RC1)}{KC}$ [m/sec]
	Note: SA is average of last two periods.
Postconditions	RC1 = RC0

Operation	(O2) calculate actual acceleration
Description	The subsystem senses rotation pulses. Counting them in two subsequent time intervals allows calculation of the car's acceleration, which is required for O4.
Associations	Class Speed
Preconditions	Measurement rate = 20 Hz;
	> 2 measurement periods since start-up;
	kilometer count (KC) set, either default or from calibration;
Inputs	Rotation pulses;
	rotation pulse count (RC1) of last measurement period;
Modifies	Increment rotation pulse count (RC0) of this period;
Outputs	Actual acceleration (A), when measurement period elapses;
	with $A = \dfrac{400000*(RC0-RC1)}{KC}$ [m/sec^2]
Postconditions	RC1 = RC0

Operation	(O3) maintain desired speed
Description	Vary throttle opening from closed to fully open as speed varies from 0.84 m/sec above desired speed, to 0.84 m/sec below it. Restrict rate of opening to 10 sec for full range.
Associations	Class Speed, class Throttle Control
Preconditions	Cruise control has been activated, calibration not ongoing and neither brake depressed nor transmission out of top gear (see dynamic model).
Inputs	Desired speed (SD), actual speed (SA)
Modifies	Throttle actuator position (VTH) with
Outputs	$$VTH = \begin{cases} 0 & \text{if} -0.84 > SD - SA \\ \dfrac{0.84 + SD - SA}{2 * 0.84} * \max(VTH) & \text{if} -0.84 \le SD - SA \le 0.84 \\ \max(VTH) & \text{if} -0.84 < SD - SA \end{cases}$$
Postconditions	$\dfrac{dVTH}{dt} \le \dfrac{\max(VTH)}{10}$

Operation	(O4) auto-accelerate
Description	Vary throttle opening from closed to fully open as acceleration varies from 0.4 m/sec^2 to 0.25 m/sec^2 below it. Restrict rate of opening to 10 sec for full range.
Associations	Class Speed, class Throttle Control
Preconditions	Cruise control has been activated, calibration not ongoing and neither brake depressed nor transmission out of top gear (see dynamic model).
Inputs	Actual acceleration (A)
Modifies	Throttle actuator position (VTH) with
Outputs	$$VTH = \begin{cases} 0 & \text{if} -0.4 < A \\ \dfrac{0.4 - A}{0.4 - 0.25} * \max(VTH) & \text{if} -0.25 \le A \le 0.4 \\ \max(VTH) & \text{if} -0.25 > A \end{cases}$$
Postconditions	$\dfrac{dVTH}{dt} \le \dfrac{\max(VTH)}{10}$

Operation	(O5) recalibrate
Description	Update the internal conversion factor that is used for calculations with the rotation pulses.
Associations	Class Rotationmeasure
Preconditions	Kilometer count (KC) has a valid old value, may be default; calibration has been enabled and cruise control is deactive; calibration counter (CC) has been reset;
Inputs	Rotation pulses counted between start/stop calibrating;
Modifies	Increment CC for every rotation pulse.

Outputs	Kilometer count (KC), when stop calibrating command occurs
	  if lower limit $\leq$ CC $\leq$ upper limit
	  then set KC = CC

Postconditions	KC is either new or remains as before

Operation	(O6) generate 1-km pulse
Description	The lifetime odometer in the console has to be driven by 1-km pulses for counting.
Associations	Class Lifetime Distance
Preconditions	Lifetime counter (LC) has been assigned with kilometer count (KC);
Inputs	Rotation pulses
Modifies	Decrement LC for every rotation pulse;
Outputs	1-km pulse, when LC becomes $\leq$ 0;
Postconditions	Reassign LC with KC;

Operation	(O7) generate 100-m pulse
Description	The distance odometer in the console has to be driven by 100-m pulses for counting.
Associations	Class Relative Distance
Preconditions	Distance counter (DC) has been assigned with kilometer count (KC);
Inputs	Rotation pulses
Modifies	Decrement DC by 10 for every rotation pulse;
Outputs	100-m pulse, when DC becomes $\leq$ 0;
Postconditions	Reassign DC with KC + DC (note DC is negative overflow);

10.2.3 Dynamic Model

A) Analysis of Events

The analysis of events starts examining the class diagram shown in Figure 10-6 and pays particular attention to the associations of the environment classes crossing the application subsystem boundary. By considering if the object of the environment class autonomously interacts across the boundary, we identify the events and list them in Table 10-3. The remainder of this section will describe these events further.

Note that this is at an abstract level and results in logical events only. Later, in the discussion of the hardware wrapper, we analyze and design details of how these events relate to real inputs at the physical boundary.

Table 10-3. Event List.

Event	Description
(E1) rotation pulse	Senses rotation of the drive shaft.
(E2) activate cruising	Driver desires to be relieved of maintaining speed.
(E3) deactivate cruising	Driver wants manual control of speed back.
(E4) start accelerating	Driver desires higher maintained speed.
(E5) stop accelerating	Driver is satisfied with achieved speed, maintain this now.
(E6) resume cruising	Driver desires to continue maintaining speed just as before braking.
(E7) enable calibration	Maintenance will make a calibration of system.
(E8) disable calibration	Calibration done, return to normal operation mode.
(E9) start calibrating	Car is at beginning of a known 1-km distance.
(E10) stop calibrating	Car arrives at end of a 1-km distance.
(E11) brake depress	Driver presses brake to reduce speed.
(E12) top gear shift out	Transmission shifts out of top gear.
(E13) throttle update	Period to update position of throttle has elapsed. Reposition throttle actuator.
(E14) take measurement	Measurement period has elapsed. Compute actual speed and acceleration.

It may come as a surprise that a few external events, like releasing the brake and shifting into top gear, are not listed, although they exist in the real world and a notification at the hardware boundary occurs. However, they do not cross the application subsystem boundary. Only the software of the hardware wrapper will make use of those notifications. See the discussion of the hardware wrapper for more details.

We group the events into a hierarchy. Figure 10-7 shows this grouping using the regular inheritance notation of class diagrams.

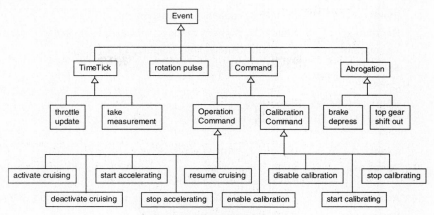

Figure 10-7. Event grouping.

The following event sheets capture all further data on the events.

Event	Command
Response	Subsystem performs some processing, see subevents
Associations	Event is represented by class Command
Source	Driver pressing buttons at physical command interface
Contents	Command identifier, equal to event number
Response Time	See subevents
Rate	See subevents

Event	Operation Command
Response	New position of throttle actuator
Associations	Class Throttle Control
Source	See Command
Contents	See Command
Response Time	Max. 0.5 sec
Rate	Spontaneously, max. burst 1–2 Hz

Event	Calib Command
Response	See subevents
Associations	Class Rotationmeasure
Source	See Command
Contents	See Command
Response Time	See subevents
Rate	Exceptional, intervening time > 1 min

Event	(E7)/(E8) enable/disable calibration
Response	State of subsystem changes, indicated by calibration indicator
Associations	Class Rotationmeasure, statechart Calibration
Source	See Command
Contents	See Command
Response Time	Not critical
Rate	See Calib Command

Event	(E9)/(E10) start/stop calibrating
Response	State of subsystem, internal counter and conversion factor modified, indicated by calib indicator
Associations	Class Rotationmeasure, statecharts Calibration and Conversion
Source	See Command
Contents	See Command
Response Time	10 ms, critical since affects accuracy of system
Rate	See Calib Command

Event	Abrogation
Response	Nullify throttle actuator
Associations	Class Abrogation Sensor, class Throttle Control
Source	Driver depresses brake or transmission shifts out of top gear
Contents	None
Response Time	Max. 10 ms, very critical
Rate	Occasionally, intervening time > 10 sec

Event	(E1) rotation pulse
Response	Update rotation counting
Associations	Class Rotation Sensor, class Rotationmeasure
Source	Rotation of drive shaft
Contents	None
Response Time	4 ms (= two third of max. rate)
Rate	0 to 1500 Hz

Event	Time Tick
Response	See subevent
Associations	Class Timer
Source	10-ms periodic interrupt from hardware timer
Contents	None
Response Time	See subevent
Rate	See subevent

Event	(E12) throttle update
Response	Update throttle actuator
Associations	Class Throttle Control
Source	See Time Tick
Contents	None
Response Time	Max. 1 sec
Rate	Ongoing at 2 Hz, but response necessary only if statechart Cruise is in state active.

Event	(E13) take measurement
Response	Update actual speed and acceleration value
Associations	Class Speed
Source	See Time Tick
Contents	None
Response Time	Max. 1 sec
Rate	Ongoing at 20 Hz

B) Analysis of States

When considering major state behavior of the application, we identify the concurrent statecharts and their elementary states as listed in Table 10-4. Figures 10-8 through 10-10 show these statecharts.

Table 10-4. Statechart list.

Statechart	Elementary States	Associations
Cruise	(S1.1) inactive (S1.2) active (S1.2.1) maintain (S1.2.2) accelerate (S1.3) suspended	Class Throttle Control, class Cruise Indicator, event Operation Command
Calibration	(S2.1) disabled (S2.2) enabled (S2.2.1) ready (S2.2.2) measure	Class Rotationmeasure, class Calib Indicator, event Calib Command
Conversion	(S3.1) default (S3.2) calibrated	Class Rotationmeasure, class Calib Indicator, event Calib Command

As you can see in Figure 10-8, some transitions of statechart **Cruise** refer in the condition clause to the elementary states of a statechart **Abrogation**. This statechart associates mainly with class **Abrogation Sensor** from the environment. You will find this statechart, as well as details about the related class **Abrogation Sensor**, in the hardware wrapper description. Here, in the analysis of the application, we simply assume the ability to test statechart **Abrogation**, telling if actually neither the brake is depressed nor the transmission out of top gear.

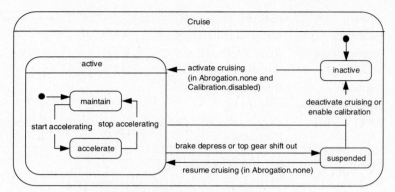

Figure 10-8. Statechart Cruise.

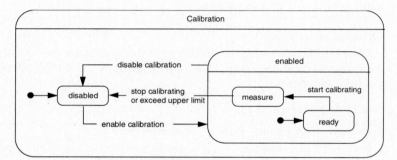

Figure 10-9. Statechart Calibration.

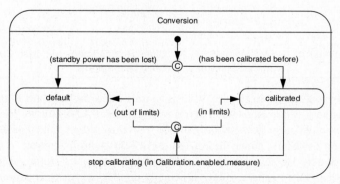

Figure 10-10. Statechart Conversion.

Table 10-5 shows the actions table corresponding to all three statecharts. There, we list the actions an event will trigger in a given state besides triggering the state transition as specified graphically in the statecharts of Figures 10-8 through 10-10. Also, events triggering an action but not a transition are included, for example, the throttle update event.

We add at the end of Table 10-5 the state Sx, called collective other. Since class Rotationmeasure and class Speed continuously consume the events rotation pulse and throttle update without being associated with any of the defined states, we add the actions of these events under state Sx.

Table 10-5. Actions table.

Elementary State	Event	Actions/Activities
(S1.1) Cruise.inactive	\<enter\>	(1) cruise indicator off
		(2) nullify throttle actuator
	\<exit\>	(5) set desired speed = actual speed
(S1.2) Cruise.active	\<enter\>	(3) cruise indicator on
(S1.2.1) Cruise.active.maintain	\<enter\>	(6) perform operation O3
	throttle update	(6) perform operation O3
(S1.2.2) Cruise.active.accelerate	\<enter\>	(7) perform operation O4
	throttle update	(7) perform operation O4
	\<exit\>	(5) set desired speed = actual speed
(S1.3) Cruise.suspended	\<enter\>	(2) nullify throttle actuator
	\<ongoing\>	(8) cruise indicator blink 2 Hz
(S2.2.1) Calibration.enabled.ready	\<enter\>	(9) calib. indicator blink 4 Hz
	start calibrating	(10) reset calibration counter (O5)
(S2.2.2) Calibration.enabled.measure	\<enter\>	(11) calib. indicator blink 2 Hz
	rotation pulse	(12) count pulses (O5)
(S3.1) Conversion.default	\<enter\>	(13) calib. indicator on
	disable calibration	(13) calib. indicator on
	stop calibrating	(14) set kilometer count (O5)
(S3.2) Conversion.calibrated	\<enter\>, disable calibration	(15) calib. indicator off
	stop calibrating	(16) set kilometer count (O5)
(Sx) collective other	rotation pulse	(17) perform operation O1
	take measurement	(18) perform operation O2

C) Enhanced Analysis of Events and States

Table 10-6 shows the significance table. It summarizes the significance of each event from the event list, Table 10-3, in each of the elementary states of statecharts Cruise, Conversion and Calibration shown in Figures 10-8, 10-9 and 10-10, respectively. Note that we include the collective other pseudo state Sx here too.

For obtaining the significance of an event in a compound application state, you have to apply the OCTOPUS significance calculus on the values assigned to the elementary states of the concurrent statecharts.

Table 10-6. Significance table.

Elementary State	Event													
	E1	E2	E3	E4	E5	E6	E7	E8	E9	E10	E11	E12	E13	E14
S1.1	1	e	0	0	0	0	1	1	1	1	0	0	0	1
S1.2.1	c	0	e	e	0	0	e	1	0	0	c	c	c	c
S1.2.2	c	0	e	0	e	0	e	1	0	0	c	c	c	c
S1.3	c	0	e	0	0	e	e	1	0	0	0	0	0	c
S2.1	1	1	1	1	1	1	e	0	0	0	1	1	1	1
S2.2.1	c	0	0	0	0	0	0	e	c	0	1	1	1	1
S2.2.2	c	0	0	0	0	0	0	e	0	c	1	1	1	1
S3.1	1	1	1	1	1	1	1	1	1	e	1	1	1	1
S3.2	1	1	1	1	1	1	1	1	1	e	1	1	1	1
Sx	c	1	1	1	1	1	1	1	1	1	1	1	1	c

Based on the significance values shown in Table 10-6, we also perform an event laxity analysis. It makes no sense to merge any of the nine command events, E2 through E10, with any of the five others. From the noncommand events, only events E11, **brake depress**, and E12, **top gear shift out**, are sensible candidates to merge. Checking with the laxity rules reveals the technical correctness of a new compound event, E20, **abrogation**, combining E11 and E12. Moreover, the two events E11 and E12 both trigger the same sole transition in statechart Cruise, indicating that the application does not need to distinguish between them. Because compound event E20 can be used equally well, we totally substitute events E11 and E12 with event E20 from now on. This reduces the noncommand events to the four events E1, E13, E14 and E20.

Regarding the command events, we produce a complete event laxity matrix for all of them as shown in Table 10-7, because the requirements specification explicitly demands some variance in the command interface. When designing the hardware wrapper, we may wish to reduce the need for input signals and buttons by choosing a mapping of physical events to a set of command events, optionally including a few compound command events instead of the pure ones. Of course, any merger of command events produces a command of which the meaning can be understood only bound by the context of its occurrence. Hence, it becomes a context-bound command.

Table 10-7. Event laxity matrix of command events.

Event	2	3	4	5	6	7	8	9	10
2		x	x	x	x		x	x	x
3							x	x	x
4				x	x		x	x	x
5					x		x	x	x
6							x	x	x
7							x	x	x
8									
9									x
10									

Not all feasible compound command events make sense from the point of view of the user interface. For example, it is a bit strange to combine the start accelerating event E4 with the disable calibration event E8, although the matrix in Table 10-7 indicates its technical correctness. On the other hand, the laxity analysis clearly tells us that a perhaps desired combination of two events, like E2 and E7 into a merged activate/enable event, would lead to a conflict. This fact was not obvious at the beginning.

The list shown in Table 10-8 records a selection of first- (and higher-) order compound command events that we consider reasonable. From the list shown in Table 10-8, we are able to pick a consistent and complete, but reduced, set of command events. Some alternative sets of compound command events are marked in the columns 1, 2 and 3.

Table 10-8. Selection of compound command events.

Compound Event	Merge	Some Possible Sets			
		1	2	3	...
(E21) toggle cruising	E2 + E3		x	x	
(E22) toggle calibration	E9 + E10				
(E23) activate cruising/start calibration	E2 + E9				
(E24) deactivate cruising/stop calibration	E3 + E10				
(E25) toggle cruising/calibration	E2 + E3 + E9 + E10	x			
(E26) start accelerating/calibration	E4 + E9		x		
(E27) stop accelerating/calibration	E5 + E10		x	x	
(E28) start accelerating/resume cruising	E4 + E6	x			
(E29) resume/start calibration	E6 + E9				
(E30) start accelerating/calibration or resume	E4 + E6 + E9			x	

Column 1 of Table 10-8 yields to an alternative set that consists of the five command events E5, E7, E8, E25 and E28 only, called command event set CES1. This set will be used later in the hardware wrapper for control signal assignment CSA1. Table 10-9 summarizes this set of command events.

Table 10-9. Command event set CES1.

Event	Description
(E5) stop accelerating	Driver is satisfied with achieved speed, maintain this now.
(E7) enable calibration	Maintenance will make a calibration of system.
(E8) disable calibration	Calibration done, return to normal operation mode.
(E25) toggle cruise/calibration	Context-bound command: either E2 activate cruising or E3 deactivate cruising or E9 start calibrating or E10 stop calibrating.
(E28) accelerating/resume	Context-bound command: either E4 start accelerating or E6 resume cruising.

D) Subsystem-Environment Interaction Scenarios

Figures 10-11 through 10-13 show some typical interaction scenarios between the entities of the environment as defined in Figure 10-6 and the target application subsystem.

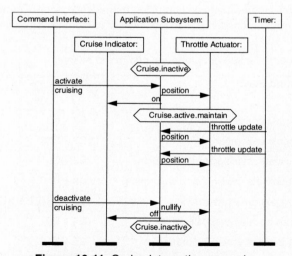

Figure 10-11. Cruise interaction scenario.

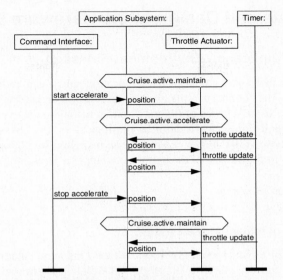

Figure 10-12. Accelerate interaction scenario.

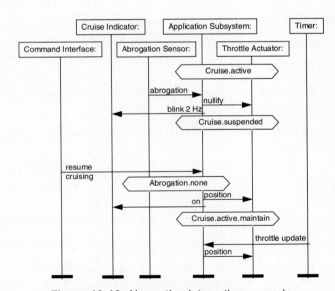

Figure 10-13. Abrogation interaction scenario.

10.3 Analysis and Design of the Hardware Wrapper

10.3.1 Application Environment Revisited

We revisit the object model of the application subsystem and look at its environment as defined by the boundary in the application object diagram shown in Figure 10-6. We systematically list all classes of Figure 10-6 that belong to the environment of the application object model. For each we describe the logical vs. the physical view and the mapping between those views. When explaining the mapping, we deliberately make a few forward references to the models of the hardware wrapper as presented in the subsequent sections.

Class Rotation Sensor
Logical view:

* Source of rotation pulse event E1

* Event E1 directed to all Rotationmeasure instances, that is, the singular instances of classes Speed, Lifetime Distance and Relative Distance

Physical view:

* Sensor at drive shaft continuously produces pulses

* Rate of pulses varies as speed of car varies from 0 to 1500 Hz

* Pulses drive interrupt logic of processor at line INT0

* Falling edge of pulses interrupts processor

mapping of views:

* All subclasses of class Rotationmeasure possess an entry for notification of one rotation pulse

* Interrupt service routine for INT0 calls this entry for each of the singular instances of those classes

Class Timer
Logical view:

* Source of throttle update event E13 and take measurement event E14

* Event E13 directed to the singular instance of class Throttle Control

* Event E14 directed to the singular instance of class Speed

Physical view:

* Timer hardware periodically produces pulses at 100 Hz

* Pulses drive interrupt logic of processor at line INT1

- Falling edge of pulses interrupts processor

- Interrupt service routine ticks time scheduling of the operating system, which in turn may make soft interrupts

Mapping of views:

- Interrupt service routine for INT1 divides 100 Hz to 20 Hz and calls the take measurement entry of the singular instance of class Speed at 20 Hz representing event E14

- The operating system schedules a periodical process representing event E13 at 2 Hz

Class Indicator
Logical view:

- Can be set on, off, blink 2 Hz or blink 4 Hz

Physical view:

- Line at output port, either at +5 V or current sink of max 50 mA

- May be connected to LED + resistor or something similar

Mapping of views:

- Subclasses Cruise Indicator and Calib Indicator of class Indicator associate each with a distinct bit in the output port; see wrapper object model

- Wrapper class Indicator provides interface and functionality to manipulate this bit

- The operating system schedules a periodical process at 4 Hz, which calls any instance of wrapper class Indicator (or its subclasses) for blinking

Class Command Interface
Logical view:

- Source of event Command and subevents, optionally reduced command event set (e.g., command event set CES1)

- Event Calib Command and subevents directed to class Rotationmeasure

- Event Operation Command and subevents directed to the single instance of class Throttle Control

Physical view:

- Switches connected at the control signal lines of the input port

- Detect either falling edges of signal or both falling and raising edges

Mapping of views:

- Alternative assignments of commands to control signals (control signal assignment or CSA) with optional usage of a reduced command event set as analyzed in 10.2.3C (see Figure 10-14 for the specific alternative CSA1 using CES1)

- Each control signal is represented by a distinct wrapper class derived from wrapper base class InputWatcher; see wrapper object model

- Interrupt service routine for INT1 polls all the singular instances of those classes with the actual value of its associated bit from the input port

- Edges in the signal are mapped to events depending on the instance

Note about CSA1: Control signal 1 represents compound event E25. Pressing the corresponding multifunction button activates or deactivates cruising or, if control signal 3 has enabled calibration, it starts or stops calibrating. As long as the button of control signal 2 is held down, auto-acceleration is done; unless cruising has been suspended, in which case pressing the button means resume cruising (compound event E28) and the following release of the button is ignored.

Class Abrogation Sensor
Logical view:

- Internal state follows state of the car's brake or transmission; see statechart in the wrapper dynamic model

- Actual state can be tested

- Source of event E20

Physical view:

- Switches at brake and transmission connected via two lines to input port

- Detect falling and raising edges of these two signal lines

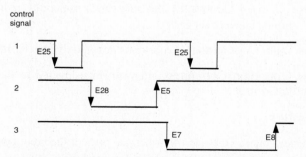

Figure 10-14. Control signal assignment CSA1.

- Raising edge in brake or transmission line assigned to brake depress or top gear shift out

- Falling edge represents brake release or top gear shift in

Mapping of views:

- Wrapper class Abrogation Sensor associates with two distinct bits in input port; see wrapper object model

- Interrupt service routine for INT1 polls the singular instance of this class with the two bits from the input port

- Edges in the signal update the state of statechart Abrogation

- A raising edge in either the brake or transmission signal is mapped to event E11

Class Throttle Actuator

Logical view:

- Repositions on request

Physical view:

- Eight lines of output port connected to D/A converter

- Analog voltage amplified to drive actuator

Mapping of views:

- Write digital position value into corresponding 8 bits of output port

Class Speedometer

Logical view:

- Displays speed as computed by class Speed

Physical view:

- Eight lines of output port hold digital speed value

- These lines may be connected to a digital display unit or a D/A converter driving an analog meter

Mapping of views:

- Class Speed writes new digital speed value into corresponding 8 bits of output port whenever the take measurement event E14 has triggered computation of new value

Class Odometer

Logical view:

- Counts and stores number of pulses from class Distance (or subclass)

- Displays this value

Physical view:

- Electromechanical counters connected to lines of output port

- 60-ms pulses in these lines drive the counter

Mapping of views:

- Request an output pulse whenever interrupt service routine for INT0 passes class Lifetime Distance and 1 km has been counted, or INT0 passes class Relative Distance and 100 m has been counted

- If output pulse is requested the corresponding bit in output port has to be set and cleared

10.3.2 Object Model and Other Content of the Hardware Wrapper

The result of the former section is an object model of the hardware wrapper. Figure 10-15 shows its class diagram. Note that compared to the class diagram of the application subsystem shown in Figure 10-6, we take the reverse view here. The hardware wrapper is in focus now and thus inside the boundary, whereas the classes of the application subsystem are shown outside.

As you can see in Figure 10-15, the class diagram shows some of the attributes of the wrapper classes in more detail. You will also note that a few member functions are repeated downwards in the inheritance hierarchy. In this way we indicate the use of virtual member functions.

Besides the classes already known from the application environment a few new classes have been added. The new classes ISRINT0 and ISRINT1 represent the two interrupt service routines for INT0 and INT1, respectively. Further, the class Operating System represents the underlying operating system. We add these three classes to show the important role they play.

The application class Distance inherits the wrapper class OutputPulser from across the boundary. This is how this class and, it follows, its subclasses Lifetime Distance and Relative Distance, get the wrapper support. In all other cases, the application subsystem gets its support from the wrapper by object interactions, either in the form of a request for service originating from the application object, or the wrapper detects an event and directs it to the appropriate application object.

Whereas some of the classes of the application environment have been kept and refined in the wrapper class diagram, other classes have such little content that they can be mapped into other parts. We list these missing classes in Table 10-10 and explain how they are represented in the hardware wrapper.

Table 10-10. List of classes mapped into other parts.

Class	Mapped into
Rotation Sensor	ISRINT0 triggered by an interrupt at line INT0
Timer	ISRINT1 implements the periodic activation of class Speed. Periodic activation of class Throttle Control is done by the time scheduling of the operating system that is ticked by ISRINT1
Throttle Actuator	Class OutputPort writing into a bit-field of output port
Odometer Life-time Odometer Relative Odometer	Wrapper base class OutputPulser writing into one bit of output port based on periodic activation by the operating system
Speedometer	Class OutputPort writing into a bit-field of output port

Next, we examine the wrapper class diagram shown in Figure 10-15, to see if all the associations which cross the boundary of the application class diagram shown in Figure 10-6 can be matched to a corresponding association crossing the boundary in Figure 10-15. Wherever classes are bounded by associations bearing the same names in both figures, the matching is obvious. However, since the above-listed classes do not appear in the wrapper object model anymore, we have to make sure that their associations are represented, either by associations with the new wrapper classes or by some other means. We summarize these facts in Table 10-11.

Table 10-11. Association replacements.

Association	Original Classes	Replacement
sense rotation	Rotation Sensor Rotationmeasure	'do counting' between ISRINT0 and class Rotationmeasure
visualize measurement	Speed Speedometer	'make output' associated with class OutputPort instead of class Speedometer
count and display	Distance Odometer	inheritance from class OutputPulser and 'make output' associated with class OutputPort
periodic activation	Timer Speed	'do measurement' between ISRINT1 and class Speed
periodic activation	Timer Throttle Control	'periodical scheduling' by operating system instead of class Timer
drive position	Throttle Actuator Throttle Control	'make output' associated with class OutputPort

10.3.3 Functional Model of Hardware Wrapper

The analysis of the application subsystem identified services that the hardware wrapper will provide. The following operations describe these services.

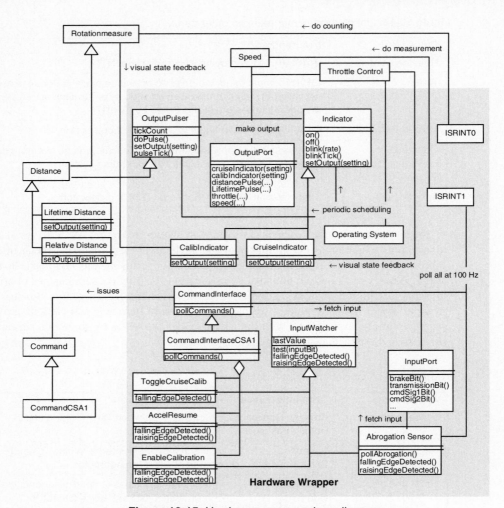

Figure 10-15. Hardware wrapper class diagram.

Operation	(WO1) indicator management
Description	Manipulates visual, binary indicator that is driven by output port line
Associations	Class Indicator and all its subclasses
Preconditions	For each indicator a bit in output port is exclusively assigned Blink tick occurs every 270 ms
Inputs	On, off or blink rate request
Modifies	Internal state, see statechart Indicator Blink tick counter
Outputs	Setting of bit in output port
Postconditions	

Operation	(WO2) odometer pulse
Description	Produces a pulse in the line connected to the odometer display unit
Associations	Class OutputPulser and all its subclasses
Precondition	Bit of output port exclusively assigned No pulse ongoing Pulse tick every 30 ms
Inputs	Length of pulse in units of 2 ticks
Modifies	Counter for pulse ticks
Outputs	Bit of output port set for a specified number of ticks
Postconditions	Bit reset

Operation	(WO3) abrogation status
Description	Makes external state of brake and transmission internally available as a summary state
Associations	Class AbrogationSensor
Preconditions	Input bits of brake and transmission signal continuously polled and changes reflected in statechart Abrogation
Inputs	State request
Modifies	
Outputs	Actual state
Postconditions	

The analysis of the application subsystem has identified events that drive the application subsystem. In the following, we describe operations of the hardware wrapper that generate some of these events based on a primitive event (see the dynamic model in the subsequent section for more information about primitive events).

Operation	(WO4) poll input for commands
Description	External command buttons drive the bits of the input port, changes shall be detected and mapped into events
Associations	Class InputWatcher, class CommandInterface and its aggregates
Preconditions	Saved bit value from last cycle Assignment of commands to control signal lines selected
Inputs	(P15) poll input
Modifies	

Outputs	Command events depending on selected assignment, e.g. for CSA1 it is
	
	if falling edge detected:
	    (E25) toggle cruising/calibration
	    (E28) start accelerating/resume cruising
	    (E7) enable calibration
	
	if raising edge detected:
	    (E5) stop accelerating
	    (E8) disable calibration

Postconditions	Save actual bit value for next cycle

Operation	(WO5) poll abrogation
Description	External switches at brake and transmission drive bits of the input port, changes in the external state shall be detected and optionally mapped into events
Associations	Class InputWatcher, class AbrogationSensor
Preconditions	Saved bit value from last cycle
Inputs	(P15) poll input
Modifies	Internal state, see statechart Abrogation
Outputs	If raising edge in brake or transmission signal detected and in state Abrogation.none: (E20) abrogation
Postconditions	Save actual bit value for next cycle

10.3.4 Dynamic Model of Hardware Wrapper

A) Analysis of Events

From the point of view of the hardware wrapper, we identify the primitive events as listed in Table 10-12. As you can see, this table also proves that all events crossing the application boundary are mapped to one primitive event. Some events, like E1, E13 and

E14, are identical to primitive events. The others are computed by the hardware wrapper based on a primitive event.

Table 10-12. Primitive event list

Primitive Event	Description
(P1) rotation pulse	Forwarded as event E1
(P13) throttle update	Forwarded as event E13
(P14) take measurement	Forwarded as event E14
(P15) poll input	Check all input bits for changes and derive the events E25, E28, E5, E7, E8 and E20
(P16) pulse tick	Starts and stops output pulses
(P17) blink tick	Basic indicator blinking period elapsed

A primitive event is either a hard interrupt (done directly by one of the interrupts from the hardware) or a soft interrupt (done indirectly by the time scheduling of the operating system). Figure 10-16 shows the grouping of primitive events.

B) Analysis of States

For a few wrapper classes we like to add a statechart specification. These statecharts are shown in Figures 10-17 and 10-18. The name of each statechart indicates the class to which it belongs.

C) Interaction Scenarios

The interaction scenarios highlight how instances of the wrapper classes perform the request from the application subsystem in conjunction with the interrupt service routines and the scheduling of the operating system. See Figures 10-19 and 10-20.

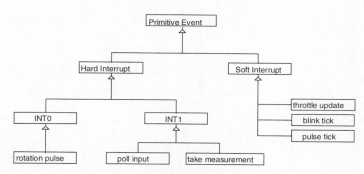

Figure 10-16. Primitive event grouping.

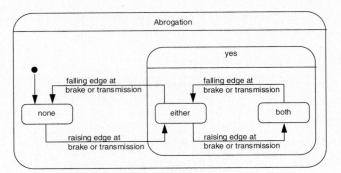

Figure 10-17. Statechart Abrogation.

10.3.5 Design of the Hardware Wrapper

The hardware wrapper of Cruise Control is driven by the two interrupts INT0 and INT1. They generate all primitive events either directly, via the interrupt service routines ISRINT0 and ISRINT1, or indirectly, by ticking the operating system. We systematically develop the event threads of all primitive events as listed earlier in Table 10-12 and document them in Figures 10-21 and 10-23 with help of the object interaction graph notation. All objects are singular instances of their classes. We interchangeably use the class name starting with a small letter to identify the corresponding object. For details, please refer to the class outlines given at the end of this section.

Figure 10-21 shows the event threads of the primitive hard-interrupt events: rotation pulse, take measurement and poll input. They are derived from either interrupt service routine ISRINT0 or ISRINT1 and are denoted by solid arrows due to their synchronous invocation nature.

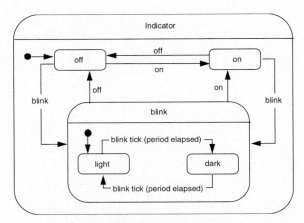

Figure 10-18. Statechart Indicator.

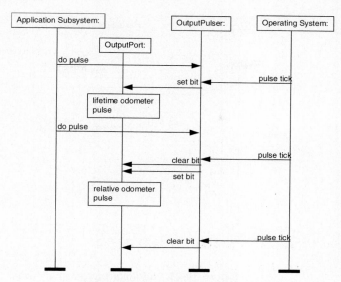

Figure 10-19. Odometer pulses.

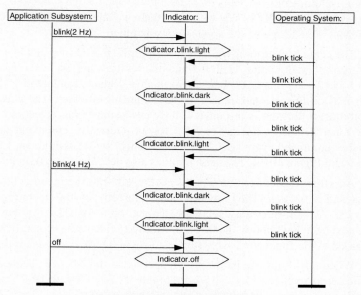

Figure 10-20. Indicator blinking.

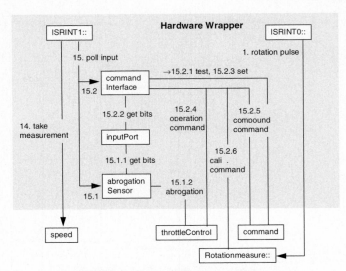

Figure 10-21. Hard-interrupt event threads.

As you can see in Figure 10-21, interrupt service routine **ISRINT0** solely generates the **rotation pulse** event, which is simply forwarded to the application subsystem. Also, the **take measurement** event is forwarded to the application subsystem, but by interrupt service routine **ISRINT1**. We will pick them up and identify their corresponding event threads when designing the application subsystem.

The event **poll input** is the only other primitive hard-interrupt event. It is derived from interrupt service routine **ISRINT1** and divides itself into the two object interaction threads 15.1 and 15.2. Figure 10-21 generalizes object interaction thread 15.2. Its exact structure depends on the selected variant of the command interface. The class from which object **commandInterface** is instantiated fully encapsulates this selection. Figure 10-22 shows the inner details of interaction 15.2 for an alternative command interface that accomplishes command event set CES1 using control signal assignment CSA1. Refer to Table 10-9 and Figure 10-14. The class outlines also describe this alternative.

All other remaining primitive events are soft-interrupt events: **throttle update, pulse tick** and **blink tick**. They are generated indirectly by the operating system (see Figure 10-23). All soft-interrupt events are denoted by a dashed arrow because they involve a context switch. Of those, the **throttle update** event and the **pulse tick** event is simply forwarded to the application subsystem, and we will look for its event thread later.

When qualifying the hardware wrapper event threads, we decide on the asynchronous kind for interactions 15.1.2, 15.2.4 through 15.2.6 in Figure 10-21 because these become events of group **Command** of the application subsystem. Their corresponding event threads will be determined when designing the application subsystem. Unless this has been done, we can put only a general place holder into the class outlines where these events are issued. However, the class outlines as given here at the end of this section antic-

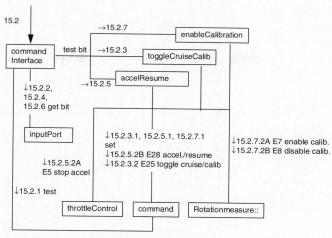

Figure 10-22. Detailed interactions for CES1/CSA1.

ipate the result of the application subsystem design in respect to these generated events and state the final mechanism by scheduling a specific target process.

Figure 10-24 merges all wrapper event threads from Figures 10-21 and 10-23 in their qualified form. Grouping the objects results in the two object groups **WG1** and **WG2**, as marked in Figure 10-24. Although the generated application events, as well as the forwarded events, naturally define the root of more object groups, we defer their definition until application subsystem design.

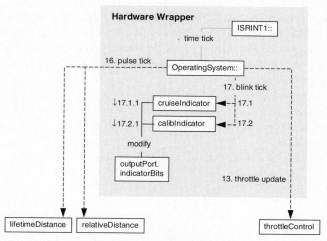

Figure 10-23. Soft-interrupt event threads.

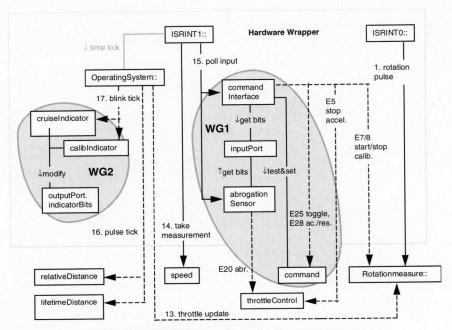

Figure 10-24. Object groups of the hardware wrapper.

Group **WG1** defines the coverage of the interrupt service routine for **INT1** inside the hardware wrapper. A process is not needed for this group. Note that there exists an additional part of this interrupt service routine in the application subsystem which will be defined by the event thread of the forwarded **take measurement** event. At the lowest machine level, the interrupt vector associated with **INT1** is simply directed to the start of interrupt service routine **ISRINT1**, which in turn calls the other objects as defined by group **WG1** and forwards the **take measurement** event to the proper target in the application subsystem. See the outline of the interrupt service routine **ISRINT1**.

Group **WG2** identifies the need for an extra wrapper process, called process **blinker**. See the process function outline.

As you can easily see in Figure 10-24, none of the wrapper groups overlaps with each other. Consequently, the hardware wrapper does not contain shared objects, and synchronization is not an issue here. This situation will change when the application subsystem is considered too.

Below are the outlines of the process function and the interrupt service routines:

```
interrupt service routine ISRINT0
    // invoked each time a rotation pulse is sensed
    forward 'rotation pulse' event to app subsystem;
endisr;


interrupt service routine ISRINT1
    // runs periodically at 100 Hz
    raise at 20 Hz 'take measurement' event and forward it to app subsystem;
    AbrogationSensor::pollAbrogation();   //enter via static part
    commandInterface.pollCommands();        //enter via virtual interface
    OperatingSystem::tick();   //just a placeholder, depends on usage
endisr;


process function Blinker
    loop forever
        disable interrupt;
        if    schedule time not elapsed
        then wait for time schedule;
        enable interrupt;
        put process on time list for resched after 270 ms;
        Indicator::blinkTick();   //enter via static part
    endloop;
endprocessfunction;
```

Below are the class outlines of the hardware wrapper:

```
class  OutputPulser
    // sync save even in ISR, but a request during ongoing pulse is dropped
    int tickCount;
    virtual fct setOutput(setting);   //subclass defines where in output port
    function requestPulse(lenghtInTicks)
        disable interrupt;
        if    tickCount <= 0  //no pulse ongoing
        then tickCount = lenghtInTicks;
        enable interrupt;
    endfunction;
    function pulseTick(); //invoked by process PulseFormer every 60 ms
        disable interrupt; //sync tickCount access
        if    tickCount <= 0
        then setOutput(0);   //stop pulse
        else setOutput(1);   //start pulse if not yet done
             decr tickCount;
        endif;
        enable interrupt;
    endfunciont;
endclass;


class Indicator
    // app must serialize usage, no local sync done
    static int blinkCount;  //shared by all instances
    int blinkRate;
    statechart Indicator state;  //local to each instance, no external access
    virtual function setOutput(setting);  //subclass defines where in output port
    static function blinkTick()    // invoked by process blink every 250 ms,
```

```
        incr blinkCount;              // shared by all instances
        cruiseIndicator.doBlinking();  //list all instances here
        calibIndicator.doBlinking();
    endfunction;
    function on()
        setOutput(1);
        statechart state = on;
    endfunction;
    function off()
        setOutput(0);
        statechart state = off;
    endfunction;
    function blink(rate)
        blinkRate = rate;
        setOutput(1);
        statechart state = blink.light;
    endfunction;
    function doBlinking()
        disable context switch;  //sync blinking with interface
        if   statechart state == blink
        then if   modulo(blinkCount, blinkRate) == 0
             then if   statechart state == blink.light
                  then setOutput(0);
                       statechart state = blink.dark;
                  else setOutput(1);
                       statechart state = blink.light;
                  endif;
             endif;
        endif;
        enable context switch;
    endfunction;
endclass;


class  InputWatcher
    Bit lastValue;
    virtual function fallingEdgeDetected();
    virtual function raisingEdgeDetected();
    function test(inputBit)  //allowed only in ISR
        if   lastValue != inputBit
        then lastValue = inputBit;
             if   inputBit == 0
             then fallingEdgeDetected()
             else raisingEdgeDetected();
        endif;
    endfunction;
endclass;


class  ToggleCruiseCalib inherits InputWatcher
    fct fallingEdgeDetected()
        //originate event E25 for command;
        command.id = toggleCruiseCalib;
        schedule process command;
    endfct;
endclass;
```

```
class  AccelResume inherits InputWatcher
    function fallingEdgeDetected()
        //originate event E28 for command;
        command.id = accelResume;
        schedule process command;
    endfunction;
    function raisingEdgeDetected()
        //originate event E5 for throttleControl;
        command.id = stopAccelerating;
        schedule process command;
    endfunction;
endclass;


class  EnableCalibration inherits InputWatcher
    function fallingEdgeDetected()
        //originate event E7 for Rotationmeasure::;
        command.id = enableCalibration;
        schedule process command;
    endfunction;
    function raisingEdgeDetected()
        //originate event E8 for Rotationmeasure::;
        command.id = disableCalibration;
        schedule process command;
    endfunction;
endclass;


class  AbrogationSensor inherits InputWatcher
    static statechart Abrogation state;  //shared by all instances
    static function pollAbrogation()  //invoked by INT1, shared by instances
        brake.test(inputPort.brake());          //access the instances
        transmission.test(inputPort.transmission());
    endfunction;
    function fallingEdgeDetected()
        if   statechart state == yes.both
        then statechart state = yes.either
        else statechart state = none;
    endfunction;
    function raisingEdgeDetected()
        if   statechart state == none
        then schedule process throttle;
             statechart state = yes.either
        else statechart state = yes.both;
    endfunction;
endclass;


class InputPort
    bit cmdSig1Bit, cmdSig2Bit, cmdSig3Bit, cmdSig4Bit, brakeBit, transmissionBit;
    function cmdSignal1() returns bit-value
        return cmdSig1Bit;  //final implementation may inflate this
    endfunction;
    . . . ditto all others
endclass;
```

```
class  CommandInterface
   // interface for command variants
   virtual function pollCommands();   //invoked by INT1
endclass;


class  CommandInterfaceCSA1 : CommandInterface
   // one specific alternative of the command interface
   ToggleCruiseCalib toggleCruiseCalib;   //compound event E25
   AccelResume accelResume; //event E5 and E28
   EnableCalibration enableCalib; //event E7 and E7
   function pollCommands();   //invoked by INT1
      if   command.id == none
      then toggleCruiseCalib.test(inputPort.cmdSignal1());
           if   command.id == none
           then accelResume.test(inputPort.cmdSignal2());
                if   command.id == none
                then enableCalib.test(inputPort.cmdSignal3());
           endif;
      endif;
   endfunction;
endclass;


class OutputPort
   bitField speedField, throttleField;
   bit cruiseBit, calibBit, distanceBit, lifetimeBit;
   function speed(setting)
      disbale interrupt;   //make subparts mutually exclusive
      speedField = setting;   //final implementation may inflate this
      enable interrupt;
   endfunction;
   function throttle(setting)
      disbale interrupt;
      throttleField = setting;
      enable interrupt;
   endfunction;
   function cruiseIndicator(setting)
      disbale interrupt;
      cruiseBit = setting;
      enable interrupt;
   endfunction;
   . . .
endclass;
```

10.4 Design of the Application Subsystem

10.4.1 Event Threads and Object Groups

The design of the hardware wrapper gives us a clear understanding of the events entering the application subsystem. For each event we build an event thread based on the knowledge we obtain from the scenarios and the object model. Using the object interaction graph notation in each step of the procedure, we produce Figures 10-25 and 10-26. The

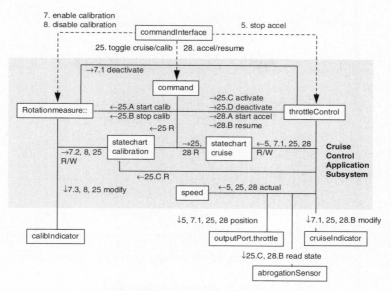

Figure 10-25. Command event threads.

event threads are accompanied by developing class outlines showing a bit more detail (see Section 10.4.4).

Figure 10-25 shows all event threads of event group Command. The assumed set of command events is according to control signal assignment CSA1. However, this selection is fully encapsulated in the class from which object command is instantiated. For another control signal assignment, another variant of this class would be used. The class outlines include only the variant according to control signal assignment CSA1.

Events of group CalibrationCommand manipulate data shared by all instances of any subclass of base class Rotationmeasure. The processing of these events is statically packed in the base class. In Figure 10-25 we indicate this fact by using the class name qualifier for a related pseudo object to which the events direct.

Figure 10-26 shows the event threads of all other events. This includes the events E1 and E13 forwarded from the interrupt service routines ISRINT0 and ISRINT1, respectively. The corresponding event threads are part of the interrupt service routines.

The rotation pulse event has to be broadcast to all instances of any subclass of base class Rotationmeasure. This we achieve by a function that is statically declared in class Rotationmeasure.

We recognize that both figures explicitly show the access of statechart Cruise and Calibration by several objects. However, statechart Conversion does not appear, and class Rotationmeasure can most likely encapsulate it.

Although we instantiate only one object from class OutputPort, Figures 10-25 and 10-26 treat this object as separate boxes, each devoted to another subpart. This can be justified because class OutputPort aggregates bit-fields that are used for independent pur-

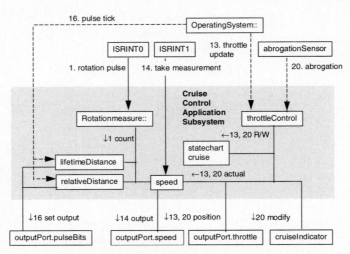

Figure 10-26. Noncommand event threads.

poses. However, the microscopic implementation of writing a single bit into the physical register of the output port would break this independence. Therefore, we enforce mutual exclusiveness between those writings by disabling and enabling the interrupt when manipulating the output port. See the outline of class OutputPort.

Qualification of the event threads cannot justify asynchronous interaction at any place. The noncommand event threads are rather short anyway and require completion as fast as possible. Introducing some asynchronous interaction inside any of the command event threads makes no sense because a command always has to be completed before the next one starts. Based on this decision, we determine the object groups by applying the rules of the fair set.

The fair set of object groups related to the noncommand event threads is kept as is (see Figure 10-27). Groups G1 and G3 are subparts of the corresponding interrupt service routines, and as such they can be neither merged nor split. A merger of groups G4 and G2 would limit the concurrency too much. A split of group G4 would introduce many shared objects.

Applying the rules of the fair set of object groups on the command event threads results in three groups with many shared objects. Here, we merge the groups into one because concurrency between the commands is not required and sharing of objects is reduced. Figure 10-28 shows this final group G5.

10.4.2 Process Outlines

Due to the fact that the hardware wrapper only forwards the rotation pulse event, group G3 will be executed by the interrupt service routine for interrupt INT0. In a similar way, the take measurement event will pass as part of the execution thread of interrupt INT1 from the hardware wrapper to the application subsystem, and covers group G1. Groups

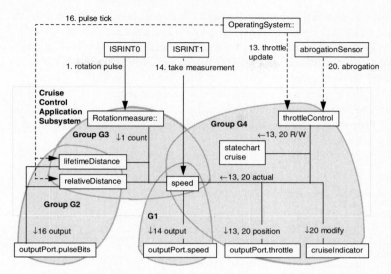

Figure 10-27. Object groups of noncommand event threads.

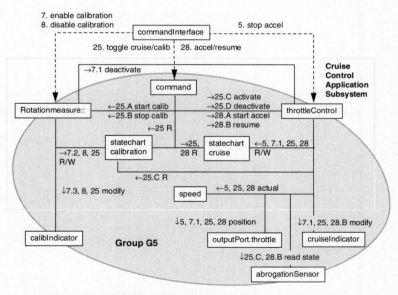

Figure 10-28. Object groups of command event threads.

G2, G4 and G5 require operating system processes for execution. We call them process `pulseFormer`, process `throttle` and process `command`, respectively.

Process `throttle` will be scheduled periodically at 2 Hz, and this scheduling represents the **throttle update** event. Whenever an **abrogation** event is detected in the hardware wrapper, process `throttle` will also be scheduled.

Upon detection of a command, the hardware wrapper will store a command identification and schedule process `command`.

Process `pulseFormer` runs periodically every 30 ms, and starts or stops a pulse for the lifetime or relative odometer.

See the following process function outlines for more details:

```
process function Command  //associates with G5
    loop forever
        disable interrupt; //makes free of command and wait atomic
        command.id = none;
        wait;
        enable interrupt;
        disable context switching;
        if    command is of compound kind
        then command.crackCompound()
        else switch command.id
            enableCalibration: Rotationmeasure::enableCalibration();
            disableCalibration: Rotationmeasure::disableCalibration();
            startCalibrating: Rotationmeasure::startCalibrating();
            stopCalibrating: Rotationmeasure::stopCalibrating();
            activateCruising:  throttleControl.activateCruising();
            deactivateCruising: throttleControl.deactivateCruising();
            startAccelerating: throttleControl.startAccelerating();
            stopAccelerating:  throttleControl.stopAccelerating();
            resumeCruising:    throttleControl.resumeCruising();
            endswitch;
        endif;
        enable context switching
    endloop;
endprocfunction;



process function Throttle  //associates with G4
    loop forever
        disable interrupt; //make test and wait atomic
        if    abrogation
        then enable interrupt;
            throttleControl.suspendActivation();
        else if   throttle update time elapsed
            then enable interrupt;
                put process on time list for resched after 500 ms;
                throttleControl.updateActuator;
            else //neither abrogation nor throttle update actually valid
                await abrogation or throttle update;
                enable interrupt;
        endif;
    endloop;
endprocfunction;
```

```
process function PulseFormer  //associates with G2
   loop forever
      disable interrupt;  //make test and wait atomic
      if   schedule time not elapsed
      then wait for time schedule;
      enable interrupt;
      put process on time list for resched after 30 ms;
      lifetimeDistance.pulseTick();
      disable interrupt;
      if   schedule time not elapsed
      then wait for time schedule;
      enable interrupt;
      put process on time list for resched after 30 ms;
      relativeDistance.pulseTick();
   endloop;
endprocessfunction;
```

10.4.3 Shared Objects and Synchronization

The selected grouping of objects and their execution by independent execution paths results in shared objects. We list all shared objects in Table 10-13.

Table 10-13. Table of Shared objects.

Object	Shared Between Groups	Solution
speed	(1) G1 - G3 (2) G1 - G4 (3) G1 - G5 (4) G3 - G4 (5) G3 - G5 (6) G4 - G5	Uncritical Disable interrupt Disable interrupt Uncritical Uncritical Disable interrupt
throttleControl	(7) G4 - G5	Disable context switch
outputPort.throttle	(8) G4 - G5	Disable context switch
cruiseIndicator	(9) G4 - G5 (10) G4 - WG2 (11) G5 - WG2	Disable context switch Disable context switch Disable context switch
calibIndicator	(12) G5 - WG2	Disable context switch
Rotationmeasure::	(13) G3 - G5	Disable interrupt
statechart Cruise	(14) G4 - G5	Disable context switch
lifetimeDistance, relativeDistance	(15) G2 - G3	Disable interrupt
command	(16) G5 - WG1	Atomic
AbrogationSensor::	(17) G5 - WG1	Atomic

Note that the static part of class **Rotationmeasure** is shared too, as well as statechart **Cruise**. We also added any sharing with wrapper groups to Table 10-13. In the following, we take a closer look at each shared item and, if critical regarding synchronization, we design a solution.

(2) Only **G1** interleaves **G4** since **G1** is executed by an interrupt service routine. **G4** reads data produced by **G1**. This requires synchronization if the data access is not done by an atomic processor instruction. We disable/enable interrupt in the functions of class Speed that make this access.

(3) (6) Solved by (2).

(10) (11) (12) **WG2** executes the blinking. It reads and writes the state. This must be protected against the interface functions on, off and blink. We disable/enable context switching in the function doBlinking of class Indicator.

(7) (8) (9) (14) Only **G4** interleaves **G5** due to the higher priority of its process. The related processing requires synchronization. We protect all **G5** processing by disabling/enabling context switching.

(13) Only **G3** can interleave **G5** since **G3** is executed by an interrupt service routine. Both manipulate the **calibrationCount**. This requires synchronization by disabling/enabling interrupts if this access is not done by an atomic processor instruction.

(15) Similar situation to (13).

(16) Critical is the access of member **id** of object **command**. It is assumed that this can be done by an atomic processor instruction.

(17) Similar situation to (16).

10.4.4 Class Outlines

```
class  Rotationmeasure
    static int kilometerCount, calibrationCount; //shared by all subclasses
    int count;
    static function rotationPulse();    //invoked by INT0
        increment calibrationCount;
        increment speed.count;
        lifetimeDistance.countRotationPulse();
        relativeDistance.countRotationPulse();
    endfunction;
    static function startCalibrating()
        if   statechart calibration == enabled.ready
        then disable interrupt;  //make atomic, case (13)
            calibrationCount = 0;
            enable interrupt;
            calibIndicator.blink(2 Hz);
            statechart calibration = enabled.measure;
        endif;
    endfunction;
    static function stopCalibrating()
        if   statechart calibration == enabled.measure
        then disable interrupt;  //make atomic, case (13)
            if calibrationCount in limits
            then kilometerCount = calibrationCount;
                enable Interrupt;
                calibIndicator.off();
                statechart conversion = calibrated;
            else kilometerCount = default;
                enable interrupt;
                calibIndicator.on();
                statechart conversion = default;
            endif;
            statechart calibration = disabled;
        endif;
```

```
        endfunction;
    static function disableCalibration()
        calibIndicator.off();
        statechart calibration = disabled;
    endfunction;
    static function enableCalibration()
        throttleControl.deactivate();
        calibIndicator.blink(4 Hz);
        statechart calibration = enabled.ready;
    endfunction;
endclass;


class  Speed inherits Rotationmeasure
    int lastCount;
    SpeedValue actualSpeed, actualAccel;
    static function takeMeasurement()    //invoked by INT1 at 20 Hz
        if    lastCount > 0
        then calculate actualSpeed and actualAccel
             according to operations O1 and O2;
             outputPort.speed(actualSpeed);
        endif;
        lastCount = count;
        count = 0;
    endfunction;
    function actualSpeed()
        disable interrupt;   //sync access, case (2)
        auxilarySpeedStore = actualSpeed;
        enable interrupt;
        return auxilarySpeedStore;
    endfunction;
    function actualAccel()
        disable interrupt;
        auxilaryAccelStore = actualAccel;
        enable interrupt;
        return auxilaryAccelStore;
    endfunction;
endclass;


class LifetimeDistance inherits Rotationmeasure, OutputPulser
    function countRotationPulse()
        decrement count;
        if    count <= 0
        then requestPulse(1);
             count = kilometerCount;
        endif;
    endfunction;
    function setOutput(setting)
        outputPort.lifetimePulse(setting);
    endfunction;
endclass;


class  RelativeDistance inherits Rotationmeasure, OutputPulser
    function countRotationPulse()
        decrement count by 10;
        if    count <= 0
        then requestPulse(1);
             count = kilometerCount + count;
```

```
            endif;
      endfunction;
      function setOutput(setting)
            outputPort.relativePulse(setting);
      endfunction;
endclass;
```

```
class  Command
      cmdId id;
      virtual function crackCompound()
endclass;
```

```
class  CommandCSA1 : Command
      function crackCompound()
            switch id
            toggleCruiseCalib:
                  switch statechart calibration
                  enabled.ready:   Rotationmeasure::startCalibrating();
                  enabled.measure: Rotationmeasure::stopCalibrating();
                  disabled:
                        if   statechart cruise == inactive
                        then throttleControl.activateCruising();
                        else throttleControl.deactivateCruising();
                  endswitch;
            accelResume:
                  if   statechart cruise == active.maintain
                  then throttleControl.startAccelerating()
                  else if   statechart cruise == suspended
                        then throttleControl.resumeCruising();
                  endif;
            endswitch;
      endfunction;
endclass;
```

```
class ThrottleControl
      int desiredSpeed;
      function activateCruising()
            if   statechart cruise == inactive and
                  statechart calibration == disabled and
                  statechart abrogation == none
            then desiredSpeed = speedometer.actualSpeed
                  maintainSpeed();
                  cruiseIndicator.on();
                  statechart cruise = active.maintain;
            endif;
      endfunction;
      function deactivateCruising()
            outputPort.throttle(0);
            cruiseIndicator.off();
            statechart cruise = inactive;
      endfunction;
      function startAccelerating()
            if   statechart cruise == active.maintain
            then autoAccelerate();
                  statechart cruise = active.accelerate;
            endif;
      endfunction;
```

```
    function stopAccelerating()
        if    statechart cruise == active.accelerate
        then desiredSpeed = speedometer.actualSpeed
             maintainSpeed();
             statechart cruise = active.maintain;
        endif;
    endfunction;
    function resumeCruising()
        if    statechart cruise == suspended and
             statechart abrogation == none
        then maintainSpeed();
             cruiseIndicator.on();
             statechart cruise = active.maintain;
        endif;
    endfunction;
    function suspendActivation()
        if    statechart cruise == active.accelerate
        then desiredSpeed = speedometer.actualSpeed;
        outputPort.throttle(0);
        cruiseIndicator.blink(2 Hz);
        statechart cruise = suspended;
    endfunction;
    function updateActuator();
        if    statechart cruise == active.maintain
        then maintainSpeed();
        if    statechart cruise == active.accelerate
        then autoAccelerate();
    endfunction;
    function maintainSpeed()
        compute VTH according to operation O3;
        outputPort.throttle(VTH);
    endfunction;
    function autoAccelerate()
        compute VTH according to operation O4;
        outputPort.throttle(VTH);
    endfunction;
endclass;
```

11

REFERENCE MANUAL

11.1 Notation Summary

11.1.1 Use Case Sheet

Use Case	Name of the use case.
Actors	External requesters of the system services or an autonomous activity.
Preconditions	Conditions that need to be satisfied to do the use case, these do not guarantee that the use case will be successfully completed.
Description	Short statement describing the use case including time requirements and exceptions that could happen.
Sub Use Cases	References to sub use cases.
Exceptions	How the system responds to the exception cases indicated in the Description field.
Activities	References to use cases describing the activities taking place during each use case.
Postconditions	Conditions after the use case is successfully completed and the conditions that apply if the use case is terminated due to an error.

11.1.2 Operation Sheet

Operation	Name of the operation.
Description	Short statement describing the operation.
Associations	Associations to the classes and objects and possibly also to the events and states to which it is related.
Preconditions	Conditions that need to be satisfied to start the operation, these do not guarantee that the operation will be successfully completed.
Inputs	Arguments that an operation needs to perform its desired function.
Modifies	What modifications the operation causes on its arguments or on common data in the subsystem.
Outputs	What information the operation needs to supply its client.
Postconditions	Conditions after the operation is successfully completed and the conditions that apply if the operation is terminated due to an error.

11.1.3 Event Sheet

Event	Name of the event.
Response	The desired end-to-end response from the system.
Associations	Associations to the classes and objects and possibly also to the operations to which it is related.
Source	The originators of the event, for example, other subsystems or the hardware wrapper.
Contents	Data attributes that an event may hold.
Response Time	The maximum and minimum time limits concerning the giving of the response.
Rate	The rate of occurrence that can be, for example, at startup, periodic every 10 minutes, timed at 8:00 AM and 2:00 PM, occasional, exceptional, etc.

11.1.4 Class Diagram

A class labeled with class name A.

A class labeled with class name Abc and optionally with :
- A cardinality number k indicating how many objects can be instantiated from the class.
- The attributes.
- The member functions.

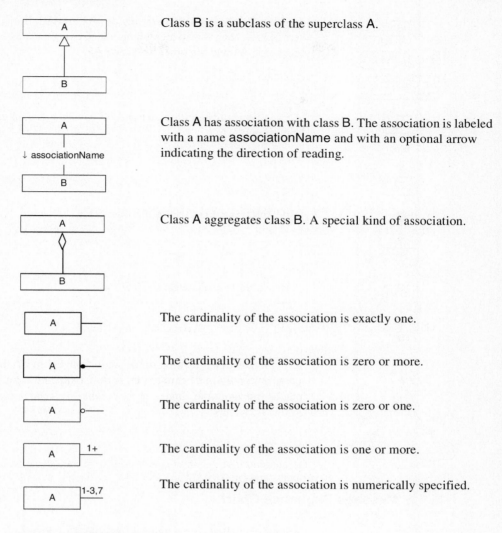

Class B is a subclass of the superclass A.

Class A has association with class B. The association is labeled with a name associationName and with an optional arrow indicating the direction of reading.

Class A aggregates class B. A special kind of association.

The cardinality of the association is exactly one.

The cardinality of the association is zero or more.

The cardinality of the association is zero or one.

The cardinality of the association is one or more.

The cardinality of the association is numerically specified.

11.1.5 Statechart

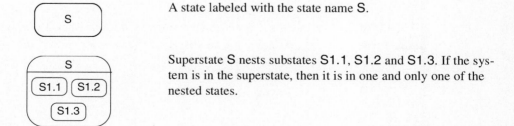

A state labeled with the state name S.

Superstate S nests substates S1.1, S1.2 and S1.3. If the system is in the superstate, then it is in one and only one of the nested states.

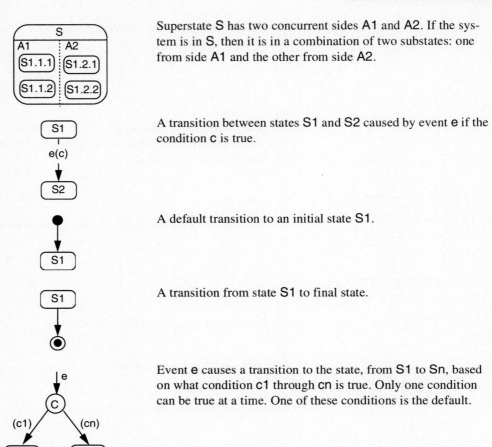

Superstate S has two concurrent sides A1 and A2. If the system is in S, then it is in a combination of two substates: one from side A1 and the other from side A2.

A transition between states S1 and S2 caused by event e if the condition c is true.

A default transition to an initial state S1.

A transition from state S1 to final state.

Event e causes a transition to the state, from S1 to Sn, based on what condition c1 through cn is true. Only one condition can be true at a time. One of these conditions is the default.

11.1.6 Message Sequence Chart

An entity labeled with a name A.

An event or a message e sent by entity A and received by entity B.

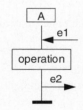

A timeout timeout is set after the reception of e1 during which e2 must be sent.

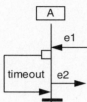

An operation operation is performed between the reception of e1 and the sending of e2.

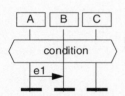

If the condition condition is true, entity A sends e1 to B. Both A and C participate in the condition, but not B.

11.1.7 Object Interaction Graph

An object.

A trigger to the controller of the object interaction thread.

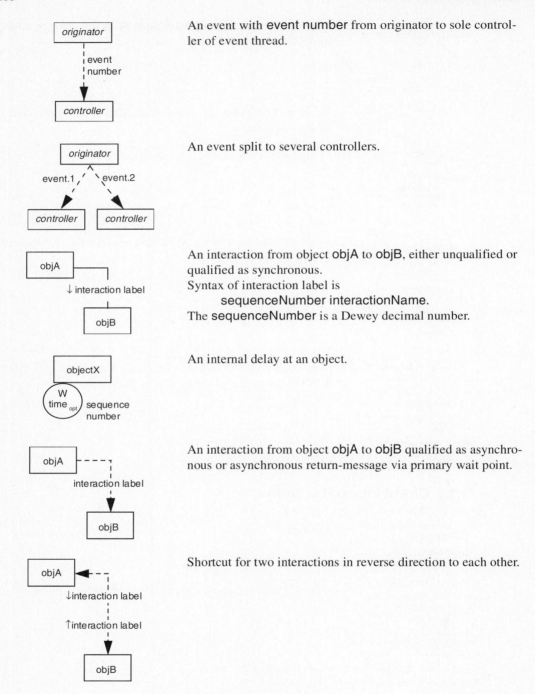

An event with **event number** from originator to sole controller of event thread.

An event split to several controllers.

An interaction from object **objA** to **objB**, either unqualified or qualified as synchronous.
Syntax of interaction label is
      sequenceNumber interactionName.
The **sequenceNumber** is a Dewey decimal number.

An internal delay at an object.

An interaction from object **objA** to **objB** qualified as asynchronous or asynchronous return-message via primary wait point.

Shortcut for two interactions in reverse direction to each other.

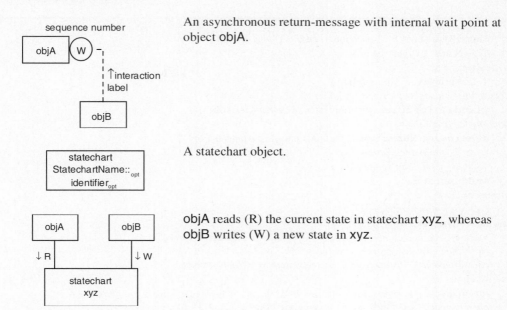

An asynchronous return-message with internal wait point at object objA.

A statechart object.

objA reads (R) the current state in statechart xyz, whereas objB writes (W) a new state in xyz.

11.1.8 Outlines Syntax

class outline ::=
 class ClassName *base spec* - opt
   data declaration - opt **;** . . .
   virtual function declaration - opt **;** . . .
   function declaration - opt **;** . . .
 endclass;
process outline ::=
 process function ProcessCodeName
   data declaration - opt **;** . . .
   execution statement **;** . . .
 endprocessfunction;
isr outline ::=
 interrupt service routine ISRname
   execution statement **;** . . .
 endisr;
base spec ::=
 inherits ClassName - list
data declaration ::=
 static - opt *type spec* - opt identifier *array spec* - opt |
 statechart *StatechartName* - opt identifier
type spec ::=

SimpleTypeName | ClassName | **ref**   (*type spec*) |
ClassName **(** *type spec* **)**
array spec ::=
    [LowerIndex **:** UpperIndex **]**
virtual function declaration ::=
    virtual function functionName **(** *parameter* - opt **)**
function declaration ::=
    static - opt **function** functionName **(** *parameter* - opt **)**
            data declaration - opt
            execution statement. **;** ...
    endfunction;
parameter ::=
    type spec -*opt* identifier **,** ...
execution statement ::=
    VerboseStatement | *object spec* **=** *expression* | **return** *expression* |
    statechart spec **=** *statechart value* |
    call statement | *if statement* | *switch statement* | *loop statement*
call statement ::=
    functionName **(** *expression* - opt **,** ... **)** |
    object spec **.** functionName **(** *expression* - opt **,** ... **)** |
    ClassName **::** *call statement*
if statement ::=
    if *expression* **then** *execution statement* **;** ... *else case* - opt **endif**
else case ::=
    else *execution statement* **;** ...
switch statement ::=
    switch *expression*
    CaseLabel **:** *execution statement* **;** ...
    ...
    otherwise case - opt
    endswitch
otherwise case ::=
    otherwise: *execution statement* **;** ...
loop statement ::=
    loop forever *execution statement* **;** ... **endloop** |
    while *expression* **do** *execution statement* **;** ... **endwhile** |
    do *execution statement* **;** ... **while** *expression* **enddo**
expression ::=
    Value | VerboseExpression | *object spec* | ClassName **::** |
    statechart expression | *expression* - opt Operand *expression*
object spec ::=
    identifier | Identifier **[** *index spec* **,** ... **]** | **this**
    functionName **(** *expression* - opt **,** ... **)** |
    object spec **.** *object spec* | ClassName **::** *object spec*
index spec ::=
    expression | *expression* **:** *expression* | **for each**
statechart expression ::=

---

statechart spec |
    expression **==** *statechart value* | *expression* **!=** *statechart value*
statechart spec ::=
    identifier | **statechart** StatechartName - opt *identifier* |
    statechart spec **.** ComponentName
statechart value ::=
    StateName | ComponentName **.** *statechart value*

11.1.9 CASE Tools

The OCTOPUS method adopts, as far as possible, the notations of the well-known OMT and Fusion methods, and applies standards, such as [Z120 '94], to the notation of the message sequence chart. The method introduces additional notations only, when required by the special constraints of embedded real-time systems. As a result, OCTOPUS can be supported by the current case tools which allow their users to add and implement new notations. Here are examples of such case tools (many others are available worldwide):

Paradigm Plus, from ProtoSoft
17629 El Camino Real 202, Houston, TX 77058, USA
Tel: +1 713 480-3233   Fax: + 1 713 480-6606

StP/OMT, from Interactive Development Environments
595 Market Street, San Francisco, CA 94104, USA
Tel: +1 415 543-0900   Fax: + 1 415 543-0145

Object Maker, from Mark V Systems
16400 Ventura Boulevard, Encino, CA 91436, USA
Tel: +1 818 995-7671   Fax: + 1 818 995-4267   Email: objectmaker@markv.com

Also other tools such as **Visio**, from Shapeware Corporation, **With Class**, from MicroGold, **Select OMT** from Select Software Tools and many others.

11.2 OCTOPUS Roadmap

Abstraction Level	Development Phase	Structural Model	Functional Model	Dynamic Model
System (Problem Domain)	**System Requirements Specification**	System context diagram	System use case diagram and use cases	System use case diagram and use cases (scenarios)
Subsystem	**System Architecture**	Subsystems diagram	Specified in the analysis functional models of subsystems ↓	Specified in the analysis dynamic models of subsystems ↓
Class	**Subsystem Analysis**	Class diagram and class description table	Subsystem operation sheets	Subsystem Event list and event groups Diagram and event sheets and statecharts and actions table and significance table and (compound events) and scenarios
Object	**Subsystem Design**	Class outlines and process outlines and inter-process message outlines	Outlines of member function which merge into the outlines in the structural model ←	Object interaction threads and event threads and object groups

GLOSSARY

abstract environment object   Originator of an event that does not belong to another application subsystem. The hardware wrapper provides an interface to it or a stub that generates the event.

action   Uninterruptable (atomic, short in time) operation that often accompanies transitions between states.

action table   Part of the dynamic model. Accompanies a statechart. Records actions or activities triggered by events.

activity   Interruptable (long in time or ongoing) operation that occurs when the system is in a certain state.

analysis object   Captures a concept, abstraction or thing that is considered relevant in object modeling.

application subsystem   Any subsystem besides the hardware wrapper. Focuses on the application domain.

application subsystem boundary   Separates the application subsystem from its environment. Defines the interface of the subsystem. Shown in the class diagram.

asynchronous communication   (between objects) A client communicates with the server by sending a service request. The client continues execution.

CES   (acronym) Command Event Set. A special term used in Chapter 10, Cruise Control System Case Study.

CSA   (acronym) Control Signal Assignment. A special term used in Chapter 10, Cruise Control System Case Study.

class description table   Accompanies the class diagram. Describes each class.

class diagram   Part of the object model. May be refined during design. It consists of classes linked by associations.

class outline   A semi-formal notation used to capture structure and behavior of a class during design.

client   (object) An object that requests services provided by the server object.

compound event   An event that indicates occurrence of one out of a set of events. Which one it means can be determined by using the system state since the laxity of these events is given.

compound state   A state formed by combining the elementary states of concurrent statecharts.

controller   (in object interaction thread) The object that receives the trigger.

design object   An extension of the analysis object. It can be distinctly identified. It is an instance of its corresponding class.

dynamic model   One of the analysis models. Includes description of events, statecharts and scenarios.

elementary state   A state that does not have substates.

environment   (of application subsystem) Everything outside the application subsystem that interacts with it.

event   Logical input communication with which an abstract environment object requests the application subsystem to perform some processing.

event list   Part of the dynamic model. It lists all events of a subsystem and describes each briefly.

event sheet   Part of the dynamic model. Formal layout, but informal content. Captures important data about the event.

event thread   An object interaction thread with an event as trigger.

explicit concurrency model   Model of concurrency during design. It describes concurrency separately from the objects by using the notion of processes as supported by real-time operating systems.

functional model   One of the analysis models. Describes the operations and their effects.

grouping of events   Events that are similar to each other are grouped into superevents. Visualized by an inheritance diagram.

hard interrupt   A real hardware interrupt. Counterpart of soft interrupt.

hard real-time system   A system in which a failure to meet time requirements is an error.

hardware wrapper   A special subsystem that always exists. Shields the application subsystems from the underlying hardware.

implicit concurrency model   Mental view of concurrency during analysis. Events are broadcast to all objects; interested objects start processing as if each had its own infinitely fast processor.

interobject concurrency   Appears between distinct objects. It means that a transaction at an object may be interrupted at some undetermined point by another object.

intra-object concurrency   Occurs in the same way as interobject concurrency, except that it relates to the operations of a single object.

laxity   (of events) A term used to express the fact that two events can be merged into a compound event without any loss of correctness.

message sequence chart   Formal notation to describe a scenario graphically.

object diagram   Optional part of the object model or built during design. It consists of objects connected by links.

object group   A conceptual union of objects and synchronous interactions formed by one or more continuous sequences of synchronous interactions between those objects.

object group process   The unique process or interrupt service routine associated with an object group. It provides the execution of the group.

object interaction   General term for any flow of control or data from object to object.

object interaction graph   A design notation to visualize object interaction.

object interaction thread   An object interaction of those objects that one thread of execution traverses. Started by a trigger at the controller object.

object model   One of the analysis models. Shows the structure of a subsystem.

object-interaction concurrency   Macroscopic view of concurrent execution of object interaction threads. Excludes inter- and intra-object concurrency. When an object has completed a transaction, any of the concurrent interaction threads continues next.

operation sheet   Part of the functional model. Formal layout, but informal content. It describes an operation.

originator   (in an event thread) The object that issues the triggering event.

preemption   Under control of the operating system, a process with higher priority can interrupt the execution of a process with lower priority, and enter the running state.

primitive event   The input event to the hardware wrapper from the underlying hardware.

process   An operating system concept. Basic unit of activity managed by the operating system. Each has its own thread of execution.

process outline   A semi-formal notation to capture static structure and behavior of an object group process during design.

process outline graph   Visualizes the object interaction threads of the different branches of an object group process.

process priority   A property of the process. Affects scheduling and preemption.

process state   The basic state of the process is either running, ready to run or waiting.

qualified event thread   An event thread, in which (a) synchronous invocation or asynchronous communication is specified for all object interactions, (b) asynchronous return-messages have been added where needed, and (c) either an internal or primary wait point is defined for the reception of any return-message.

root object   Any object group has at least one. The synchronous links to the other members of the group are tracked from it.

scenario   A sequence of events between the objects of the environment and the subsystem that is carried out for some purpose. Represented by a message sequence chart.

server   (object) An object that provides a service to a client object upon request.

significance table   Part of the dynamic model. Records significance or importance of an event in elementary or superstates.

SLT   (acronym) Subscriber Line Tester. A case study used in this book. Based on a real telecommunication product.

soft interrupt   Another process preempts the actually running one.

soft real-time system   A system in which time requirements are less critical than in hard real-time systems. An occasional failure to satisfy some time requirements may be acceptable.

state hierarchy   (in a statechart) A superstate is decomposed into substates in OR/AND fashion. In OR decomposition, the superstate is in only one of its substates. In the AND decomposition, it is concurrently in several substates.

statechart   Enhanced form of state transition diagram which uses state hierarchy to decrease the size of the representation.

subsystem   A major structuring component of systems.

synchronization   A mechanism to control the concurrent access to shared resources in multithreaded programs.

synchronous invocation   (between objects) A client calls a function in the server. The client continues execution only after the function in the server returns.

system context diagram   Like in structured analysis and design, but enhanced with the object model notation. It shows the actors around the system and how the system is related to them.

system increment   A part of the system composed of one or more subsystems which, when fully implemented, produces a partially operational system which can be tested.

system state   The compound state of the system.

unqualified interaction model   Mental view of object interaction where any server completes any request in zero time and returns to the client. No interleaving of interactions occurs; as many interactions as you like start and complete in a time window as close to zero as you like.

use case   Describes a particular way of using the system to be built as a black box. Use cases are analogous to the script of a play. They describe the role of each actor in the play and how the actors behave in a scenario.

use case diagram   Visualizes a hierarchy of use cases using the aggregation notation of class diagrams.

visibility   (of objects) The reference to an object that is needed to be able to access the object. If objects are in the same memory space, a client interacts with a server by using the runtime address of the server. If the objects are distributed in different memory spaces, symbolic referencing has to be used.

REFERENCES

[Agha '86] G. H. Agha, *Actors: A Model of Concurrent Computation in Distributed Systems*, Cambridge, MA: MIT Press, 1986.

[Booch '87] Grady Booch, *Software Components with ADA*, Menlo Park, CA: Benjamin/Cummings, 1987.

[Buroff '94] Steven Buroff and Rob Murray, C++ Oracle, *C++ Report*, November-December 1994.

[Cargill '92] Tom Cargill, *C++ Programming Style*, Addison Wesley, 1992.

[Chen '76] P. Chen, The Entity Relationship Model—Toward a Unified View of Data, *ACM Transactions on Database Systems*, Vol. 1, No. 1, March 1976.

[Coad '91] Peter Coad and Edward Yourdon, *Object-Oriented Analysis*, Englewood Cliffs, NJ: Prentice Hall, 1991.

[Coleman '93] Derek Coleman, Patric Arnold, Stephanie Bodoff, Chris Dollin, Helena Gilchrist, Fiona Hayes and Paul Jeremaes, *Object-Oriented Development—The Fusion Method*, Englewood Cliffs, NJ: Prentice Hall, 1993.

[Cook '94] Steve Cook and John Daniels, *Designing Object Systems—Object-Oriented Modeling with Syntropy*, Englewood Cliffs, NJ: Prentice Hall, 1994.

[Coplien '92] James O. Coplien, *Advanced C++ Programming Styles and Idioms*, Reading, MA: Addison Wesley, 1992.

[CORBA '93] Object Management Group, *OMG Common Object Request Broker Architecture and Specification (CORBA)*. Revision 1.2, OMG TC Document 93.12.43, December 29, 1993.

[CORBA '94] Object Management Group, *IDL C++ Language Mapping Specification*, OMG Document 94-9-14, September 12, 1994.

[Dahl '69] O. J. Dahl, B. Myhrhaug and K. Nygaard, *SIMULA Programmer's Reference Manual,* The Norwegian Computing Center, Oslo, 1969.

[DeMarco '78] Tom DeMarco, *Structured Analysis and System Specification*, Englewood Cliffs, NJ: Prentice Hall, 1978.

[Ellis '90] Margaret A. Ellis and Bjarne Stroustrup, *The Annotated C++ Reference Manual,* Reading, MA: Addison Wesley, 1990.

[Gamma '95] Erich Gamma, Richard Helm, Ralph Johnson and John Vlissides, *Design Patterns—Elements of Reusable Object-Oriented Software*, Reading, MA: Addison Wesley, 1994.

[Garlan '93] David Garlan and Mary Shaw, An Introduction to Software Architecture, *Advances in Software Engineering and Knowledge Engineering*, Vol. 1, Singapore: World Scientific Publishing, 1993.

[Gilbert '93] John W. Gilbert III and Robert G. Wilhelm, A Concurrent Object Model for an Industrial Process-Control Application, *Journal of Object-Oriented Programming*, November-December, 1993.

[Goldberg '83] A. Goldberg and D. Robson, *SMALLTALK-80: The Language and Its Implementation*, Reading, MA: Addison Wesley, 1983.

[Gomaa '93] Hassan Gomaa, *Software Design Methods for Concurrent and Real-Time Systems*, Reading, MA: Addison Wesley, 1993.

[Gomaa '95] Hassan Gomaa, Reusable Software Requirements and Architectures for Families of Systems, *The Journal of Systems and Software*, Vol. 28, No. 3, March 1995.

[Harel '87] David Harel, Statecharts—A Visual Formalism for Complex Systems, *Science of Computer Programming*, Vol. 8, No. 3, June 1987.

[Hatley '87] Derek J. Hatley and Imtiaz A. Pirbhai, *Strategies for Real-Time System Specification*, New York: Dorset House Publishing, 1987.

[Hoza '89] Bradley J. Hoza, Mark K. Smith and Stephen R. Tockey, An Introduction to Object-Oriented Analysis, *5th Structured Techniques Association Conference,* Chicago Chapter ACM, Structured Techniques Association, Chicago, May 8–11, 1989.

[IEEE '93] IEEE, *IEEE Guide to Software Requirements Specifications*, IEEE Std 830-1993, The Institute of Electrical and Electronics Engineers, 1993,

[Jacobson '92] Ivar Jacobson, Magnus Christerson, Patrik Jonsson and Gunnar Overgaard, *Object-Oriented Software Engineering—A Use Case Driven Approach*, Reading, MA: Addison Wesley, 1992.

[Johnson '92] Ralph E. Johnson, Documenting Frameworks with Patterns, *Proceedings of OOPSLA '92, SIGPLAN Notices,* 27(10), Vancouver, BC, Canada, October 1992.

[Kafura '89] D. G. Kafura and K. H. Lee, Inheritance in Actor based concurrent object-oriented languages, *Proceedings of ECOOP '89*, Cambridge, UK: Cambridge University Press, 1989.

[Karaorman '93] Murat Karaorman and John Bruno, Introducing Concurrency to a Sequential Language, *Communications of the ACM*, Vol. 36, No. 9, September 1993.

[Kronlöf '93] Klaus Kronlöf, ed., *Method Integration—Concepts and Case Studies*, New York: John Wiley & Sons, 1993.

[Lippman '91] Stanley B. Lippman, *C++ Primer, 2nd Edition,* Reading, MA: Addison Wesley, 1991.

[Meyer '88] Bertrand Meyer, *Object-Oriented Software Construction*, Englewood Cliffs, NJ: Prentice Hall, 1988.

[Meyers '92] Scott Meyers, *Effective C++—50 Simple Ways to Improve Your Programs and Designs,* Reading, MA: Addison Wesley, 1992.

[MRI '93] Microtec Research, Inc., 2350 Mission College Boulevard, Santa Clara, CA 95054, *Software Development Environment and Tools*, Doc. 101033-001, 1993.

[PAR '94] Paradigm Systems, Inc., Suite 2214, 3301 Country Club Road, Endwell, NY 13760, *Paradigm LOCATE Reference Manual*, 1994.

[Pesonen '93] Pekka Pesonen, *Object-Based Design of Embedded Software*, Technical Research Center of Finland, Espoo, 1993.

[Rumbaugh '91] James Rumbaugh, Michael Blaha, William Premerlani, Frederick Eddy and William Lorensen, *Object-Oriented Modeling and Design*, Englewood Cliffs, NJ: Prentice Hall, 1991.

[Rumbaugh '95a] James Rumbaugh, OMT: The Object Model, *Journal of Object-Oriented Programming*, January 1995.

[Rumbaugh '95b] James Rumbaugh, OMT: The Dynamic Model, *Journal of Object-Oriented Programming*, February 1995.

[Rumbaugh '95c] James Rumbaugh, OMT: The Functional Model, *Journal of Object-Oriented Programming*, March/April 1995.

[Russo '88] Vincent F. Russo and Simon M. Kaplan, A C++ Interpreter for Scheme, *Proceedings of USENIX C++ Conference*, 1988.

[Selic '94] Bran Selic, Garth Gullekson and Paul T. Ward, *Real-Time Object-Oriented Modeling*, New York: John Wiley & Sons, 1994.

[Shaw '90] Mary Shaw, Toward Higher-Level Abstraction for Software Systems, *Data and Knowledge Engineering 5*, New York: North Holland, 1990.

[Shlaer '92] Sally Shlaer and Stephen J. Mellor, *Object Lifecycles: Modeling the World in States*, Englewood Cliffs, NJ: Prentice Hall, 1992.

[Sixtensson '93] Anders Sixtensson, Cleanroom Specification, *Proceedings of the 1st Annual European Industrial Symposium on Cleanroom Software Engineering*, Copenhagen, Denmark, October 1993. Q-Labs AB, IDEON Research Park, Beta 4, S-22370 Lund, Sweden.

[Stroustrup '91] Bjarne Stroustrup, *The C++ Programming Language*, 2nd edition, Reading, MA: Addison Wesley, 1991.

[Stroustrup '94] Bjarne Stroustrup, *The Design and Evolution of C++*, Reading, MA: Addison Wesley, 1994.

[Ward '85] Paul T. Ward and Stephen J. Mellor, *Structured Development for Real-Time Systems*, Vols. 1–3, Englewood Cliffs, NJ: Prentice Hall, 1985-86.

[Wirfs-Brock '90] Rebecca Wirfs-Brock, Brian Wilkerson and Lauren Wiener, *Designing Object-Oriented Software*, Englewood Cliffs, NJ: Prentice Hall, 1990.

[Z120 '94] International Telecommunication Union, Telecommunication Standardization Sector of ITU, *Criteria for the Use and Applicability of Formal Description Techniques, Message Sequence Chart (MSC), ITU-T Recommendation Z.120*, ITU, 1994.

INDEX